CAD and the
Practice of Architecture:

ASG Solutions

Dennis Neeley and Bob Callori

CAD and the Practice of Architecture:

ASG Solutions

By Dennis Neeley and Bob Callori

Published by:

OnWord Press
1580 Center Drive
Santa Fe, NM 87505 USA

Copyright © 1993 Dennis Neeley and Bob Callori
First printing July 1993
SAN 694-0269

10 9 8 7 6 5 4 3 2 1

Printed in the United States of America

Library of Congress Cataloging-in-Publication Data

Neeley, Dennis and Bob Callori
CAD and the Practice of Architecture: ASG Solutions

Includes index.

1. ASG Architectural (computer program) 2. AutoCAD (computer program) 3. Architectural drafting 4. Computer-aided drafting
I. Title
93-83270
ISBN 1-56690-012-3

Trademarks

ASG Model Vision is a registered trademark of ASG. ASG Architectural, ASG Detailer, ASG Core, ASG COGO, ASG TOPO, ASG Roads, ASG Site, ASG Structural, ASG Electrical, ASG Mechanical-HVAC, and ASG Mechanical-Plumbing are trademarks of ASG. AutoCAD, AutoCAD AEC Architectural, AutoCAD Training Center, and AutoShade are registered trademarks of Autodesk, Inc. AutoFlix, Autodesk Animator, and Autodesk 3D Studio are trademarks of Autodesk, Inc. Pella is a trademark of the Rolscreen Company. CON DOC is a registered trademark of the Professional Systems Division of the American Institute of Architects. R:BASE is a registered trademark of the Microrim, Inc., and dBASE is a registered trademark of Borland International.

Other products and services that are mentioned in this book are either trademarks or registered trademarks of their respective companies. OnWord Press and the authors make no claim to these trademarks.

Warning and Disclaimer

This book is designed to provide information about ASG Architectural 6.0 and the implementation of computer-aided drafting in architectural practice. Every effort has been made to make this book complete and as accurate as possible; however, no warranty or fitness is implied.

The information is provided on an "as-is" basis. The authors and OnWord Press shall have neither liability nor responsibility to any person or entity with respect to any loss or damages in connection with or rising from the information contained in this book.

About the Authors

Dennis Neeley, AIA, received his Bachelor of Architecture degree in 1967 and a Master's one year later from the University of California, Berkeley. He began architectural practice with Terry Lofrano in 1970, and the firm expanded rapidly into development and construction. In 1984 the partners decided to downsize in order to concentrate on architecture and to implement CAD in their office. Unsatisfied with the available architectural applications, they purchased AutoCAD and began development of architectural-specific software. As demand for their product grew, they formed Archsoft Inc. to sell copies. Later the partners licensed the application to Autodesk, Inc., which marketed it as AutoCAD AEC Architectural, now the ASG Core and application modules. In 1989 Dennis Neeley became president and CEO of ASG.

Dennis Neeley has written prolifically on the automation of the AEC professions for *Architectural Record* and other design and construction publications. He is a monthly contributing editor for *CADENCE* magazine. Neeley has lectured throughout the country on CAD, education, and the future of the architectural and engineering professions, serving as AEC Expo keynote speaker in 1991.

Bob Callori, AIA, is a graduate of Kent State University, Ohio, School of Architecture. He is a registered architect and CAD instructor at UC Berkeley Extension for the Interior Design and Interior Architecture Certificate program. He is the author of *AutoCAD Release 12 Instant Reference*, published by SYBEX, and has been a technical editor for numerous AutoCAD books. Bob's CAD management skills have included the design of resort hotels and office buildings. For several years Bob has functioned as the co-chairman of the San Francisco AutoCAD User Group, ASG Bay Area User Group, and San Francisco American Institute of Architecture Computer Forum.

OnWord Press...

OnWord Press is dedicated to the fine art of practical software user's documentation.

In addition to the authors and ASG personnel, who developed the material for this book, other members of the OnWord Press team helped to make the book that ends up in your hands.

Thanks to Laura Sanchez, Denice Anderson, Margaret Burns, Frank Conforti, Scott Deshaies, Lynne Egensteiner, Betsy Fogelman, Tim Guerrette, Kris Kuipers, Carol Leyba, John Messeder, Julie Mullen, Dan Raker, David Talbott, and Tierney Tully.

Contents

Part 1: CAD and the Practice of Architecture   1

Dennis Neeley

Part 2: ASG Architectural 6.0 Tutorial   125

Bob Callori

Session 4: Roofs   229

Session 5: Draft Elevation   247

Session 6: Annotations and Tags   263

Session 10: Eye View   417

Index   435

Picture Credits

Illustrations on pages 54, 74, 75, 101, 105, and 107, courtesy of Bailey and Associates, Architects. Illustrations on pages 81 and 82, courtesy of Robert Bernstein, President, CADesign. Illustrations on pages 8, 16, 56, and 58, courtesy of Hornberger + Worstell, Inc., Architects. Illustrations on page 94, by LaserCAMM, courtesy Scale Models Unlimited. Ilustrations on pages 9, 12, 24, 25, 57, 59, 60, 62, 84, 85, 86, 88, 92, 106, 108, and 112, courtesy of Neeley/Lofrano, Architects. Illustration on page 90, courtesy of Sandy & Babcock, Inc., Architects and Planners. Developer: Kanabe Resort Company. Illustrations on pages 7, 9, and 87, courtesy of St. Mary's College of California, Campus Architects Office. Illustration on page 14, courtesy of Toft & DeNevers, Structural Engineers. Illustration on page 28, courtesy of Vertex, a division of ASG, created for 3M Corporation. All other illustrations courtesy of ASG.

Part 1

CAD and the Practice of Architecture

Dennis Neeley

Acknowledgment

Writing the words for this book was the easiest part. The words come from experience, knowledge, and my vision of the future. Once the words are written come the time-consuming and tedious tasks of proofreading, modifying, formatting, and adding illustrations. Thanks to the help of many dedicated people, this book moved from words to reality.

I want to thank the many employees of ASG who have put their time and efforts into the creation of this book. I want to thank our technical employees Alan Steel, Allen Preger, Jim Forester, Wen-Yang Lin, Jojo Guingao, Terry Dorsey, Cynthia Mah, Fred Weaver, and Jan Yoder for many of the excellent graphics that I have used for illustrations within the book. Thanks go to Mark Neeley for scanning the drawings, David Kline for spending many hours desktop publishing the document, Stewart Sabadell for providing both graphics and encouragement, and Wendy Shattuck for her efforts on the book while maintaining her marketing responsibilities.

Special recognition needs to go to Edith Thacher, Technical Documents Manager, who has taken on the responsibility for meeting our commitment dates and coordinating information between ASG and the publisher. Her dedication to detail has insured that the illustrations have been gathered, titled, and properly placed within the document.

It was important to me that the book contain illustrations from the real world of architecture. Many of the graphics have come from my architectural firm, Neeley/Lofrano. Drawings created by Terry Lofrano, Gordon Crespo, Jose Alfonso, John Cole, Cynthia Wong, Tom Clark, Sany Jamal, and Vince Hose are found throughout the book. The other graphics have come from the offices of Sandy and Babcock, Warren Bailey, and Ed Thorpe at Saint Mary's College.

OnWord Press has been excellent to work with. Dan Raker has trusted from the beginning that this was a valuable book and has encouraged me to publish the document. Editor Laura Sanchez has provided direction and support necessary to bring the book to reality. Kris Kuipers has taken the electronic files provided by ASG and has been responsible for the final desktop publishing.

It has been a pleasure to work with Bob Callori. I believe that the concept of combining an overview discussion with an in-depth tutorial is unique and valuable. Without Bob's portion of the book, there would not have been a book. Bob has also provided valuable input to my writing.

There is a small group of people to whom I owe a lifetime of thanks. Terry Lofrano has been my friend for over twenty-four years. He has taught me much about life and architecture. In many ways he is the unsung hero of CAD, for without his knowledge, critiques, and encouragement, there never would have been ASG Architectural. For many years he has taken on extra responsibilities to allow me the time to devote to CAD. His belief and confidence in what is being accomplished has provided me with support and conviction.

My wife Karen has stood by me for over twenty-five years. She understands my love of architecture and my conviction that CAD and electronic information is the future of my profession. She has provided me with the time to follow my convictions, she has encouraged me when the odds were bad, she has allowed me to take risks, and she has brought me back to reality when appropriate. And finally, my son Mark, who at nine years old learned to use our first CAD product in less than five minutes, and an hour later had drawn up a house floor plan, thereby convincing me that the architectural profession would never be the same. Today, as he is preparing to enter college, he is more knowledgeable of computers and software than I. Yes, we are in the middle of a revolution.

Thank you all, for without you there would be no book.

Dennis Neeley
April, 1993

Chapter 1
Using CAD in the Architectural Office

"When we first purchased CAD, I thought that it would be nothing more than an electronic drafting board. I am amazed at what CAD is able to do."

This chapter reviews the effects of CAD — computer-aided design or drafting— upon the basic architectural design process. The rest of part 1 is organized around this design process and gives detailed examples of how CAD can be used from the preliminary programming and design phases to facilities management.

The Design Process

When CAD was first introduced into the Neeley/Lofrano, Architects, office in 1984, we considered it simply a more efficient way to draw. However, we quickly realized that CAD was much more than an electronic drafting board. It was, we discovered, the route to a qualitatively new and better way of organizing our time and energy.

The traditional architectural design process consists of the following seven phases:

1. Programming (feasibility study)

2. Preliminary design (schematic design)

3. Design development

4. Presentation and approvals

5. Contract documents and bidding

6. Construction

7. Facilities management

In the traditional hand-drawn process, moving from one phase to the next often requires redrawing. At the start, the preliminary programming and design phases are rough and are intended only to sketch out

5

The traditional architectural design process.

the concept and feasibility of a project. The design development phase refines and modifies those designs, and this phase, changes are expected, changes that often leave hand drawings in sad shape. Architecture presentation drawings are next required both for the private client and for the design review by public agencies.

After the contract documents and bidding stages are finalized, the construction documents phase often finds a firm starting the drawings all over again to reflect the final decisions on the design of the project; in addition, during construction, the contractor often maintains "as built" drawings of the constructed project. Finally, the contract documents and the "as built" drawings are turned over to the facilities manager, with the facility being managed and modified over the life of the building.

While CAD does not change the phases of architectural design nor the goals of each phase, it definitely changes the users approach and movement within those phases. For example, as soon as our office receives a commission for a project, we enter the survey, topography, trees, existing structures, and soils information into the CAD software, but in fact, we are now starting to receive CAD drawings from surveyors that eliminate the need to even enter this information.

As part of this early phase, information is entered on the setbacks and notes on planning, and because of CAD layering capabilities, it is easy and efficient to let the drawing warehouse information. The information in a "layer"— that is, a set of information, such as all the survey points or site electrical information— can be displayed or set aside— hidden— much as you might pick up first one and then another file of specifications elaborated in a hand-drawn design.

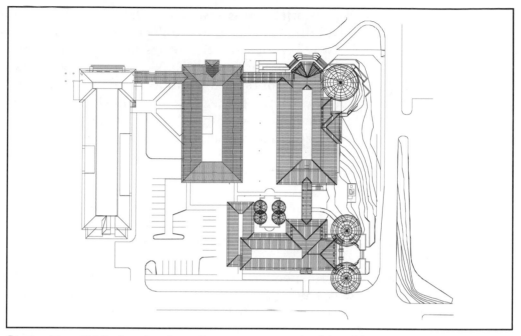

Start with a CAD drawing from the surveyor and add architectural elements.

A preliminary architectural design begins with laying out basic shapes, parking, landscaping, and area calculations. As shown above, CAD is ideal for this phase. The SPACE command can be used to create basic shapes and the areas are automatically calculated. The SPACE command also lets you set wall heights to study massing.

With hand drafting, we often fooled ourselves into believing that we had a viable solution only to find that when we drew the solution accurately, it wouldn't work. With CAD, though, the accurate solution is drawn early in the design process. Although, at times you may find this accuracy confining, you will probably decide that the advantages are well worth the trade-off.

Design development once required completely redrawing the site, parking, buildings, and so on. With CAD, you need only draw the changes. As architects are constantly checking to make sure that nothing has been overlooked, this program can help to make sure that you have not dropped a setback or forgotten a site line.

With CAD, entered information is always available and is never lost. CAD drawings are additive, that is, they aren't created from scratch each time, which had always carried the risk of losing crucial information. CAD design studies are therefore easy to make. You can save a drawing and then experiment with options for windows and roofs by making several studies and then moving ahead with the design you choose. If you later decide to reopen the solution, you can call up the saved original version and begin again from that point.

In our office, design presentation is the phase that has been most drastically changed by using CAD, which conjures up the three-dimensional, or 3D, geometry of the design. With the EYE command, we can quickly lay out perspective views, as well as walk through the EYE WALK commands, and walk around (EYE ROUND) the designs.

We often use CAD perspective geometry as the background for hand-drawn perspectives, saving hours of boring, repetitive, labor-intensive layout work. It easily and quickly provides ample views so that you can

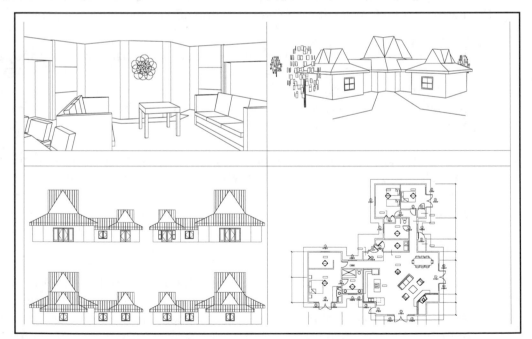

3D preliminary design studies.

Perspective views from any vantage point are created from the 3D model.

pick the best viewpoint location. Rendering and animation software absorbs the geometry to realistically render and animate your design.

Because CAD is more flexible, more dynamic, and more sensitive, clients and public organizations understand our CAD designs better than when we had used hand-drawn renderings, colored elevations, and plans. CAD can absorb more data faster and do more with them, thus approximating more closely the fluidity and perceptiveness of the human eye and feelings. As a consequence, people feel more at ease with the architectural designs presented and accept and interact with the concepts more comfortably.

The contract document phase is based on the design development phase. Here the speed capability of CAD is truly realized. Plans develop quickly, with details added from ASG Detailer or the architect's own CAD library. The software also offers many automatic routines that increase drawing speed. Backgrounds drawn for architectural and engineering drawings pop up instantaneously, and repetitive elements that draftspeople used to dread, such as windows on elevations as shown in

CAD is ideal for designs with repetitive elements.

the figure above, can now be rapidly reproduced in exactly the correct locations.

The geometry of the CAD drawing can now be automatically fed into analysis software that is interfaced with CAD applications. This interfacing saves time and increases accuracy. In many cases, the results of the analysis are the basis for an automatic drawing of the correct solution.

The drawing data can now serve as the basis for the automatic generation of the specifications, resulting in faster and more accurate specifications. The bidding phase is likewise eased by CAD applications. Now you can automatically export information from the CAD drawings into estimation software.

During construction, the architects' and engineers' drawings are used as the basis for "as built" drawings, which property owners then use as the foundation for their facilities management program.

Our firm has used 100% computer-assisted design since early 1985, and more and more architectural and engineering firms are switching to 100% CAD usage. In a few years, CAD offices will be the norm, not the exception. While CAD doesn't eliminate parts of the process, it does change how work is distributed among the phases. Of course, the upcoming generations of CAD may very well change the phases themselves.

Chapter 7, on the future of CAD, gives you some previews into the potential of CAD and a master database — a future that is not far away.

How CAD Affects Architectural Practice

"I have a small firm and we do one-of-a-kind projects.
I could never use CAD."

"We have a large firm and we use a mainframe computer.
The personal computer is not powerful enough."

"We have CAD in the office but only use it on our repetitive projects.
Most of our employees are still on the drafting boards."

"We have made the commitment to be 100% CAD and it is the best
decision we ever made."

CAD has already had a profound impact upon each of the offices described in these quotes, even in the first case, where the designer is not yet using CAD. There the potential effect is actually the greatest. Many architects and engineers who are now using CAD tell me that they wish they had switched to CAD earlier because now they see the time savings that are possible — and time, as any good financial planner knows, is money.

CAD lets you seize opportunity without fumbling. It lets the designer envision an idea and transfer it into a real plan without having to plod through intermediate steps. In the hand-drawing process, the designer creates a sketch; the draftsperson draws up the sketch; the designer checks and corrects the sketch; and then the draftsperson redraws it, incorporating all the corrections. This process is repeated over and over until the desired result is realized. CAD, however, lets the designer leap from an idea to an elaborated plan directly, without the long and error-ridden hand-drawing phase.

In the second quote that opens this section, describing an office that uses a mainframe computer, the problem lies in the type of hardware, or computer, being used to apply CAD. In the past, a mainframe was the only type of computer that was powerful and fast enough to handle CAD. Today, this is no longer true. Still, I encounter CAD managers from firms that use mainframe computers who stubbornly defend their use.

In fact, the personal computer (PC) of today is often more powerful and faster than an older mainframe. Software and hardware for PCs have made major advances because of the huge demand while mainframe software

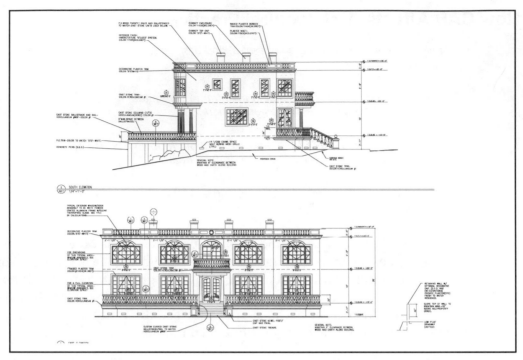

CAD lets the designer move quickly from an idea to an elaborated plan.

and hardware have remained relatively dormant, losing their place in the race as a result. Adding workstations to a mainframe is several times more expensive than is adding PC workstations. ASG has recently demonstrated software to offices that could afford to convert to PCs by simply eliminating the monthly service and maintenance charges on their mainframes.

The third quote brings up an important concern: an office that decides to use CAD must also decide (1) how much of the office will move onto CAD and (2) what projects will be drawn with CAD. Certain hard realities will influence these decisions.

First, how much money can you afford to spend? In our case, we quickly realized that if CAD really is a good idea, it should be used on all projects, and if it is to be used on all projects, then each person in our office would need a PC workstation. We calculated that if all of our projects were on an hourly basis, we could cover the cost of installing and using CAD by increasing our hourly rates $5 per hour.

I have not yet talked with any firm where this additional $5 per hour would have negatively impacted their business. Indeed, firms that have properly implemented CAD have decreased errors and increased productivity.

At any rate, even if you decide to switch totally to CAD, the switch itself is not instantaneous; you need to determine which projects, or parts of projects, are the most logical for CAD applications.

Surprisingly, this is not a difficult decision. If you're handling projects that have repetitive elements, such as motels and hospitals, put them on CAD first. The plans for all your projects are also logical candidates because, for CAD, plans are used as background drawings for other architectural drawings and for engineering drawings. Likewise, elevations that have many repetitive elements are good candidates. In truth, as application software and hardware have developed muscle power, CAD is worth using all the time on all projects.

We discovered very early on that ways of working that we had thought quite efficient were, in fact, painfully inefficient once we were drawing with CAD. Before, we started creating background drawings before we were 100% sure of the design; we even started blocking out elevations before we had made our final dimension decisions. We used to firm up dimensions before we reached complete agreement with our structural consultants, because we thought by jumping the gun in this way we were being efficient and fast. Of course, we also spent time redrawing when the final decisions were made.

With CAD, in contrast, the backgrounds take only minutes to draw. The elevations are partially generated from the plans. Engineers are called in earlier, and the structural information they provide is quickly reflected in the CAD drawings, as shown in the following drawing. Now we spend more time planning and investigating before we begin drawing, and once we do start drawing, we become accurate much earlier than before and without difficulty. The rewards are that projects are more efficiently developed and require fewer revisions, which translates into savings of time and money.

The last quote at the start of this section is from the architect whose office is now committed to CAD. As an architect, you probably want to

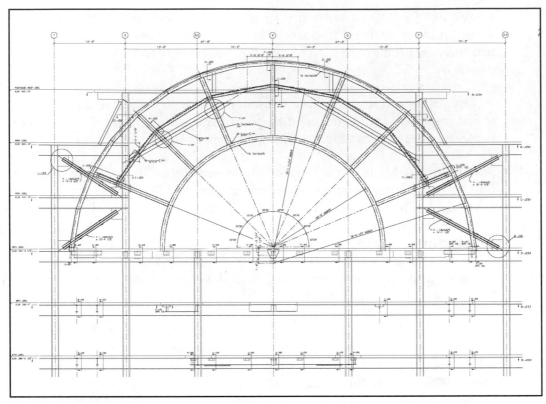

Structural CAD drawings may become the basis of architectural details.

design and manage. You want to make decisions that help create buildings and interiors.You don't want to spend time proving that you can
draw a wall and can draw a window in that wall. You also don't want to
spend your evenings checking dimensions, knowing that no matter how
carefully the drawings are checked, some error will slip by, a ghost that
will come back to haunt you and your firm when someone tries to use
it in the field. With CAD software, the dimensions calculate and are
noted automatically. CAD eliminates much of the busywork for the
architectural office, leaving you with more freedom and with more
confidence.

Company Size and CAD

How does the size of your architectural firm affect the decision to use CAD? Such questions are important for chief executive officers who are weighing costs and benefits. Here are some answers.

In the small firm, the user can create directly with CAD, an extremely efficient process because ideas flow directly from your mind into the drawing. New CAD users are amazed at the quantity and quality of drawings that can be created in a single day.

In the medium-size firm, there are two basic methods of using CAD: the designers use it to create preliminary designs and design development drawings while the contract documents are turned over to the draftspeople to be drawn; in other firms, the designers still use hand sketches and drawings, which are then drawn up in CAD by the draftspeople. As CAD becomes faster, more powerful, and easier to use, both designers and drafters will surely be using CAD for all applications.

Large firms that have implemented the ASG suite of integrated applications have benefited from improved productivity. These firms most often have networks installed to allow for the easy transfer of drawings from one group to another. For instance the civil department starts with the site and then shares its drawings electronically with all the other disciplines that need site drawings as a base for their work. Plans created by the architects are the basis of electrical, plumbing, structural, heating, ventilation, and air-conditioning, fire safety, and interiors.

Through the use of integrated software, employees may be easily trained on several applications. Integrated software is also easier for the CAD administrators to install and maintain.

Manual Drafting/CAD

Some hand drafters object to the impersonal and graphically "flat" look of some CAD drawings. While this concern is valid, the impersonality can be overcome. The impersonal feel has several roots. One is subjective: many drafters have expressed their creativity in their drawing and lettering skills, in their ability to manipulate lines, and in their organizational skills. CAD drawings though, can be made as "artistic" as you

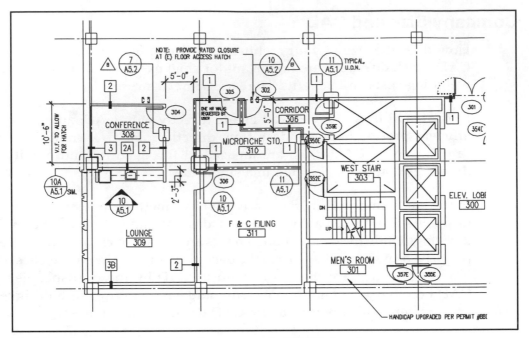

Variable line weights and shading are part of CAD drawing.

like. Hundreds of lettering styles are available — even hand-lettering fonts. CAD software can also draw in various line widths, so the drawings don't need to feel "flat." We find that the urge to hand draw to express individuality and creativity fades quickly when the draftsperson no longer needs to spend the entire day redrawing a repetitive element tens or even hundreds of times. Once CAD itself is seen as the medium for artistic expression, it can easily become as favored and pleasurable a tool as, say, an expensive drafting pen set.

Moreover, CAD allows more drawing comfort than hand drawing. Employees with bad backs no longer need to lean over a drafting table. In addition people who are not able to draw by hand, such as those with physical disabilities, can use CAD to create perfect drawings.

In the past, pregnant women in our office found it difficult to hand draw the last few weeks before delivery. Today, they can sit in any position and draw with CAD. Many drafters who have been injured and who no longer are able to draw by hand have constructed individualized devices through CAD that allow them to draw once again.

Similar devices for the disabled range from voice commands to special keyboards to unique pointing devices that are operated by hand, by head, or even by eye movement. Drawings by disabled people may take longer to create, but once completed, they are perfect; the lines, dimensions, and text are the same in CAD no matter how they are generated.

Drawing Management

Drawing management deals with the assignment of layer names; with drawing names, drawing storage, revision procedures, and the mixing of hand drawing with CAD on the same sheet; with plotting; and with networking workstations. The following is a broad overview of drawing management.

Layer Names

If you are ever at a meeting of CAD experts and energy is dragging, just mention "layer names" and you will instantly provoke a lively discussion. To understand why, note that CAD allows drawing elements, such as lines, walls, doors, notes, fixtures, trees, and so on, to each be placed on unique "layers." This feature is powerful because it lets you dissect the drawing at any time to create background drawings, just as surgical texts offer many different drawings of the human body, each showing the elaboration of a full system— or layer— such as musculature, lymph nodes, skin, and bones.

The problem arises with the need to name the many systems or layers of architectural data in a way that conveys similar meanings to all users. ASG Architectural offers prenamed layers; however, tens of thousands of people who use ASG Architectural have added and named their own layers and modified the preassigned layers. These modifications are fine as long as the drawing stays within the architectural office, but as soon as such a drawing is sent out to consultants or owners, the problem of creative layer naming becomes crucial. If your consultant works for ten architects, he or she may work with ten different layering schemes. As a result, the consultant is constantly trying to keep track of each office's in-house standard, an inefficient activity.

```
┌─────────────────────────────────────────────────────────────────────┐
│ Version 6.0 for R11          PARTNER(tm)          (c) 1985-92 ASG     │
│ ┌─────────────────────────────────────────────────────────────────┐ │
│ │                      Edit Layer Template                        │ │
│ │  Major Minor1 Minor2   Group     Basic        Alias Clg_name    │ │
│ │  ↱                                                               │ │
│ │  FL00  ASBL   0100    │ APPLIANC ARAPPLIANCE    500  A_FLOR_APPL │ │
│ │↓ FL01  EXST   0200    │ APPLIANC ARAPPLSPEC     501  A_FLOR_IDEN │ │
│ │  FL02  PROP   0300    │ APPLIANC ARSCABINET     502  A_FLOR_CASS │ │
│ │  FL03  PRO1   0400    │ APPLIANC ARDCABINET     503  A_FLOR_CASD │ │
│ │  FL04  PRO2   0500    │ APPLIANC ARCABINET      504  A_FLOR_CASE │ │
│ │  FL05  PRO3   0600    │ APPLIANC ARDCAB2D       505  A_FLOR_CA2D │ │
│ │  FL06  PERM   0700    │ APPLIANC ARSCAB2D       506  A_FLOR_CA2S │ │
│ │  FL07  TEMP   0800    │ DOOR/WND ARDOOR         515  A_DOOR      │ │
│ │  FL08  DEMO   0900    │ DOOR/WND ARHEADER       516  A_WALL_HEAD │ │
│ │  FL09  NEWC   1000    │ DOOR/WND ARDOORSPEC     517  A_DOOR_IDEN │ │
│ ├─────────────────────────────────────────────────────────────────┤ │
│ │↕  1/117  ↔  1/10 │217K free│              Major                  │ │
│ └─────────────────────────────────────────────────────────────────┘ │
│ ┌─────────────────────────────────────────────────────────────────┐ │
│ │ ASG Path: C:\ASG5\                              231K free        │ │
│ └─────────────────────────────────────────────────────────────────┘ │
└─────────────────────────────────────────────────────────────────────┘

┌─────────────────────────────────────────────────────────────────────┐
│   F10: Save and exit      Ctrl-PageUp: Top          Tab: Next        │
│   Esc: Quit without saving Ctrl-PageDown: Bottom  Shift-Tab: Previous│
└─────────────────────────────────────────────────────────────────────┘
```

The user may determine the names of CAD layers.

Element	ASG Layer Name	AIA Layer Name
Wall	ARWALL	A_WALL
Door	ARDOOR	A_DOOR
Window	ARWINDOW	A_GLAZ_FRAM
Plumbing fixture	MPFIXTURE	P_FIXT
Electrical receptacle	EEPOWER	E_POWER_WALL

ASG has been seeking to set layering standards. Because of our thousands of users, our layer standard, is in many cases, the de facto standard. However, the American Institute of Architects (AIA) has published a layer-naming guideline and several consultants have promoted their own layer guidelines. It would be wonderful if we could all agree on a consistent set of layer names, but that will never happen. Realizing that it is unlikely that any standard will ever exist, ASG has created tools to allow you to convert one set of layer names to another automatically, one answer to the layer-naming controversy.

In your office, the most important layer-naming decision is selecting which standard you are going to use and remaining consistent thereafter. All ASG products have a coordinated layer-naming-scheme; thus, if you adopt the ASG system, you are assured of consistency and can avoid layer-naming conflicts.

Drawing Names

The name you give a drawing is a crucial tool for software users, so it must be thought out carefully or you will quickly create a frustrating mess. At first, most CAD users name their drawings to reflect the actual drawing, but you only have eight alphanumeric spaces for the name, so additions become the rule, not the exception.

For example, if you are working on a three-story building, you may find it logical to name the first-floor plan FLOOR1. If you have several projects under way, though, you must also indicate the individual client: SMITHFL1. Soon you may have a revision and want to keep a copy of the plan as it was before the revision, so now you have to shorten the name Smith and the drawing becomes SMIFL1R1.

We have now created an almost meaningless name, with little relation to the previous drawing name, although it is supposed to function as the foundation of a whole system. Obviously, drawing names are crucial and should follow a logical pattern from the moment you introduce CAD. The ASG system for layering names will help set up such a pattern.

ASG proposed the following system, which has proved workable over several years. Our system produces a drawing name, such as AB01A201. The AB represents our client. We started with AA, AB, AC, and so on, and we have a list that relates the two letters to our clients' names. The first 01 indicates the revision number on the drawing. The note A2 indicates that the drawing is an architectural drawing and that it is a floor plan. We have adopted, with a minor modification, the naming system of the Northern California chapter of the AIA, where the final 01 indicates that this is the first sheet of floor plans. Here is an example AB01A201:

An "Exploded" Layer Name Example

Client	Revision No.	Type of Drawing	Type of Plan	Sheet Number
AB	01	A	2	01

Type of Drawing	Type of Plan
A Arch	0 Title
C Civil	1 Site
L Landscape	2 Floor plans
S Structural	3 Sections - elevations
E Electrical	4 Detail plans
M Mechanical — HVAC	5 Interior elevations
P Mechanical — Plumbing	6 Reflected ceiling
	7 Vertical circulation
	8 Interior details
	9 Exterior details

With a system such as this, you can be sure that your layer names make sense and are useful.

Drawing Storage

One of the first questions I am asked by architects who are considering a switch to CAD is, "How can you entrust your entire livelihood— and that of many others— to some magnetic charges on a plastic disk?" In our office, we have a consistent system of backups. The reality is that it is safer to have disk copies stored in several locations, as well as to have paper plots, than it is to have all your original drawings lying in a drawer in your office. You are only protected if you have taken precautions to be protected, but with CAD, you are better protected from loss than with paper drawings.

In a Non-networked Office

My office has used a non-network system — of standalone PCs — that has protected us as well as allowed us to avoid the question, "Who has the original?" We start a drawing, and when we are done working on the drawing, it is saved on the computer hard disk. At the same time, it is saved on a floppy disk, which is considered the original and is stored in a fireproof file. The next time the drawing is to be worked on the draftsperson checks out the floppy, loads it into the computer, and continues work. The copy stored on the computer hard disk is used only as a backup copy in case the floppy copy is corrupted.

We let the floppy be the original because that keeps two people from working on the same drawing at the same time — if you have the floppy, you have the drawing. If employees are allowed to work off the hard disk, it is too easy for one employee to work off the hard disk copy and

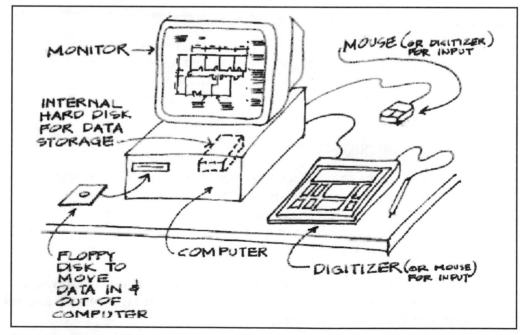

Standalone computers.

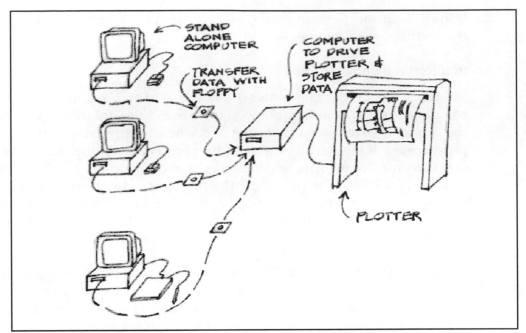

Non-networked computers.

another to work off the floppy. Then at the end of the day, you have two originals, each different, and one will need to be tossed out. On a regular basis, we copy the floppies and take the safe copy out of the office to protect it against fire or theft. Because of those precautions, we have never lost a drawing.

In a Network Office

If your office has a network, the process is simplified, as shown above. The file server computer stores all the drawings. You check out the drawing and work on it at your workstation after the drawing is electronically transferred to you. The network operating system can be set up to ensure that only one person has the drawing at any one time. Backup copies can be stored on your workstation hard disk, and files on the network server hard disk should be saved onto disk, tape, or CD ROM (compact disk, read-only memory) at regular intervals and taken out of the office for storage.

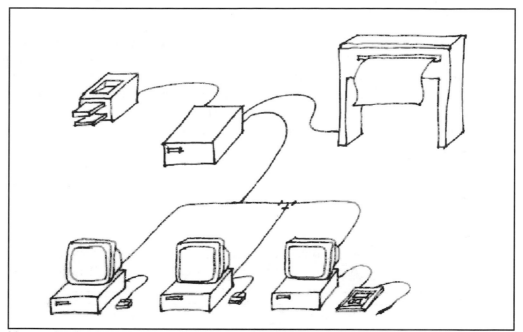

Networked computers, printers, and plotters.

Hand Drawing Mixed with CAD

Now, let's say that you are almost ready to go to bid. You have 50 sheets in the set. Touchup work is needed on several sheets, but if you make the corrections in CAD, it will take ten hours to replot the sheets. What should you do? You probably pull out your pencil and add the information to the existing plots, by hand.

The crucial question is what to do next. You can move on another next project and file the mixed CAD/hand drawing in the flat file or you can go back to the computer and make the changes and add the information to the CAD drawing. The second path is by far the most efficient in the long run. The real value of CAD is that it creates an accurate database of information that can be used for years into the future. If the hand-entered information is *not* added to the CAD drawing, that drawing will remain incomplete and have less long-term value.

Plotting

Plotting can be a weak link in your use of CAD. However, you may also find that it forces you to plan more efficiently and to make better, calmer presentations. With hand drafting one hour before a meeting, you can call out to the drafting room to stop drawing and to copy a set of the drawings; one hour later you will walk into the meeting with copies in hand. With CAD, while you follow the same process, but you place your call one day earlier. If you are using a pen plotter, plotting a complicated drawing will take 30 to 60 minutes. If you are using an electrostatic or ink jet plotter, the plot will take five to ten minutes; with an electrostatic plotter, the second plot of the same drawing can usually be made in only one to three minutes.

At first, we were annoyed by this forced change to our normal operating style, but, we soon found that we planned for the plotting process and

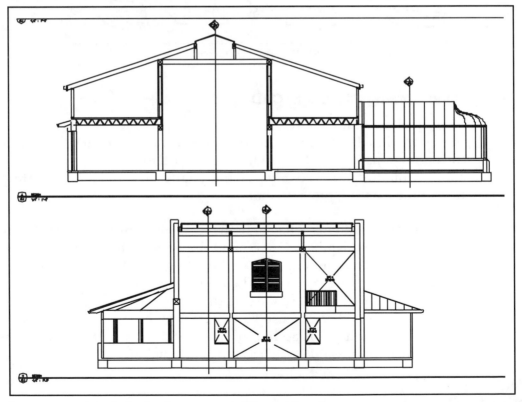

Layers may be plotted using several different line types.

stopped drawing when necessary. The side benefit of stopping the draw-ing process earlier was that we entered meetings more relaxed and better prepared because we had not been rushing around until three minutes before the meetings making last-minute decisions and changes in the drawings.

Mainframes, Workstations, and Networking

When I first became involved with CAD in 1984, there were simple distinctions among mainframe, mini, and micro computers. The micro, or PC, was inexpensive (less than $10,000 for both hardware and soft-ware), a standalone machine (non-network), not very powerful because it had limited storage capacity (20 Mb, or megabytes), and not very fast (0.1 mips, or millions of instructions per second). The micro was man-aged individually by the user, which allowed the expression of personal style.

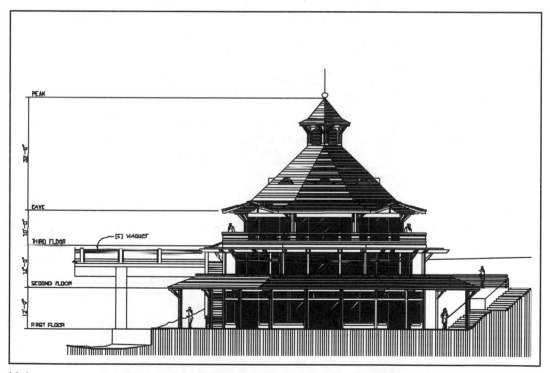

Using a computer does not limit the complexity of your drawing.

The mini was more expensive ($30,000 to $60,000), usually networked so that several users could easily communicate and share files, and moderately powerful, with storage capacities of 100 Mb and speeds of 1 to 5 mips. Although some CAD packages were available, the cost discouraged CAD usage, so minis were predominantly used for word and data management.

The mainframe computer was CAD's cradle. Hardware and software were expensive ($150,000). The computer was powerful, with speeds of 1 to 5 mips; storage capacity was limited only by your checkbook ($1,000 per megabyte). The mainframe computer was based on a networking system, with a host computer providing the computing power and satellite workstations connected to the host.

Today, the situation is very different. The separation between micro and mini has disappeared, with the price of each ranging from $3,000 to $16,000, depending on the exact configuration. The power of these computers exceeds the main frame power of just a few years ago (1 to 60 mips), with an internal hard disk storage of more than 500 Mb.

The mainframe computer is still a viable solution but only in unique situations. The micro and mini can operate either as standalone workstations or as part of a network. Nowadays, the network may be set up so that each computer is still the center of the computing power, with the network simply used to transfer information and to store data and drawings. In addition, the network may be set up with a host micro or mini and satellite terminals that are used only for input, with the host doing the computing.

The networking of the workstation computer, whether micro, mini, or mainframe, brings each user tremendous power for accessing programs and data. Chapter 7 discusses many of the features that you will find in the next few years, features that will forever change the architectural profession. The network will be an important part of this future.

Chapter 2
Basic CAD Features

"When I read my first hardware and software brochures, it was like I was reading a foreign language— actually worse, because I knew the words but had no idea of what they meant in the context of the brochure."

Users must understand certain fundamental concepts in order to work with the computer, or hardware, and the programs, or software. This chapter gives an overview of what you need to know in order to use and understand CAD.

CAD Basics

The PC workstation is revolutionizing the architectural design profession. Since the earliest days of construction, ever since the labor was divided among planners and builders, the planners have had to make drawings to convey the design to the builders, hand drawings that are laborious, slow, repetitious, and prone to errors.

In the last five years, the PC and CAD software have together started a revolution that will forever change the method by which drawings, schedules, and specifications are developed. CAD drawings are created efficiently, base information is easily shared without wasteful redrawing, and errors are decreased because of the inherent accuracy of the CAD drawing.

Each year, PC power continues to increase without driving up the cost. Each year, PC software increases in both speed and functionality. Within the next ten years, the computer will dominate all the drawing professions, with the PC and CAD able to give you the ability to design, present, and create drawings in a fraction of the time you presently need and with spectacular results.

The PC frees the architectural designer from the constraints of the office. Today, you can take the computer to your client to document the program requirements, and then take it on to the site itself to work on preliminary design. You may even find, as I have, that on some days you are more efficient staying at home and working on the computer there, saving hours of commuting time and becoming part of the telecommuting trend that may change our needs for transit and increased highway construction, thus conserving our natural environment and resources. Whether from your home or from anyplace else that has a phone, you can call up your host computer at work to look at, check, and work on drawings.

Integrated CAD Solutions

Drawings are the medium of expression for the architect's work. They transmit the design first to the client, next to the approval agencies, then to the contractors for construction, and finally to the facilities managers who maintain the building. Hand drawings have no "intelligence" and are a static medium, but "smart" electronic drawings are associated with data and they are dynamic: they can change even as you watch them by flipping, rotating, angling, and showing movement. They can also be transferred from discipline to discipline, from surveyors to architects, and from engineers to city planners.

ASG Architectural is one of several AEC application software packages developed by ASG, each standardized and integrated to the others, ensur-

You may now receive manufacturer specifications and detail information electronically.

ing that what is drawn by one professional can be used and elaborated on by other design consultants. ASG products also include interfaces to analysis software. CAD is fast moving toward the day when all the information you need to design and document a project will be available on your computer. Standardization and integration also ensure that once you have learned one application, you will be well on the way to mastering other applications.

The Vertex Division of ASG has created electronic catalogs for the manufacturers of several building products, with the goal of providing the user with the capability to design and reference information electronically. Manufacturers provide information, details, and specifications that may be electronically imported into your contract documents.

CAD software is moving away from a simple replacement for the parallel bar toward an automatic drawing tool, and you are now able to draw a few lines, have that information transferred into analysis software, and have the results fed back into the CAD software for the automatic creation of the drawings. In the future, you'll do less actual drawing; instead, you'll direct the software to develop solutions you will then study and refine.

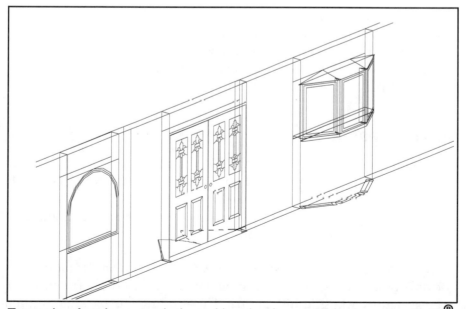

Example of various symbols and levels of complexity from the Pella® designer.

Drawing Speed

Speed is a constant topic among CAD users — I am continually asked if CAD is faster than hand drawing. The general answer is yes. However, there is no simple answer to this question because there are several variables. First, the draftsperson must know the software. Some employees are faster than others at working with the software, just as some employees are faster than others at hand drawing. One-of-a-kind complex drawings are slower to create than either repetitive drawings or drawings that use other drawings as backgrounds.

Next, various computers run at different speeds and calculate differently, thus affecting the time you need to draw and move that drawing around. Various graphics boards process the data differently, producing major speed differences. Various versions of the AutoCAD software run at different speeds. The size of your drawing too has a major effect on the speed with which you perform operations. Finally, CAD drawing involves selecting one item after the other in sequence. The coordination and the logical organization of these sequential steps in the software also heavily affect drawing speed.

As a rule, *always buy the fastest computer available*. The faster the hardware solution, the more work you can complete. First, though, take the time to learn to be efficient. Put your drawing management system in place before you create flurries of drawings. It does no good to produce piles of drawings created quickly if they are wrong or if you don't store them where you can find them.

AutoCAD® Basics

Personal computer CAD, or PC CAD, created in the early 1980s, was at first advertised as having 80% of the power of mainframe CAD at 20% of mainframe cost. Several vendors brought PC CAD to the market at about the same time, but one company— Autodesk, with its product, AutoCAD— quickly dominated the marketplace.

AutoCAD was easily customized, which led to the development of hundreds of add-on specialty programs that increased the functionality of the basic AutoCAD graphic engine. These add-on programs automated the basic AutoCAD commands and features, and by customizing AutoCAD,

Basic AutoCAD® menu before application is installed.

operations that would formerly have taken several minutes and scores of individual steps could be completed in seconds and with only a few steps.

Although application software simplifies the use of AutoCAD and decreases your need to understand its commands, you still must know Auto-CAD before you start to work with the applications, with many learning from the following ways:

1. Many people have learned AutoCAD by simply loading the software and drawing.

2. There are several excellent books designed to teach you AutoCAD.

3. ASG and others have video tapes on how to use AutoCAD.

4. Many software dealers provide AutoCAD classes.

5. Hundreds of Authorized AutoCAD Training Centers® (ATC) across the country are devoted to teaching AutoCAD and CAD applications.

Although this book is not intended to teach AutoCAD, the next few pages introduce the basic features, commands, and functions the user will need to understand. One advantage of application software is that many of the commands are automated and simplified, which makes AutoCAD easier to use. Also, because AutoCAD is a generic graphic engine used by all drawing disciplines, it is not necessary to know all the AutoCAD features to become proficient with applications such as ASG Architectural.

Layers

One of CAD's most important features is its ability to assign different categories of objects and lines to different layers within the drawing. All doors can be assigned to one layer, all plumbing fixtures to another, and all notes to yet another.

Think of each layer as a clear sheet and of the CAD drawing as an unlimited stack of clear sheets or layers. You can draw on any sheet you wish and then look down through the stack to see all the sheets and a final drawing. If you want to create a presentation drawing, you can pull out the sheets that show the notes, dimensions, and section and elevation targets. At any time, the user can turn a layer on or off, thus displaying that aspect of the drawing while simultaneously suppressing the rest.

Layers are constantly manipulated during the drawing session (1) to study objects on various levels of the building, (2) to create presentation drawings from contract documents, (3) to show several proposed designs, and (4) to simply turn "off" or "freeze" layers to make it easier and faster to work on the drawing.

AutoCAD can either turn layers on or off or *freeze* or *thaw* the layers, and while both functions may seem to have the same results, the difference is worth noting. In a large drawing, the speed of the computer falls off as the drawing size grows. If you turn layers off, the layer database continues to be carried with the drawing database, so no drawing speed is gained.

However, if you freeze layers, the database for the selected layers is no longer carried with the drawing database, so the computation accelerates. The price you pay for using the freeze or thaw commands is that when you thaw a layer, it requires a "regen," or regenerate, instead of just a "redraw" phase. The regen process rebuilds the database, which takes several times longer than the redraw process if you have a large drawing.

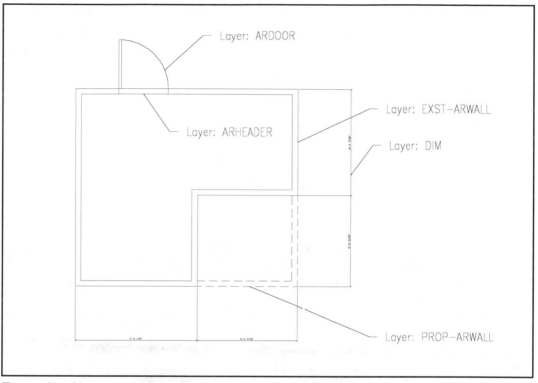

Example of layer names.

As noted earlier, when you are using ASG Architectural, layers are automatically created and given the preprogrammed names. You can rename the layers and you can also create new layers or move objects and lines from one layer to another. The layer names supplied with the program are single names. However, you can create an elaborate hierarchy and assign up to four parts to each layer name.

ASG applications use a unique four-node layer-naming scheme that lets you further identify the layer names. Instead of simply naming a layer Wall, you can identify the wall with any four attributes such as (1) *First Floor*, (2) *New*, (3) *Full Height*, and (4) *Wall*, which can then be used to search for items in the drawing. You can look at all the new walls on the first floor or at all the new full-height walls on the first floor.

Scale and Units

AutoCAD creates all drawings at full size within the AutoCAD database. If you plotted an AutoCAD drawing at a scale of 1:1, it would plot out at full size. To plot out a drawing at an architectural scale of 1/4 inch=1 foot, you plot the drawing at 1:48.

While working on a drawing, keep in mind that you are looking at a full-scale drawing and then "zooming" in and out for closeup or distance views. The size of the image on the monitor has no relation to scale: it is simply how close or how far you have moved from the image. At first, a few users find this "not to any practical scale" difficult to comprehend, but this concern quickly becomes unimportant as you use CAD.

AutoCAD works on the basis of a unit of measure. When working on ASG Architectural with the imperial setting, the unit of measure defaults to 1 inch. If you have chosen the metric setting, your choice of units is millimeters or meters. With the imperial setting, when you are asked to enter a distance, you may enter either 12 or 1' to indicate 12 inches. Because the

Dialog box prior to entering attribute data; the attributes are linked to the drawing element.

default unit of measure is inches, note that you do not need to enter the inch mark (") after the number 12.

Attributes and Entity Handles

CAD's ability to attach attributes to CAD symbols is one of its most powerful features. When a hand drawing is completed, you have graphite on paper and that's just about all. The CAD drawing, however, is both a drawing and a database. The attributes attached to the symbols are used to develop (1) bills of materials, (2) schedules, (3) estimates, and (4) specifications that accurately represent the drawing.

AutoCAD automatically gives each distinct line and/or object in the AutoCAD drawing a unique alphanumeric code. The application developer and the user can use this unique alphanumeric code or "entity handle" to manipulate the objects and populate the database.

The combination of attributes and entity handles is the foundation for the database of the drawing, which is used to unleash the power of CAD.

Parametric Design

As you draw with AutoCAD, lines and objects are added to the drawing in three basic ways:

1. At times, you may add lines directly by selecting the LINE command and by then indicating the starting and end points for the line. It will be drawn.

2. At other times, you may select a predrawn symbol, such as a bathtub, and then pull the symbol into the drawing and specify where the symbol should be inserted. Then you rotate the symbol to the correct orientation and it is added to the drawing.

3. Finally, sometimes the process appears the same as in the second example, but the internal functioning of the applications software is quite different. The difference is one of precision. Although you may be able to specify a size for a predrawn symbol, the symbol is just a representation. In this process, the symbol is drawn to the exact size you specify from a parametric formula, which describes the object or objects to be drawn. When you indicate that you want to draw an object of a specific size, the software first finds the formula,

references a look-up table of sizes for the object, and then parametrically — that is automatically — creates the drawing. The door or window you draw is so accurately sized that you can figure wall lengths, frame sizes, and so on.

With parametrically created objects, you can see that by changing or adding to the look-up table, you can easily modify your drawing. Parametrically created symbols also don't require that you store hundreds of predrawn shapes; thus, using parametrics decreases the amount of information that must be stored in your computer. Through the use of look-up tables, it is easy to add, delete, or modify numbers for new models of objects. It is also possible to link one parametric function to another. Without a doubt, parametric design is shaping the future of CAD and the future of architecture.

Blocks and Write Blocks

With AutoCAD, you can identify objects within the drawing to be saved and reused, either in the current drawing or in any drawing. "Blocked" items are specific to the drawing you are working on, such as, all the suites of a motel. "Write Blocked" items are saved on your hard disk and may be recalled and inserted into any drawing, such as, all the master suites of a given franchise motel type. As you use this powerful function while drawing, you will quickly recognize the massive amounts of time and energy that this recycling capacity saves for your office.

Drawing Commands

The first step that most people venture to take with CAD is to draw lines — first free-form lines and then lines with increasing accuracy. The free-form line is easy; just start and stop and start and stop. The lines can be drawn at any angle and at any length. If staying on a 90 degree orientation is important, you can switch on the ORTHO toggle, after which all lines are drawn either horizontally or vertically.

If exact lengths are important, you can enter the exact distance and orientation in the following format: @10'3<90. This draws a line 10 feet 3 inches straight up on the monitor. The AutoCAD convention is that zero (0) degrees is to the right on your screen. Angles are defined in a counterclockwise direction, so that 270 degrees is down. You can modify this base

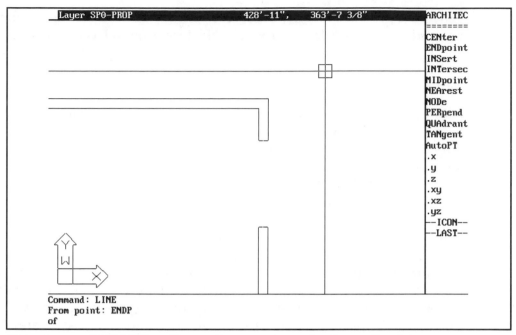

Object snap (OSNAP) settings allow precise selections of points.

setting, but I would recommend not changing it because this has become a standard.

AutoCAD has many commands, most of which are easy to understand and use. Commands such as COPY, MOVE, TRIM, and ERASE all do exactly what you would expect. Luckily, you will rarely need to use the most complicated AutoCAD commands, such as the ARC command; when you do need to, though, it has been automated and simplified by ASG software.

For example, the AutoCAD perspective-generating command (D view) requires several minutes and some skill to create a perspective view. In fact, very few seasoned AutoCAD users could exactly set the target point and height and the view point and height. With the EYE commands in ASG Architectural, it takes only a few seconds to select the perspective target and to start the computer generating the perspective.

One of the most important capabilities of AutoCAD is the OSNAP, or object snap feature, which can be used to accurately lock on to a desired location of an object. OSNAP locations, shown on the side screen in the illustration above, are provided for endpoints, centers, midpoints, intersections, and so on, and the feature lets you accurately locate one object in relation to another.

Settings

AutoCAD has hundreds of thousands of users. Over the years, these users have asked for many changes to AutoCAD, often suggesting additions that are needed by a majority of AutoCAD users; at other times, they ask for additions needed by only a few. Autodesk has added hundreds of these features, among them the opportunity to choose how you will set up AutoCAD to best suit your drawing style.

AutoCAD and ASG software come out of the box with certain "default" settings so that you can go straight to work. After you become familiar with the software, you may find that you want to change these settings. For example, earlier I indicated that an angle of zero (0) draws a line to the right on the page. However, if you would rather that a zero angle draw a vertical line up on the page, you can set AutoCAD to do so. In our software, ASG

Dialog boxes allow you to easily set up the drawing environment.

has assembled all the settings in one location on the settings menu. This simplifies how you locate and change settings.

Toggles

With several functions, you have just two choices: "Yes, I want a given feature" or "No, I do not want this feature." These choices or toggles — off/on choices — are listed on the toggles menu shown below.

In ASG Architectural, for example, you can draw all objects as either two- or three-dimensional objects. When the toggles menu appears, you find the option "2D/3D." If you select this menu item, the software lets you then flip the insertion mode from 2D to 3D, or the reverse. The prompt area on the monitor displays the current status so that you can "choose it on" or "choose it off."

Editing

AutoCAD gives you several options that define the characteristics of objects you insert into your drawing, such as layer, line color, object elevation,

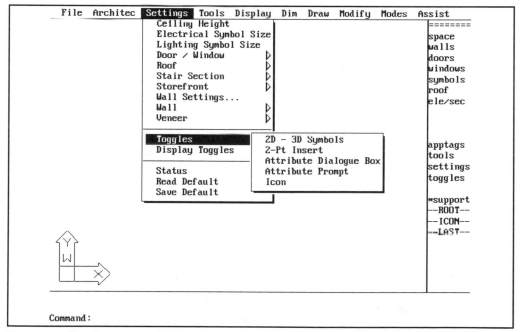

The software is customizable by the user with settings and toggles.

thickness (extruded height), and others, or you may want to change the characteristic from the way it was originally inserted into the drawing, for instance, perhaps you put the object on the wrong layer. The CHANGE command lets you make such modifications, thus providing the kind of flexibility for which CAD is justly famous.

The Interface

Application software must have a whole collection of features to be truly useful: It must have symbols to use, it must draw the objects you want, it must be reliable, and, most of all, it must be easy to use. The first CAD software I considered using was based on mainframe hardware. The salesperson said that I could really only expect to become productive as an architect with this program after four to six months of training. I felt this lag time was absolutely unacceptable; in fact, it was also unnecessary. The interface had been poorly thought out and was not designed for a practicing architect but for someone who was totally specialized in making CAD drawings.

In designing software, our goal at ASG is to make the draftsperson productive *in the first week.* We also aim to have the head of the project feel just as comfortable using the software as the full-time draftsperson does. ASG software of today has more features than that mainframe software I once considered, yet it has remained easy to learn and use. The difference is the interface—the method by which you tell the computer what you want to create. In software design, interface design is just as important as the code that triggers the functions.

The interfaces that are available include (1) the keyboard, (2) the screen menu, (3) the pulldown menus, (4) the icon menus, (5) the tablet menu, and (6) the on-screen tablet menu. Just as you have a favorite color, chair, or automobile, so also will you have a favorite interface with the software. A good interface lets you choose your own preferred method of using the software. ASG Architectural lets you choose, from all the possible AutoCAD interfaces, the one that is the most comfortable for you. You can even move between interfaces at any time as you work.

In addition to the interface, you can choose tools to enter information into the drawing. Your choices include (1) the mouse, (2) the keyboard, (3) the stylus, (4) the puck, and (5) the track ball, all of which are discussed in the following sections.

Input Devices

The Keyboard. The first versions of CAD provided only one interface, the keyboard. On this device, if you wanted to draw a line, you typed in LINE and then typed the starting and ending coordinates, or the relative distance and angle, and the line was drawn. To help simplify the keyboard process, often the software used a key letter instead of requiring that the entire word be typed in. For example, with AutoCAD, you could simply type in D, instead of DYNAMIC when you wanted to give the *dynamic* ZOOM command.

A few early CAD users still prefer the keyboard; they can enter information quickly because they have memorized not only the keyboard but also the key letters for the commands they use. However, for beginners and most seasoned users, the keyboard is not the most effective way to learn and use CAD. The other interfaces require less memorization, so you are free to devote your energy to learning the software.

The Digitizer and Template with Stylus or Puck. A digitizer is an electronic pad that senses the location of a stylus— a penlike pointing device— or of a puck— a puck-shaped pointing device— as you move the device over and around the digitizer, which may be subdivided into a drawing area or selection areas.

Over the digitizer, you can lay a graphic template that shows the various commands you need. The selection areas, which look like little boxes, can be programmed so that when you point at them, or select them, the computer software performs a function. For instance, if you pick, or point at, the box for LINE, the software performs the same function as if you had typed in the word LINE.

For both the beginner and the experienced user, the template is a great way to enter information. The commands appear in a graphical format and are printed right on the template so that you don't need to memorize the correct key word or letter to call up a command. Therefore, if you don't use CAD every day, the template lets you easily stay productive because all the commands are easy to find. The one disadvantage is that you must constantly look back and forth between the monitor screen and the digitizer. The digitizer interface does not limit your selections to only the digitizer; you are able to have selections from the pulldown, screen, and onscreen icons.

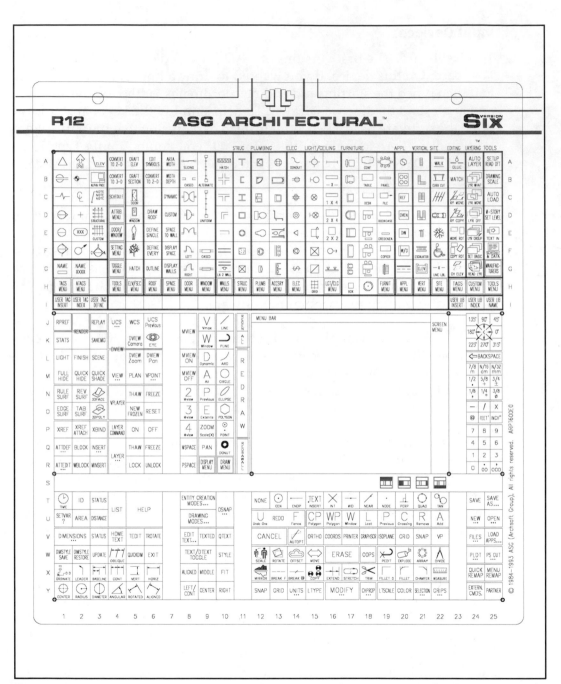

Digitizer template overlays allow you to run the software by simply picking one of the boxes.

All ASG applications of AutoCAD use a standardized digitizer template layout, which is shown below. The bottom portion of the template is the same on all ASG products and is filled with AutoCAD commands while the top section is specific to the ASG application. The template design that ASG uses has become the standard within the industry. In addition, ASG originally designed the layout and authorized Autodesk to adopt the design for their "General" template.

The Mouse or Track Ball. The mouse looks like the puck but works on a different principle. The digitizer is an exact pointing interface while the mouse is a relative pointing interface. The mouse doesn't need a digitizer pad; instead, it has a small ball that rolls around on the bottom of the device. As you move the mouse around on the table surface, the ball also moves and the crosshairs, or target, on the screen also move, following the mouse. The mouse doesn't work with a template, but, like the digitizer pointing device, the mouse lets you select options listed on the screen and draw on the screen.

A track ball is conceptually the same as the mouse— it's sort of an upside-down mouse— except that the ball is on the top and you roll the ball around

Onscreen icons may be picked to run the software.

with your fingers or hand. Both the mouse and the track ball have buttons for "return" and "select."

Visual Interfaces

Here we discuss the monitor icon interface, the pulldown interface, and the screen menu, as well as combined approaches.

The Monitor Icon Interface. An AutoCAD icon— a little picture or graphic symbol— interface can be called up on the screen. The interface is still limited in scope and the images are slow to display; however, if you are just beginning to learn CAD or have forgotten a command and need a graphic image to remind you, the icon interface is excellent.

It is also helpful if you are inserting symbols and would like to see exactly what will appear in your drawing. ASG has introduced a tablet view on-screen interface that reproduces the same layout found on the digitizer template overlay. The on-screen icon interface will probably become the interface of choice because the display will be graphic and hence fast— and less tiring to use than the digitizer because you won't need to look back and forth.

The Pulldown Interface. Along the top of the screen is displayed a menu bar, a line of spaces that may be programmed with key words or letters. When you choose one of these key words or letters by first highlighting and then selecting it, another menu is pulled down and displayed below this key word, offering you further selections. If you select one of these words, letters, or short phrases, the software either performs an operation or displays yet another pulldown menu from which you are invited to select an operation. The network of pulldown menus is very efficient and tightly coordinated.

All ASG applications use a standardized pulldown interface. The first, or furthest left, pulldown is devoted to AutoCAD commands and general ASG functions and features. The next three menus are specific to the ASG applications. The remaining pulldown menus in the series are the same on all ASG applications and are filled with AutoCAD drawing commands.

The Screen Menu. Located down the right side of the monitor screen is the area reserved for the screen menu. In concept, the screen menu operates the same way as does the pulldown menu. First, a screen menu is displayed;

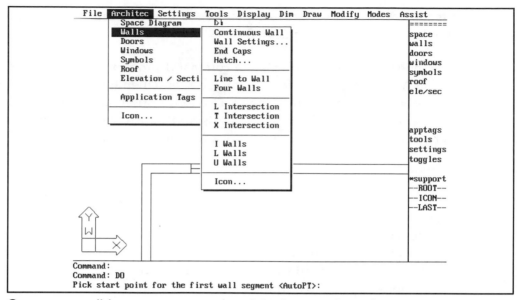

On-screen pulldown menus may be picked to run the software.

when you highlight and then select a word or letter, either a command is executed or another screen menu is displayed. From this second menu, you again make a selection that yet again either performs a command or calls up another screen menu. Just as with the pulldown menu, the screen menu design is governed by clear logic and organization.

The screen menu is limited: only eight letters or numbers may appear on a single line; therefore, the "words" offered by a screen menu are often so cryptic that they are hard to figure out. Most users who prefer the screen menu interface are experienced users familiar with these cryptic notations. When properly designed and in the hands of an experienced user, the screen menu interface is one of the fastest interfaces with which to draw.

Whether you are using a digitizer, an icon interface, or a pulldown interface, you will always make certain selections from the screen menu.

AutoCAD Information and Prompts. AutoCAD shows information about your current drawing at the top and bottom of the monitor screen. At the top left, the current layer name is displayed. Just to the right of the layer name is the current status of some possible toggles, such as ORTHO, OSNAP, or GRID, and at the upper right are shown the coordinates of the crosshairs on the drawing, which may be set to be absolute or to be relative to the last drawing point specified.

At the bottom of the monitor is the command prompt area that first tells you that AutoCAD is ready for a "command" and then shows your response "line." ASG Architectural uses the area to ask questions and to tell you what is happening. If you follow the requests and information displayed, you will be able to perform most operations without reference to the manual.

The Combination Interface

Most users employ a combination of all the interfaces. I have often observed a draftsperson working with the template on the digitizer pad, drawing with one hand and typing in commands with the other. In addition, many of the ASG routines point you to the screen menu from which you will make a selection. All of the interfaces are available and you may experiment with them to choose the one — or the combinations — that is the most productive and comfortable for you.

Standardization

All ASG interfaces are standardized. The templates are designed to place the basic AutoCAD commands in the bottom portion of the template and to devote the top to the discipline-specific commands. All the AutoCAD commands are placed in exactly the same template location for each ASG product.

The pulldown menus are each laid out the same way. At the left side of each is found the FILE heading. The next three locations to the right are devoted to the discipline-specific commands and will therefore vary from product to product. The rest of the pulldown locations are devoted to the basic AutoCAD commands. These pulldown menus are the same for all ASG products. The screen menus follow this same concept. Some of the screen menus are discipline-specific while others are consistent throughout the entire product line.

This standardization is critical to the efficient use of CAD. Once you have learned one ASG product, you have learned a large portion of all ASG products. Most users do not limit themselves to one application, so the standardization greatly decreases the time needed to learn additional application products.

```
┌─────────────────────────────────────────────────────────────────────┐
│ File Architec  Settings  Tools  Display  Dim  Draw  Modify  Modes  Assist │
│     New...          │                                          ========│
│     Open...         │                                          setup   │
│     Save...         │                                          layering│
│     Save As...      │                                                  │
│     Recover...      │                                          AutoLoad│
│                     │                                                  │
│     Plot...         │                                          annotate│
│                     │                                          drawing │
│     ASE          ▷  │                                          editing │
│     Import/Export ▷ │                                          eye     │
│     Xref         ▷  │                                          multi-st│
│     AutoCAD Tools ▷ │                                          toolbox │
│                     │                                                  │
│     About ASG...    ┌──────────────────────┐                  QuickMap │
│     Setup           │  Setup...            │                  Menu Map │
│     AutoLoad        │                      │                           │
│     Re-Map          │  DimVar Status       │                  *support │
│     Manufacturer    │  Read Dimensions     │                  --ROOT-- │
│                     │  Save Dimensions     │                  --ICON-- │
│     Exit AutoCAD    │                      │                  --LAST-- │
│    ┌─┐              │  Read Default        │                           │
│    │Y│              │  Save Default        │                           │
│    │W│              └──────────────────────┘                           │
│    └─┴──→  ╳                                                           │
│                                                                       │
│───────────────────────────────────────────────────────────────────────│
│                                                                       │
│ Command:                                                              │
└─────────────────────────────────────────────────────────────────────┘
```

ASG Core is the foundation for the suite of integrated applications.

ASG Core®

All ASG application products require that ASG Core be loaded into the computer. Really two products in one, first, and most importantly, ASG Core is the integrator of the entire ASG applications product line. As you add applications, Core will be updated to include the application in the selection menu so that when AutoLoad is selected, you will be presented with the available applications. ASG applications use program routines found in Core in order to operate.

ASG Core is also a collection of utilities that will automate the use of AutoCAD. You will find routines for setting up the drawing scale and sheet size, and you will be able to control layers through Core, which contains programs for building your own templates, screen menus, and libraries of shapes.

Chapter 3
Programming, Preliminary Design, and Design Development

"With hand drawing, I am convinced that during the design of a building as much time is wasted redrawing and rewriting information as is spent in productive work."— Manager of an architectural office

The organization of this chapter follows the phases of the architectural design process and demonstrates how CAD can be used to automate that process. Obviously, each project is unique, with each process modified for its specialized requirements. By following the basic design process, you can develop a good understanding of how to use CAD. In addition, the tutorial in Part 2 will take you through the preliminary steps of creating a drawing.

The Programming Phase

The initial programming of each project begins with gathering information and efficiently entering it into the architectural design, so that it can be useful during the entire designing, building, and managing process. CAD can substantially eliminate the need to redraw graphical information or recopy alphanumeric data, both of which characterize the traditional hand-drawing process. We have found that the sooner the information is transferred into CAD the better.

The Site

All projects start with the site. Information is needed on the boundaries, setbacks, easements, existing buildings, utilities, topography, soil conditions, roads, trees, and other physical aspects. Once this information is entered into the CAD drawing, it never needs to be drawn again; with ASG COGO®, the electronic field data automatically creates the drawing. By manipulating layers, you can easily use the boundary drawing for the architectural site plans, as well as the utility plans for the mechanical and electrical consultants. CAD reduces the amount of drawing needed for location maps and phase drawings.

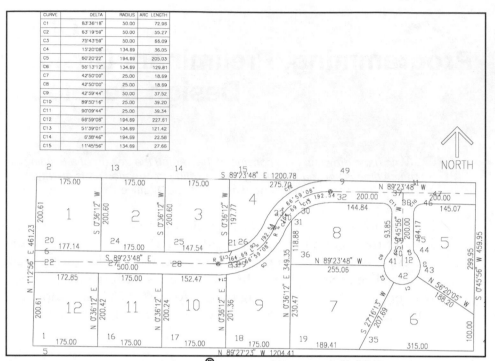

CURVE	DELTA	RADIUS	ARC LENGTH
C1	83°36'18"	50.00	72.98
C2	63°19'59"	50.00	55.27
C3	75°43'59"	50.00	66.09
C4	15°20'08"	134.89	36.05
C5	60°20'22"	194.69	205.03
C6	55°13'12"	134.89	129.81
C7	42°50'00"	25.00	18.69
C8	42°50'00"	25.00	18.69
C9	42°59'44"	50.00	37.52
C10	89°50'16"	25.00	39.20
C11	90°09'44"	25.00	39.34
C12	66°59'08"	194.69	227.61
C13	51°39'01"	134.69	121.42
C14	6°38'46"	194.69	22.58
C15	11°45'56"	134.69	27.66

Surveys created with ASG civil® software forms the basis of an architectural site plan.

ASG Core and ASG Architectural have several features that simplify the base site drawing for architects. However, if you are doing extensive site work, I recommend ASG COGO and ASG TOPO®, which are specifically designed for surveyors and civil engineers.

Boundaries

Using ASG Architectural, the boundary information is best entered in a rather roundabout method. Earlier I noted that AutoCAD creates drawings based on units of linear measurement. The default unit of ASG Architectural is the inch. For example, when you enter 22, the software will interpret this entry as 22 inches. Most surveys give dimensions in a decimal format, such as 225.75' is 225'9", or 225 feet 9 inches.

Naturally, you don't want to spend your day converting tenths and hundredths of a foot into inches and fractions thereof, so instead of converting the surveyor's units to feet and inches, you can simply enter 225.75 and the angle and a line will be drawn. Yes, the line is 225.75 *inches* long, not 225.75

feet (not yet, anyway). Continue to enter distances and angles until the boundary is completed. You now have a miniature version of the boundary. Now, move to the AutoCAD SCALE command, highlight your boundary drawing, and enlarge the drawing by a factor of 12— you now have a boundary drawing at the correct size.

Line Types and Line Labels

Both ASG Core and ASG Architectural provide you with a comprehensive set of line types that can be used to indicate fences, existing buildings, setbacks, and so on. The process to select and use the line types is simple. You can also label lines with an automatic break function that breaks the line and inserts a label.

Topography

Several types of lines can be used to represent topography. Note that AutoCAD has a command SKETCH that at first may seem the logical choice— but isn't. The SKETCH command will ask you for the increment at which you wish to locate points, usually several hundred or thousand to the inch. As you sketch, each point must be stored in the database. Clearly, you will quickly fill your drawing database with thousands of coordinates for the points on the sketched line. You could use LINEs; however, these

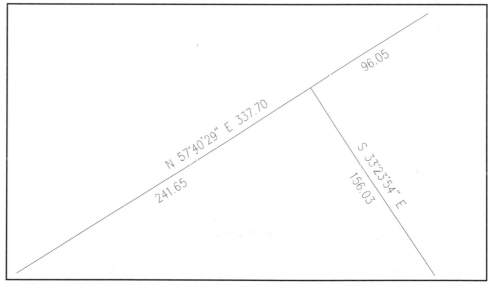

CAD boundary lines.

lines don't lend themselves to the normal curves found in a topographic drawing, and each segment of the line is an independent entity.

The most logical choice is the PLINE or polyline, command, which lets you locate points along a broken line— although the entire line is a single entity within AutoCAD. Polylines can also be modified automatically into curved lines. Furthermore, we often assign elevations to the topography lines so that we can later use the drawing for elevation studies.

The process of assigning elevations to AutoCAD lines is important and can be done in two ways. You can set your drawing level with the multistory command found in ASG Core and all elements that you draw are inserted on the chosen elevation. You can also set the elevation using the AutoCAD CHANGE command, which lets you change an existing line or object to a new elevation.

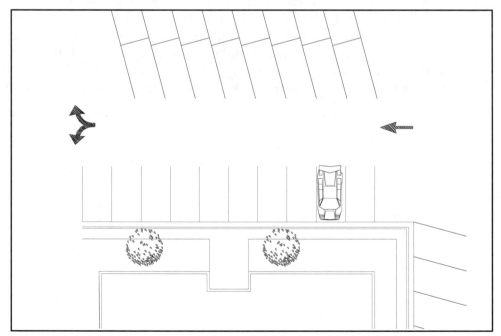

Site design is automated with CAD.

Curbs, Gutters, and Sidewalks

Under the site symbols section, you will find functions that automatically draw curbs and gutters. The software gives you prompts, or requests, for the size of the curb, the gutter, the landscape strip, and the sidewalk. Then you set starting and end points and the drawing is created. In addition, you can add driveway cuts and ramps for the disabled automatically with other selections available in this section.

Site Symbols

ASG Architectural provides a full complement of symbols available for highway markers, trees, playing fields, cars, boats, and parking layouts as shown in the previous illustration.

Once the site information is complete, the drawing can be used as needed for other architectural drawings or for other consultants by turning on and off (or Freeze and Thaw) layers or by transferring information to other drawings.

Building and Organizational Information

During the programming phase, the architectural office gathers basic information on area requirements, relationships, and goals of the project. As it progresses, the information gathered becomes more specific and complex. Eventually, the program shows exact areas, people, equipment, room layouts, and relationships. CAD is the ideal medium for both storing and manipulating this information.

Organizational Information

CAD is very useful for creating organizational charts for your clients. We leave meetings laden down with slips of paper and individual department charts and go back to our office, where we put together that company's organizational chart in CAD. Throughout the project, we update this chart as needed.

Area and Spatial Requirements

The client shows you either (1) areas that are needed for the facility or (2) needs that must be accommodated, which you convert into area and space. At the same time, the relationships between the spaces are indicated.

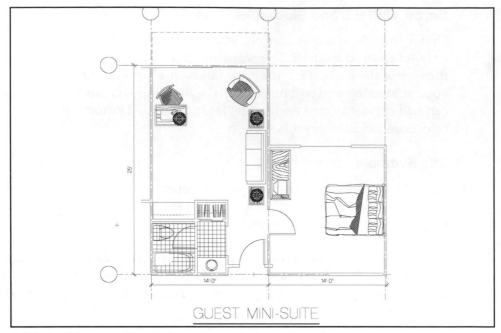

ASG Architectural includes 3D symbols to design interiors.

Several functions are available on ASG Architectural that help record these program requirements. If you want to create a relationship diagram with equal-size bubbles, use the basic drawing command to create circles or bubbles that may be labeled and then arranged, given the program requirements. We often use the SPACE command to create bubbles, because the software automatically calculates and annotates the areas of the bubbles. The use of bubbles for the preliminary design phase of the project will be discussed in the following section.

Workspace Requirements

During the programming phase on interior projects, it is common to discuss workspace requirements. Typical layouts are determined for secretaries, managers, and top management. Special equipment rooms are discussed and specific requirements determined. We immediately convert this information to CAD, which lets the client review and confirm the basic layout. Drawing accurate spaces gives an accurate calculation of the building's total space requirements. ASG Architectural has several predrawn furniture symbols that help with office layouts. These can be inserted either as two-

or three-dimensional symbols. Specific attributes, such as manufacturer, model, finish, or cost can be attached to the symbols at any time.

Equipment

We have worked on several biotech laboratories that are dense with complicated technical equipment requiring specific electrical connections and special air, gas, and waste connections. Not only are the types of connections crucial but so are the exact locations. Before CAD, we had to manage pages and pages of fixture cuts and notes on the equipment. Today, we immediately draw up the equipment in CAD and accurately locate all the utility connections, the service sizes, and the connection requirements, as shown in the following illustration. All the information we ever need is attached to the CAD drawing. During the layout phase, it is easy to check for clearances and to check that all the proper services have been provided to the equipment.

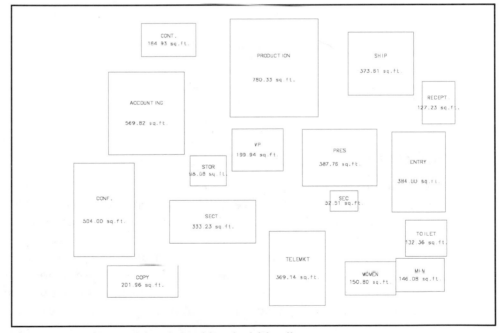

The design process begins with a bubble diagram.

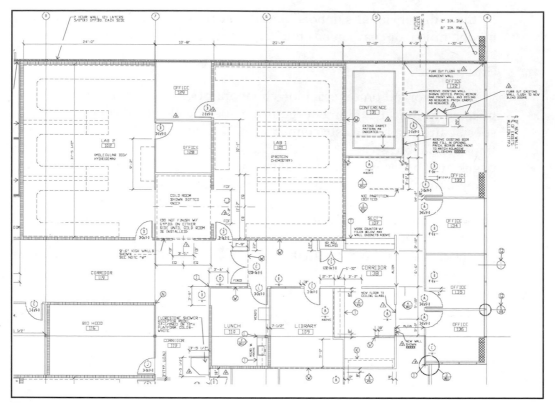

Floor plan of biotech laboratory.

The Preliminary Design Phase

The preliminary design phase is the experimental phase where you move back and forth from concept to program requirements. This phase may take several forms: It may be a quick study to determine the approximate size of the potential development to help determine if the project is even remotely feasible or it may be the first series of physical massing solutions for the project. The preliminary design can show the basic layouts and the architectural concept. By definition, the preliminary design is whatever information is needed to let the client and the architect move into the next phase.

Some parts of this phase must stay fluid and uninhibited while other segments are frankly tedious and analytical. So far, CAD is not always well suited for the spontaneous needs of the preliminary design phase, although it is excellent for other parts of this phase. In hand drafting, you tend to

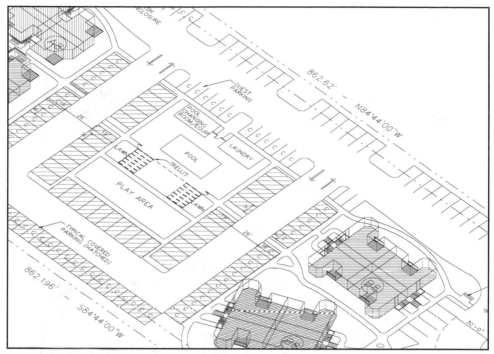

Preliminary site and massing study.

move from the simple to the complex as you move through the designing process. CAD does not require this progression; although with CAD it is difficult to be loose, it is fast and easy to assemble simple pieces and to study complex relations. This program provides important functions that can help in this phase.

The AutoCAD STRETCH command is one of the most useful commands at your fingertips. During the preliminary design phase, it is easy to "push and pull" a bit on the design and then quickly look at results with the EYE commands.

Bubble Diagrams

Bubble diagrams were created as part of the programming phase. In the preliminary design phase, the bubbles are moved around to study various solutions. When you are satisfied with a basic layout, you can automatically convert the bubbles to a wall drawing; for this feature to work, all the bubble lines must align. Often we use the bubbles to determine basic location, and

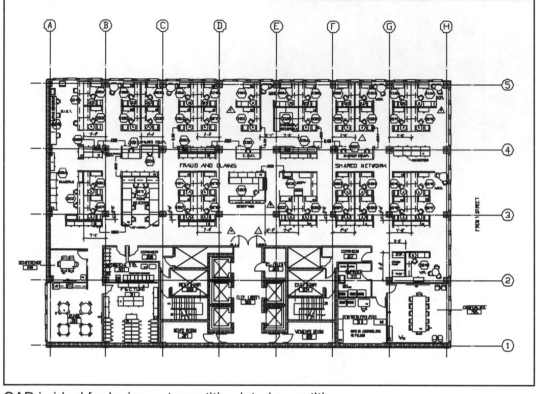

CAD is ideal for laying out repetitive interior partitions.

we don't worry about overlaps. This initial drawing is saved as a block and then reinserted; new bubbles that align are created on top of the block, then the original block is erased and the new bubble drawing is converted in a very quick process.

Mass Studies

During the preliminary design phase, the architect studies the basic massing of the project. With hand drawing, the process begins with the massing ideas, sketches, and thumbnail perspectives. Often foam board study models are made, torn apart, and remade as the designer modifies the design.

ASG Architectural has functions that let the designer quickly study the building massing. As you create walls, using either the basic WALL command or the SPACE command, you assign wall heights. The visualization

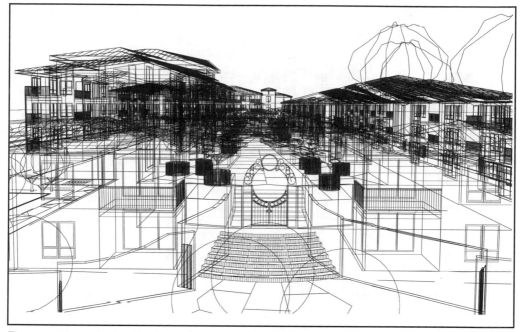

Perspective study of a housing complex prior to its hidden line removal.

commands, such as PRODUCER, EYE, EYE WALK, or EYE ROUND, let the designer easily create perspective views and walk through and around the structure. These visualization commands are further discussed in chapter 4.

Site Plans

The site plan information is developed in the programming phase, so you always start with an accurate base drawing. We draw the building masses and move them around on the site drawing. With hand drawings, we used to end up with piles of sketches; now we can save the electronic studies as drawing files for electronic review and only print out those solutions that have merit.

Parking layouts become a crucial factor during the project design. The balance among parking, building coverage, and hard and soft surfaces is crucial to the project's economic viability. In most projects, the number of parking spaces determines the area allowed for the building. Before CAD, we used to spend days on large projects simply laying out parking, trying 90-, 60-, and 45-degree angles along with other combinations to arrive at the

Housing complex with hidden lines removed.

most efficient layout. The process was time-consuming and not much fun.

ASG Architectural has a parking layout function that can save hours of time on each project. You can preset the size and the angle of the spaces. You then indicate the starting location for the row of spaces, either single or double rows, and then the ending location or the number of spaces in the row; the software draws the layout. You can adjust the location of parking rows by using the AutoCAD MOVE command. CAD is ideal for parking lot layouts.

Landscaping

During the preliminary design phase, the landscaping is diagramed. ASG Architectural's site symbols section offers a full complement of tree and bush shapes. We often use AutoCAD FILL PATTERNS to indicate the landscaped areas. The AutoCAD MULTIPLE COPY command lets you lay out a forest in seconds.

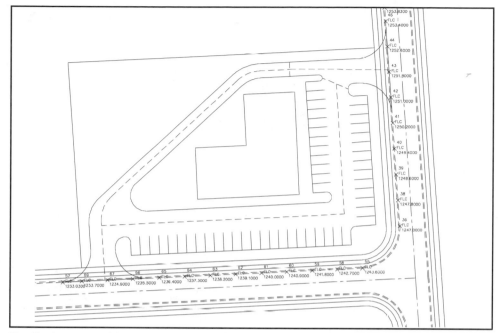

Preliminary parking layout study.

Preliminary Design Plots

CAD creates accurate drawings that tend to look like final design solutions. During the preliminary design phase, this finished appearance may not work to your advantage. At this stage, the designer is looking for feedback and wants to encourage change to improve the design. If the drawings look too complete, some people hesitate to suggest modifications.

We have found that with pen plotters you can use an old felt-tip plotter nib to make the lines look looser and less formal — more open to change. We have also used various color nibs; when we later print out the tracing, the different colors each give off a different intensity, creating a more varied visual appearance — one, again, more open to change.

Internal Design Review

During design development, the drawings are constantly being reviewed. In the past, we marked hand drawings up with a red pen and the next day a draftsperson would make the corrections. This process would be repeated until the design was acceptable. With CAD, it is most efficient to have the

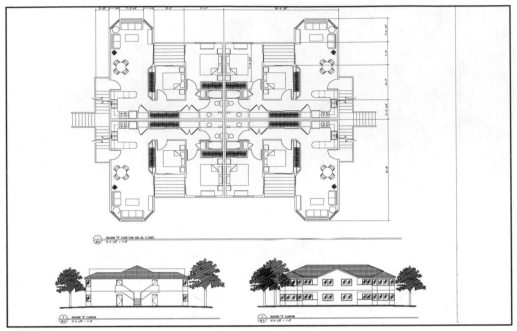

Preliminary drawings progress to design development drawings.

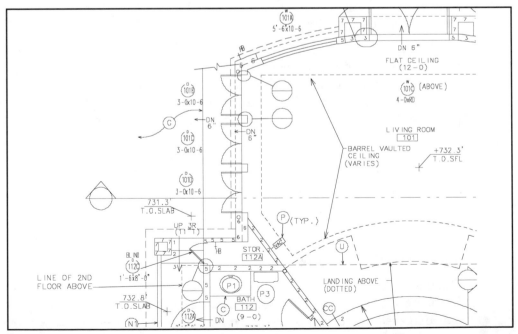

Partially completed drawing may be "marked up" electronically.

principal or project architect look at the electronic version of the solution and make the corrections directly on the drawings. At other times, we write the notes for correction on a special note layer. The draftsperson then erases the notes as he or she makes the indicated changes.

The Design Development Phase

In the design development phase, the architect makes definite decisions about all aspects of the project. The site plan is finalized and the exterior design and materials are studied and agreed upon. The interior layout and design are also determined. If the project is an interior project, the design development drawings now indicate in complete detail the layout, architectural detailing, materials, lighting, and other design elements.

This phase is a time for study. Before CAD, it often required the complete redrawing of the site plans, building plans, and the interior and exterior elevations from the preliminary design. With CAD we have found that the preliminary design drawings can usually be modified to reflect needed changes. In addition, in this phase, the architectural elements are drawn.

Walls, Doors, and Windows

Walls, doors, and windows are the basic elements of the architectural drawing. ASG Architectural gives you several ways to create these essential features. The process, which is quite simple, can be learned in minutes. Because ASG Architectural is a "mature" software product, the designers have had several years to add the many features requested by users, so don't feel overwhelmed by the multitude of options available. Just start drawing walls and inserting doors and windows by using the ASG default settings.

Default settings are "out of the box" settings selected because experience shows that most users choose these basic settings. The software could be shipped with no default setting, but this would require new users to make a number of decisions while they are still unfamiliar with the software. After you have some experience with the software, you can use the settings and toggles to set up the software to your exact specifications.

You can modify the width of the walls and set their height. You can decide if the walls should be drawn based on the centerline or on either the inside

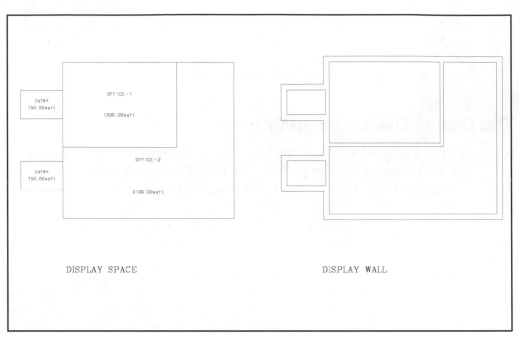

ENTRY
150.00sqft

OFFICE-1

1200.00sqft

ENTRY
150.00sqft

OFFICE-2

2100.00sqft

DISPLAY SPACE   DISPLAY WALL

Single-line diagram is automatically converted to a wall drawing.

or outside face of stud (FOS) or face of material. You can automatically indicate veneers and preselect hatching patterns. With doors, you can set the swing and the attribute, or specifications, prompts. Finally, you can also choose to draw in two or in three dimensions.

Space Diagrams

Spaces can be created (1) by defining the space by length and width or by length and square footage; (2) dynamically by forming a rectangle on the screen; or (3) free-form with lines and arcs. There are several advantages to creating spaces instead of drawing walls one at a time.

During the early design phase, you can use the space diagrams just as you would use a hand-drawn bubble diagram. Working from your program, you can quickly create the spaces in the approximate size you want and then electronically move them around until you have the most favorable layout. Just as you can save the hand-drawn studies, you can save the electronic studies either as "views" inside the drawing or as separate drawing files.

```
————————————  – – – – –        Center

————————————  – – – – –        Wall  Outer

————————————  – – – – –        Wall  Inner

════════════  – – – – –        Veneer  Outer

════════════  – – – – –        Veneer  Inner
```

The user controls wall settings.

As you work with the spaces, the lines will probably overlap. When you have your desired layout, you have several ways to convert the diagram to a floor plan with walls. First, you can use the basic WALL command and trace over the diagram. Second, you can also change the overlapping diagram to a "Block" and then lay out the space again based on the diagram, taking care not to overlap the spaces.

If the completed space diagram has been carefully created and the lines of the various diagrams do not overlap, you can take advantage of a great time saver. The software can automatically convert the space diagram to a floor plan with wall thickness. You now have the choice of an interior wall thickness and an exterior wall thickness. This feature can help you create a plan in a matter of minutes that would have taken hours to create with AutoCAD alone and even more hours if drawn by hand.

Drawing Walls

To draw walls with the pulldown interface, move the pointing device to highlight the "Architec" option on the top menu bar. When you select this

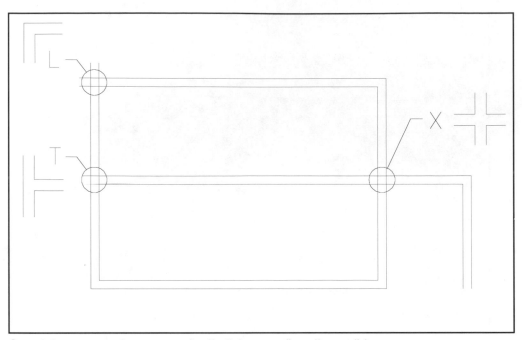

Special commands automatically "clean up" wall conditions.

heading, a pulldown menu is displayed. Select the Walls option, and the next pulldown is automatically displayed. Now select the Continuous Walls option and use the pointing device to locate the wall.

You can continue to draw wall sections until you select the Return button or the Enter key. You may toggle on and off the ORTHO command by pressing F8 or by selecting from the pulldown menu. You may draw walls in free-form, have them snap to a preset grid, or enter exact dimensions and angles. You may also draw in 2D or 3D.

Cleaning Up

Periodically, you will end up with walls that are crossing each other and the lines go through the intersection. ASG's automatic cleanup commands result in the desired intersection, as shown in the following picture.

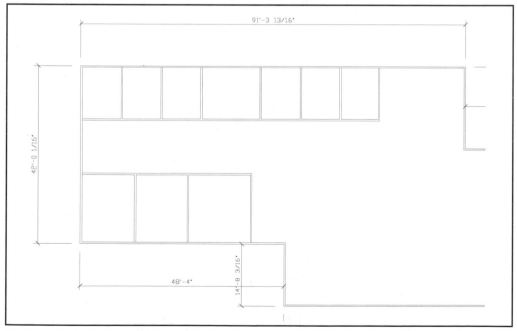

Dialog box is used to set the wall environment.

Series of chained spaces

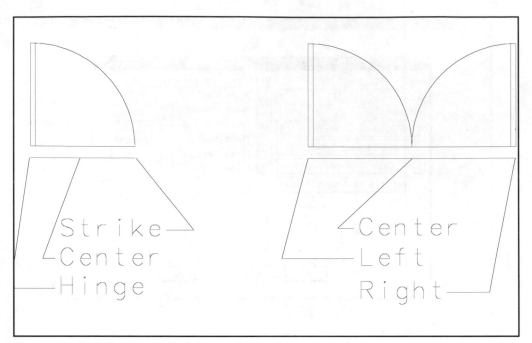

Many symbols have multiple insertion points.

Single Swing, Single Leaf Left Door	Single Swing, Single Leaf Right Door
Double Swing, Single Leaf Door	Double Swing, Single Leaf Right Door
Single Swing, Double Leaf Door	Double Swing, Double Leaf Door
Cased Opening	2-Lite Sliding Glass Left Door
3-Lite Sliding Glass Door	4-Lite Sliding Glass Door
2-Lite Sliding Glass Right Door	Garage Door
Pocket Left Door	Picket Right Door
Single Bi-fold Left Door	Single Bi-fold Right Door
Double Bi-fold Door	Window

Under many headings — for example, "Doors" — there are multiple symbols to pick from.

Wall Settings

You may draw walls based on the centerline or on the inside or outside face of material or studs. To set the wall height, width, alignment, and type, select the Wall settings dialog box.

Chaining

When you are drawing repetitive spaces, the chaining commands offer you speed. With these commands, you can easily add walls between walls and add "L" or "U" shapes. The dimensions given for the spaces created may be based on the centerline or on clear dimensions.

Doors and Windows

You can choose from two methods by which to insert the doors and windows into your drawing. You can insert these features into walls one at a time or you can select the Quick Mode option. With Quick Mode, you insert one symbolic door or window and then simply copy the symbol without stopping to actually insert the symbol into the wall. The advantage of the Quick Mode option is that you can easily COPY or ARRAY the symbol before the automatic insertion. The actual insertion operation can be done while you're on a lunch break or while you work on something else.

Just as with walls, you have a multitude of options to chose from for the actual graphic representation of doors and windows. The doors may be drawn as either two- or three-dimensional representations. The door can be shown as closed or open 45 degrees or open 90 degrees. When drawing three-dimensional doors, you can also indicate door height.

The software maintains a database on each door. Some of the data are by-products of the drawing process, such as the width and height, that is, height when it has been inserted as a three-dimensional door. The software has built in prompts to request additional door specifications. In AutoCAD, these specifications are known as "attributes." If you have indicated to the software that you want to be prompted for attributes, you will be asked for door type, door material, fire rating, thickness, door finish, frame material, frame finish, hardware group, cost, and several other attributes.

These attributes can also be used to automatically create schedules; they can be exported to database software; and they can be displayed in the drawing. ASG Architectural displays the attributes as very small notations. The

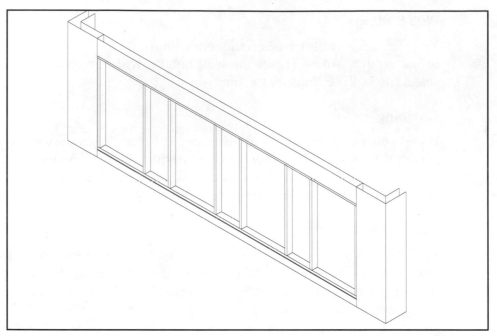

The user sets the parameters for the storefront and it is automatically drawn.

attributes, which can be found in the door number tag, are made visible to help you check the drawing at any time, plus you can check and modify them.

Storefronts

A storefront can be created between two objects or with equal spaces between the mullions or with alternating size spaces. You can insert a rectangular mullion with the dimensions of your choice or a customized shape that you have predrawn.

Roofs

ASG Architectural can create roof plans for the roof plan drawings, for the elevations sections, and for perspectives. The creation of a roof is an easy process. Simply outline the perimeter of the roof and answer the prompt for overhang, fascia depth, and slope. The roof creation is automatic.

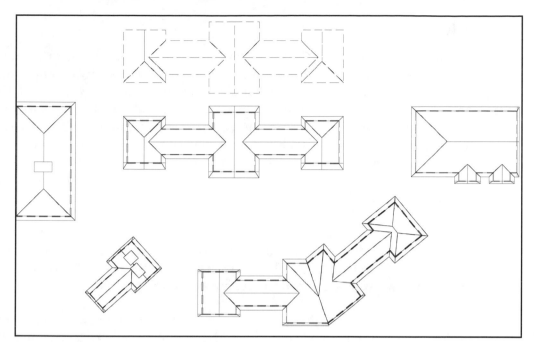

Roof studies.

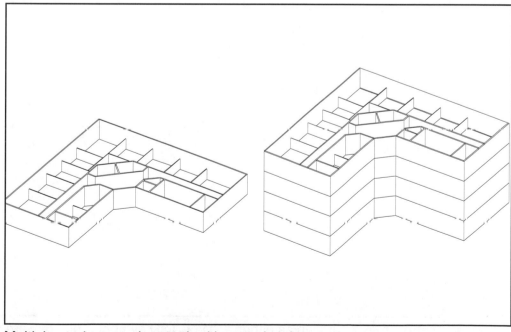

Multiple stories may be stacked in one drawing.

The Multistory Features

A few years ago, no one would ever have considered trying to create a multistory building in one drawing file on the PC. The software and hardware were not fast enough to handle large files, and the speed of the drawing manipulation would have been unacceptable. Today, the software and hardware have significantly improved in speed, and it is quite feasible to study multiple floors of a building in one drawing file. The advantages of this feature are many. Alignments can be studied, as well as the massing of the building, and presentation drawings are easy to create using the multistory features.

(**Note:** If you have created a drawing with AutoCAD AEC Architectural, you need to modify the drawing before working with the multistory features of ASG Architectural. This software automatically converts the old layers to new layers designed to accommodate the multistory features.)

Multistory is found in the Modes pulldown menu. When starting a new multistory drawing, it is easiest to first define the number of stories and the

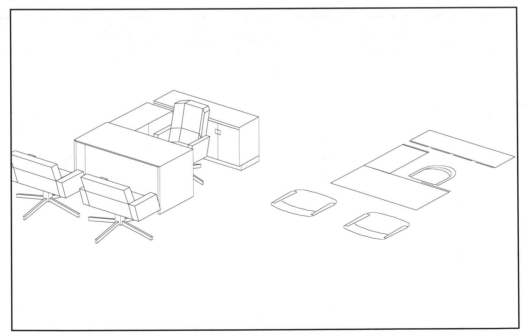

Most symbols may be drawn as either a 2D or a 3D symbol. The software will automatically convert back and forth.

floor heights. You are prompted for the floor name and its elevation above the data. For each additional floor, you are prompted for the floor-to-floor height. You can specify split or partial-height floors. After you have created a floor drawing, you can copy all or part of that drawing onto other floors.

Once the multistory building has been created, you may choose the floor that you want to work on. You can leave all the other floors visible as you work or select certain floors to be visible or display only the floor you are working on. The drawing can be dissected floor by floor and made into individual drawing files to allow for multiple drafting stations to work on the project. The individual drawing files may also be reassembled at any time to study alignments and present the multistory solution.

Symbol Insertion

ASG Architectural has a complete selection of 2D and 3D symbols, including landscaping, automobiles, boats, playing fields, plumbing, electrical, mechanical, structural, furnishings, and even people.

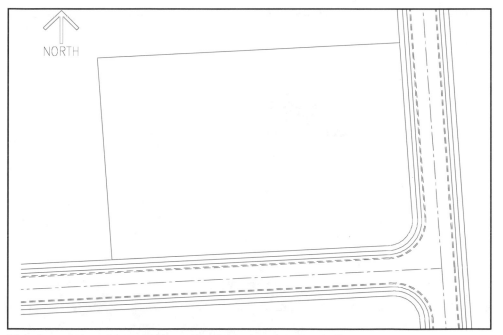

This base drawing will never need to be drawn again.

Two and Three Dimensions

One of the most powerful features of ASG Architectural is its ability to draw with either 2D or 3D symbols. An even more powerful feature is the automatic swapping of the 2D symbols for 3D, or vice versa. You can change a working drawing into a 3D presentation drawing in minutes, automatically, and you have the option of converting the whole drawing or just parts of it.

Exterior Elevations

ASG Architectural can create "draft elevations." You start with a plan that has been created with walls that have height. The software prompts you to indicate the wall that is drawn in elevation. The automatically drawn elevation can be put on the drawing you are working on or onto another drawing. You indicate the location on the sheet and the software proceeds to draw the elevation.

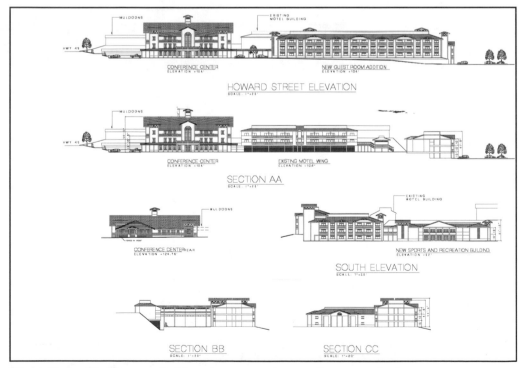

Elevations may be as simple or as complex as the user desires.

ASG Architectural contains detailed elevation symbols for doors, windows, and frames. You can also use the Pella® window and door software that was created by ASG and that is compatible with ASG Architectural. The Pella software is available to qualified design professionals at no cost from the company. An order form is included in each box of ASG Architectural. The Pella software installs realistic windows, doors, and skylights in 2D and 3D.

Consultants

During the design development process, consultants become involved in helping to determine the form and structure of the building. CAD is an ideal tool to use with consultants; it increases the accuracy of the process and decreases the time required to complete the project.

The first step in working with consultants is to give them the architectural drawings they can use both for dimensional information and for backgrounds.

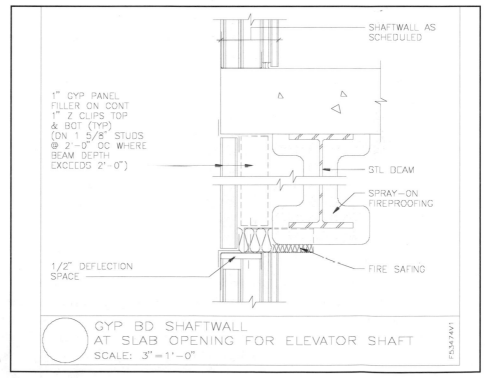

Structural detail.

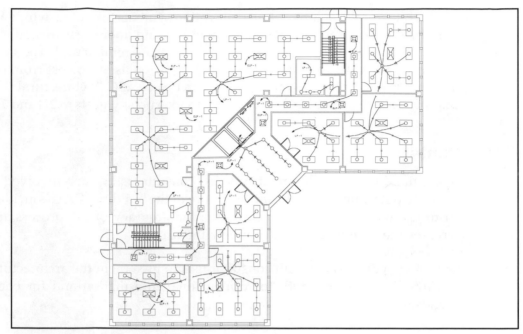

A lighting floor plan supplied by the electrical consultant.

The Civil Engineer

The civil engineer may have started the entire design process by giving you the CAD survey drawing. Now the architect sends the site design back to the civil engineer, who overlays the site drawing onto the civil drawings to study utilities, grades, streets, and boundaries. This additive process is very efficient compared with the redrawing process of hand drawing. ASG has a civil engineering series of software applications— ASG COGO, ASG TOPO, ASG Roads®, and ASG Site®— designed to automate the drawing of coordinate geometry, topography, and road design.

The Landscape Architect

The landscape architect is given both the architectural site plan as a base for the planting, irrigation, and hard-surfaces drawings and the necessary civil engineering drawings. CAD is a fantastic tool for the landscape architect, who always has to deal with repetitive elements and presentation drawings. ASG Architectural provides several landscape symbols.

The Structural Engineer

The software can draw steel, wood, and concrete shapes depending on your input. (**Note:** If you are interested in automatically creating the shapes parametrically from a data table, consider using ASG Structural®, a complete software application designed for use by both architects and structural engineers. When you draw steel shapes with ASG Architectural, you must enter height, width, flange, and web thickness. When a steel shape is drawn with ASG Structural, you are presented with the entire AISC database from which to select the steel shape. The shape is drawn automatically, to the exact dimensions stored there.)

Dimensions are crucial to the structural engineer. Using ASG Architectural, we can pass to the engineer CAD drawings that have accurate dimensions; any missing dimensions are easily determined by the DISTANCE command. Just as with the civil engineer, the structural engineer can pull the electronic architectural drawings apart to prepare the structural backgrounds. As the structural drawings are being developed, the engineer can

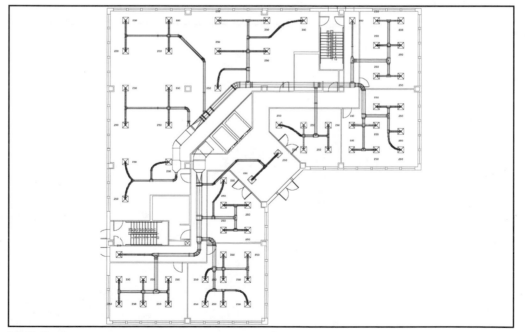

HVAC plan.

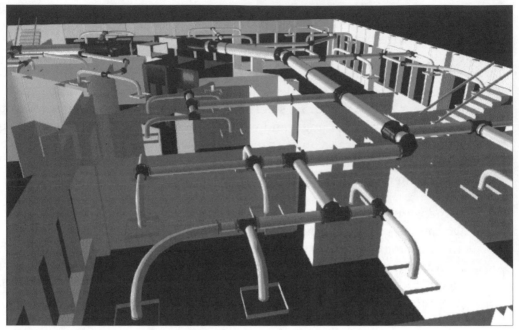

3D rendering of the HVAC system.

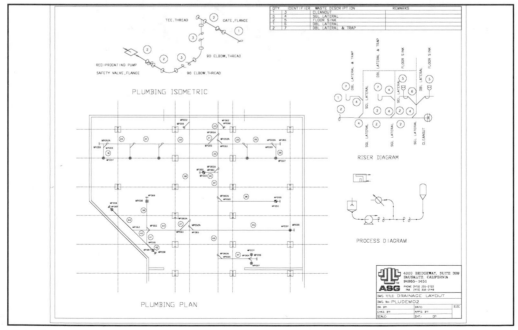

Plumbing plan.

pass electronic drawings back to the architect, which can be laid over the architectural drawings to check for conflicts.

The Electrical Engineer

The architectural drawings sometimes must show the locations of electrical receptacles, as well as telephone and lighting fixtures. An extensive library of electrical symbols is included with ASG Architectural; its set of drawings can be used by the electrical engineer to create the base electrical drawings. ASG Electrical can also be used; it was designed specifically for electrical engineers and contains hundreds of electrical symbols and automated routines, including schedule generation.

The Mechanical-HVAC Engineer

ASG Architectural contains symbols for diffusers and returns to be used in creating reflected ceiling plans. ASG Mechanical-HVAC is also available; it was designed specifically for mechanical engineers and automates the creation of heating, ventilation, and air-conditioning, or HVAC, drawings.

The Mechanical-Plumbing Engineer

ASG Architectural provides a complete set of architectural plumbing symbols. There are several automated routines for the drawing of plumbing layouts. Toilet room drawing is simplified and automated by parametric commands that create a row of toilet and urinal stalls automatically. A similar command creates the lavatory counter and automatically inserts the desired number of lavatories. ASG Mechanical-Plumbing®, created specifically for mechanical engineers, can be used in designing plumbing and fire protection systems.

The Cost Estimator

Cost estimates are required at every step of the process, beginning with the preliminary feasibility study, again during design development and contract document production to ensure that the project has stayed within the client's budget, and finally, by the contractor in the form of a bid or negotiated price prior to the start of construction. The use of CAD improves the accuracy of the estimates.

CAD easily calculates areas and keeps track of quantities, so the architect, estimator, and contractor can be more accurate in assembling the information for the estimate. ASG Estimator®, a separate conceptual estimating product designed to work with ASG Architectural, allows the designer to tag items within the drawing that are then permanently linked to a spreadsheet and R.S. Means cost database. ASG Estimator can generate, in less than ten minutes, estimates that used to take over two weeks.

Coordinating with Consultants

The use of CAD by the architect and all the consultants multiplies the advantages of CAD several times. For one thing, it is easy to distribute architectural drawings to create base drawings. When last-minute changes are made that affect the consultant's base drawings, the architect can provide new drawings that may be easily substituted for the old base information; thus conflicts can be resolved. When all the consultants have standardized on the ASG series of applications, the entire design team can be sure they are using compatible layer names and coordinated drawings.

Using CAD helps eliminate the chance of conflict. In the past, hand drawings were not accurate, so dimensions could not be scaled from the drawings. Everyone had to check and double-check long strings of dimensions. I have yet to meet an architect who would guarantee that his or her set of hand drawings contained no dimensional errors. If you draw the CAD drawing accurately — that is, if you do not override the system — the drawing is accurate, and you don't need to spend hours and hours checking dimensions.

With CAD, you won't receive that phone call from the field, after the cement for footings has already been poured, wondering if you *really* wanted a room only 6 feet long and 6 inches wide.

Chapter 4
Visualization and Presentations

"How did you create that presentation?"

Those were the first words from the design review board after we had presented our project, using electronic presentation tools. The board members — all architects — had each stood up before similar design review boards, knowing that the fate of months of work would be decided within the next few minutes, so in this review their main interest had instantly moved from the project at hand to the method we had used to make the presentation.

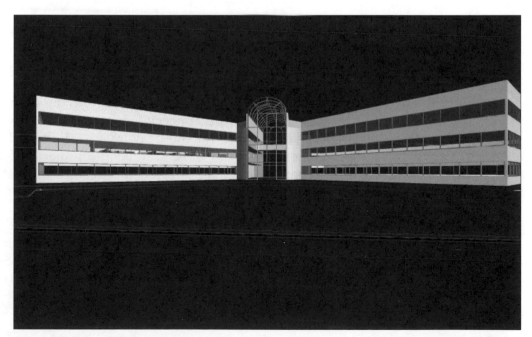

Electronic design studies are faster to create than conventional physical models or renderings.

Electronic 3D models may be easily viewed from any location.

For years, I had come to such meetings carrying rolls of colored elevations and perspectives. I would stand in front of our design, which would be pinned to the wall — several feet away from the members of the review board and even farther away from the representatives of the public. The details we had worked on for hours could only be seen by close review and thus would never be appreciated from 30 feet away. Although we had always sent copies of the drawings to the board in advance, often the members wouldn't have studied the project before the meeting. In truth, even if they had studied the design, they still lacked the personal explanations needed to understand the concept of many architectural designs.

In this case, I had used drawings at our previous meeting. The review board was ready to deny the project when I asked for a continuance to prepare a slide presentation. I was sure our design was good, but this would be my last chance.

This current session marked the first time I had arrived at a design review meeting with no colored drawings— only slides. This was early 1985 and electronic presentations were new.

The presentation easily convinced the review board to accept our design, not because we had changed it, but because this electronic presentation more clearly indicated the many facets of our project, the details, and how the project would fit into the neighborhood.

In the past, if the neighbors could not understand how the project would specifically affect them, they would give lukewarm acceptance or would oppose it. Today, with CAD, we can show them how our project will impact on their neighborhood, often gaining them as our allies in the process. Better than ever, we can now show design review boards and other city commissions more clearly how projects will affect the visual environment. The result is that our firm of Neeley/Lofrano has had more projects approved more easily than ever before— at a time when it is increasingly harder to win project approval.

After the approval of our first electronic presentation, I showed the design review board how I had created the slide presentation with video capture software. While these techniques are no longer new, such presentations are still the exception. In the future, video presentations will become standard. The rest of this chapter explores the visualization and presentation possibilities available through your computer.

Overview

CAD is a powerful tool that can be used in all phases of the architect's work. The first versions of architectural CAD software were meant to be working drawing and drafting products. As the technology improved over the years, more features were added. Today, ASG Architectural continues to be a strong drafting package, but it's now also a powerful visualization and presentation product. The early CAD users tended to be the draftspeople, but now CAD is also becoming a designer tool, with the ability to automatically create 3D geometry and the ability to easily view the design as important features.

Presentations

Often after the design development phase, or even partway through it, it is necessary to present the design for design and client reviews. However, CAD has completely changed this presentation process.

In non-CAD offices, the architect draws thumbnail perspectives for early presentations to a client. Later, the architect draws more formal

Hand sketch.

Study from a 3D model base sketch.

perspectives — sometimes plain line drawings, sometimes colored. The site plans, floor plans, and elevations are colored to show texture, colors, and shadow patterns.

These drawings are intended first to convince the designer that the design is correct, and then to show the client that it is appropriate for the project. Often the result of such client presentations is design modi-

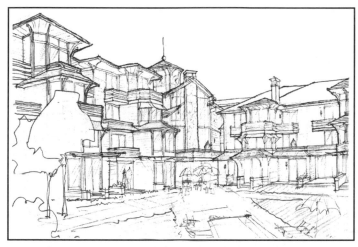

Architect's rendering based on wireframe model.

Professional rendering based on a 3D model.

fication and then another presentation. It has always seemed strange to see a large portion of our office staff spending their day coloring drawings, yet it is crucial that the client understand the project.

As a hand-drawn project proceeds, it is common to hire someone to do a professional rendering. Such drawings may be in pencil or pen, al-

Models with lines shown allow the designer to study massing.

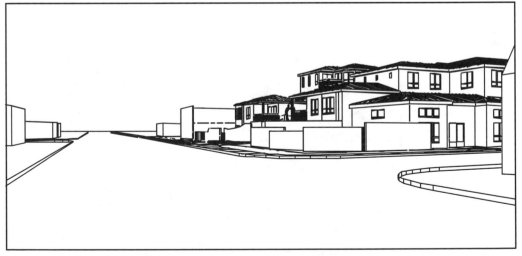

Models with hidden lines removed provide excellent representations of the design.

though most often they are in watercolor. The professional rendering shows the design, materials, and character of the project, but if the design is changed or if a change is required by a design review board, that hand-drawn perspective becomes out of date and often is rendered unusable.

Perspectives

The perspective is the traditional drawing that best represents the proposed design. The drawing can take on a multitude of representations, from the quick thumbnail sketch to the line drawing to the rendered perspective to, finally, the colored perspective drawing. Before CAD, the process of mechanically creating the accurate perspective was laborious. Often, once the layout was completed, the designer would realize that the view from another location was better and the process would begin all over again.

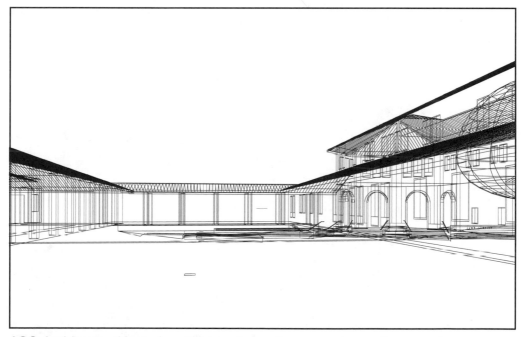

ASG Architectural includes commands to allow users to easily generate perspective views of the model.

CAD has greatly simplified this process of creating the perspective. After the 3D geometry has been created, the perspective is finished in a matter of seconds. If the location isn't right, it is simple and equally quick to select another location and flip the new perspective up on the screen. So far, the hidden lines have not been removed; you can do so by giving the AutoCAD HIDE command. The hiding process takes several seconds to several minutes, depending on the size of the drawing and the hardware you are using.

The perspectives can be used as the equivalent of thumbnail sketches or they can be used as presentation perspectives. Many architects use the CAD perspective as a base drawing for their hand-drawn perspective, a process that saves hours of work that would have been required for a mechanical layout. Colored drawings can also be created with the use of AutoCAD AutoShade® or ASG Model Vision®. You can animate the

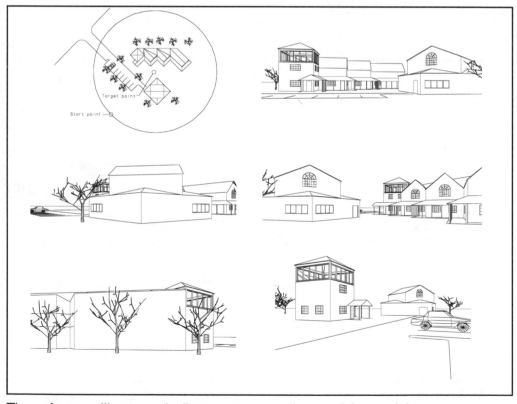

The software will automatically generate a walkaround the model.

geometry with Autodesk's AutoFlix®, 3D Studio®, or Animator® or again with ASG Model Vision.

The EYE Command

When you are designing with ASG Architectural, you have access to several commands in ASG Core that simplify the creation of quick perspective studies. These EYE commands let you pick a point you want to look *toward* and then a point you'd like to look *from*. Automatically, the perspective jumps into view on the screen. The default settings place both your "eye" and the target at 60 inches — an approximate average height for the human viewpoint — above the current base plane. For example, if you are on the fourth floor, your "eye" is thus 60 inches above that floor. You can modify the floor you are on, the target height, the height of the "eye," and even the "focus" of the lens.

The EYE WALK Command

To evaluate the design during the design process, you will often want to study several views. The EYE WALK command automatically displays step-by-step views along a straightline path between the target and the viewpoint location of the "eye." The perspective views can either display or remove hidden lines. You may also have each step, or frame, shaded using AutoShade. You determine the number of steps created, and the more steps, the smoother the animation.

Depending on the complexity of the drawing, this automatic process may take several minutes or several hours. You can also indicate that you want to create a script file, which you can then play back to study the design. With this process, you can study massing and space.

The EYE ROUND Command

The EYE ROUND command is similar to EYE WALK, but instead of steps along a straight line, the steps are taken around a circle that you draw around the target, as shown in the previous picture. The camera always looks toward the target point. For interior perspectives, draw a small circle around the target location; for exterior perspectives, draw a circle around the building. Once again, you determine the number of steps or viewpoints that will be taken. You can create a script file to play back the animation.

The model may be further enhanced with rendering software.

AutoShade®

Autodesk's AutoShade is a software color shading product that imports 3D geometry from an AutoCAD drawing and shades an image that appears in perspective view. AutoShade is relatively easy to use and produces images that will help you and your client better understand the design.

AutoCAD Animator®

You can import AutoCAD AutoShade drawings into Animator, which sequentially replays the AutoShade images, animating your design presentation. The introduction of Autodesk 3D Studio and ASG Model Vision, with substantially higher quality images, provides more appropriate tools for the creation of architectural animations.

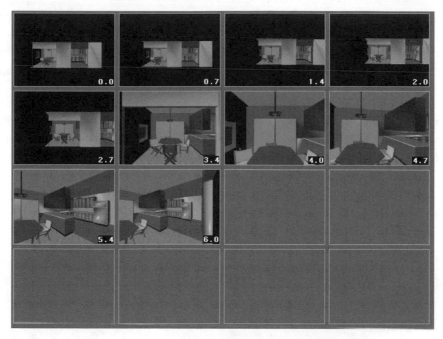

The rendered model may be animated for a spectacular presentation.

ASG Model Vision®

ASG Model Vision is a rendering and animating software application that lets you put together photorealistic renderings based on the geometry produced by ASG applications and AutoCAD drawings. The interface has been designed to allow ease of use. This software creates spectacular renderings and animations for your design studies and client presentations. With ASG Model Vision, you may texture map surfaces, show reflections, have shadows, or animate within the animation. You may even set the feeling within the rendering and animation by controlling lighting, light color, and even fog.

The primary use of ASG Model Vision is to animate your design presentations. Simply indicate the path through the space within your Auto-CAD drawing, using the application ASG Producer®, found within ASG

Core. You can have the camera rotate and tilt as it follows the path and you change the lens aperture. After the path is drawn, the information is transferred into ASG Model Vision software, where the animation is created. When the automatic process ends, you can play back the animations.

With ASG Model Vision, you may animate objects within the animation: doors can open; automobiles can move; and the assembly of parts can be demonstrated. Using this feature, you can represent the reality of the design, study the spaces, study textures, and move yourself and objects within the spaces. It's not yet quite Disney quality, which takes approximately one person year per minute of animation, but it adds the spark of life that captures the interest of the human eye.

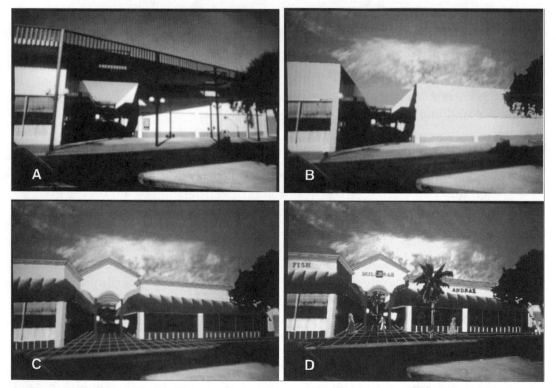

A: Existing building. B: Electronically cut away unwanted sections of existing building and addition of background sky. C: Electronically add proposed architectural elements. D: Electronically add people and signage.

Video Capture

As you work with AutoCAD, you are dealing with vector-based drawings. When a line is drawn from one point in space that has exact coordinates to another point that has yet another set of exact coordinates, these exact locations are recorded in the database. The coordinates are phrased as numerical locations so that you can summon up the exact length, angle, and slope of any line.

When you look at an AutoCAD drawing, the software builds the drawing lines up from the database. Therefore, it can be viewed from any location in space. Clearly, however, as the drawing becomes more complicated— such as one tree elaborating into a forest! — the number of locations that the software must maintain and that the computer must manipulate becomes ever greater, eventually exceeding the capacity of present-day computers.

This overload problem is recognized by software designers. Thus, they have developed another approach to dealing with computer graphics that is not based on vectors or on a numerical database. This system is similar to television. On your television or monitor, at any given moment thousands of dots, or pixels, display a color. The computer or television signal indicates which dots will be which color. The result is either a still video picture or a motion video picture, and the images are known as *raster images* or *pixel images*.

The image you see has been predetermined by camera location. You can't, in short, summon a video image onto a monitor screen showing the east side of a building and then tell the computer to show you the building from a point 50 feet to the right unless someone has already taken a picture from 50 feet to the right. (With vector-based graphics, though, the computer has absorbed the entire database of the building, so it can grant you this request.)

The advantage of rasters or pixels is that they can handle the picture of the tree or the forest. Every picture is of equal complexity to the raster/pixel system. It simply lights up the dots on the monitor screen with the correct colors. With raster graphics — often referred to as "paint and video capture" — you can set spectacular graphic results.

Laser cutter creating model piece.

The finished model.

For example, with a "paint" package, you can create a foreground using a green base color, a background using a blue, and, presto— you have a field with a blue sky. Let's say your design is for a schoolhouse building. You can locate a red square on the horizon line, put a red triangle on top of the red square, and you have a "little red schoolhouse." You can add text with a yellow line to label your drawing. If you like, you can now go in and modify individual dots.

Depending on your skill and time, you can make the field look just like grass, dot the sky with beautiful white clouds, and give your schoolhouse clapboard siding, windows, doors, and even shadows— although this is possible, really only artists can use the paint package in this manner.

Using the same example, you can take the first drawing of the schoolhouse with the blue sky and green grass and easily modify the image with *actual* video pictures. You can go outside with a video camera and take a picture of the sky, a grass field, and a red schoolhouse, then you cut in the *real* pictures.

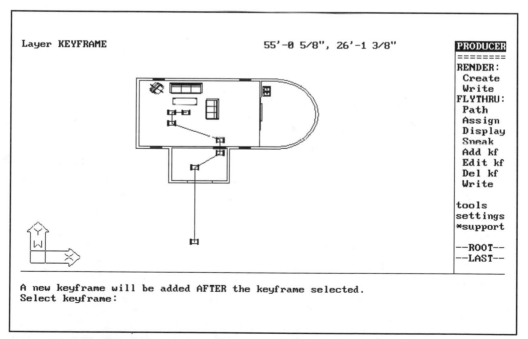

Plan with animation path.

If you now want to show your design but the project is not yet built, you
have several options. You can build a model or make a sketch and take
a video image of that model or sketch, and then cut this image into the
image of the sky or field. Once the image is in the drawing, you can color,
tint, or even add other images. Maybe your schoolhouse isn't out in the
country but in an urban setting. This is easy to handle: simply go to the
site and photograph it from the angle at which you want to show your
building.

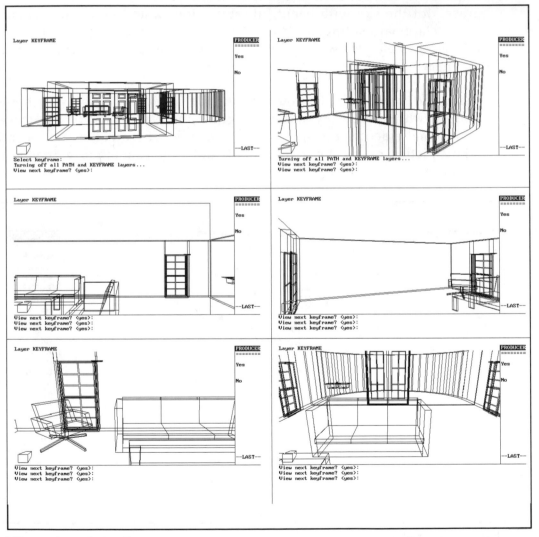

Views along the path.

There is, in fact, an easier approach than building a physical model or drawing a sketch of the school: create the drawings of the building with ASG Architectural. Photograph the site and transfer the image to the video capture software. Pinpoint the view on your CAD drawing and use the EYE command to display a perspective view. Capture this line drawing and cut it into the background drawing; use the paint program to color the perspective.

Better yet, after you have set the viewpoint, create a colored rendering automatically with AutoShade or ASG Model Vision and put that image into the background drawing. With this approach, you can quickly create very realistic images that show your design in context to the environment.

Models

While this chapter has been discussing electronic images, CAD can also provide you with physical models. The traditional model sometimes has advantages over the rendering or animation, because it can be studied from millions of vantage points by many people and can be used to great advantage for presentations and sales. Mass — real physical mass — has an aspect of liveliness and life that is hard to reproduce in electronic models.

With CAD drawings, you no longer need to cut model pieces by hand. The CAD drawing can be used to drive a laser that cuts out the entire model from illustration board or from Plexiglas. Pieces can be cut out with very fine detail. The laser power can be reduced and then used to etch texture on the surface of the material. The laser cutter moves at a rate of several inches per second and can quickly cut out a model.

CAD and Visualization

Electronic data forms the foundation for spectacular presentations. Animation will increase the quality of building design more than any other single CAD tool. Designers now can pretest their designs; the clients can preview the designs and provide more meaningful critiques; and review agencies can make more informed decisions because they have more graphical information.

I have designed buildings and spaces for years and have always thought that I had an excellent sense of the spaces being designed— but now I study the spaces and buildings with ASG Model Vision and I'm frankly convinced that animation is the most useful tool ever made available to the designer. This kind of preview for our designs prompts us to improve our designs in new ways. In the old days, these changes would not have been made; the failures would have been frustrating to acknowledge as we walked through the completed project. No more! Animation is the single greatest factor in this improvement.

Chapter 5
Contract Documents

"CAD is the ultimate overlay drafting system."

"With CAD you start the contract document phase with a running start."
—Contract managers on an architectural design team

In the traditional architecture practice, the contract document phase started with a redrawing to reflect the final decisions made in the design development phase. If the contract document phase did *not* start with new drawings, you often had to erase almost as much as you drew. With CAD, you can use the ERASE, STRETCH, TRIM, ROTATE, MOVE, and COPY commands to modify the design development drawings in order to start the contract document phase. Thus, much of the drawing is already done by the time you begin the contract work.

The purpose of the contract document phase is to generate the drawings, schedules, and specifications that let building departments check the drawings and let contractors estimate, bid, and build the structure. The design development drawings show design, materials, and spatial relationships; the contract documents add dimensions, notes, and details.

Now schedules are created for doors, windows, finishes, hardware, plumbing, lighting, beams, columns, reinforcing bars, landscaping materials, duct work, and many other items. The specifications describe in minute detail both the materials and the process to be used in supplying, storing, assembling, and applying the materials.

Dimensions

Dimensioning the drawing is simple and accurate with CAD. The Auto-CAD OSNAP commands accurately locate the dimension points. Auto-CAD gives you the choice of a running dimension or repetitive dimensions from the same base point. Dimensions can also be made at an angle. AutoCAD has associative dimensioning, which means that if you STRETCH the length of a room and if you have included the actual dimension text in the window of the items to be STRETCHed, the dimension is automatically recalculated and the new text displayed.

You have the option of setting the design of the tick mark and the location of the dimension text. Before AutoCAD puts the dimension into the drawing, you are given the chance to override the calculated dimension. However, *never* override the calculated dimension without the clear understanding that you could be defeating the inherent accuracy of the CAD drawing.

Notes

There are several different recommendations on the best way to annotate the drawings. Some architects put their notes next to the object being noted and then point to the object with a leader line with an arrowhead. Other architects use numbers or alphabet letters near the object and again use an arrow to point to the object; then they organize the notes in one location on the drawing.

In a variation of this latter "keynoting" technique, known as CON DOC®, the note near the object uses a specification number that refers to standard notes found both on the drawing and in a standard notebook. The notes are numbered to correspond to the CSI format and are also consistent with the numbering used in the specifications.

All of these forms of notation are possible with ASG Architectural. Notes can easily be typed and placed near the object. The command prompts you for the start and end points of the pointer line and automatically places an arrowhead at the end. If you want to use numerical or alphabetic notes you are prompted to give the letter or number and then the pointer line and the arrowhead locations.

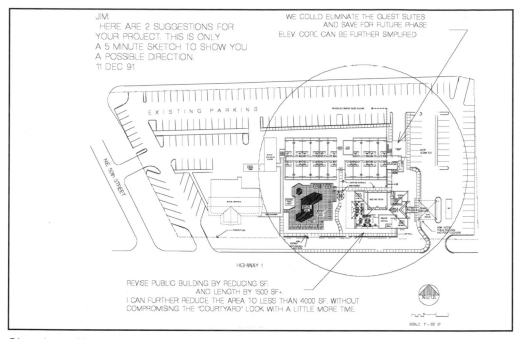

Site plan with client's electronic design review notes.

You are next asked if you want to write the note in the place that you had chosen on the drawing for writing notes. If you answer yes, you are automatically moved to the note area, where you can write your comments. Then you are asked if you want to move back to the last drawing area; if you answer yes, you are returned to your drawing.

At times, you may want to use standard notes that are typical for your office as it wastes time to type these out for every project or every sheet. ASG Core has a "Text In" and "Text Out" feature that lets text be brought into the drawing from an outside text file. This feature is extremely useful, as you also can take text out of the drawing, modify the text using a text editor, and then bring the text back into the drawing.

Using "Data Link" (found in ASG Core) you may dynamically link the note to the objects in the drawing. After creating the link, when you select a note the objects in the drawing connected to it will be highlighted. Also, if you use Data Link to create your note table, when you add a new note the table will automaticaly be regenerated with the note inserted in the correct position.

Qty	Description	Manufacturer	Part Number	Lamp Type
4	FL. FIXT. - 1X4	LITHUANIA	1PM2-2CF30-12	F20BX/SPX32
15	FL. FIXT. - 2X2	LITHUANIA	2PM4-2CF40-26	F40BX/SPX35
5	FL. FIXT. - 2X2 EM	LITHUANIA	2PM6-4CF60-18	F40BX/SPX45
85	FL. FIXT. - 2X4	LITHUANIA	2PM3-2CF40-16	F40BX/SPX35
10	FL. FIXT. - 2X4 EM	LITHUANIA	2PM4-3DF40-20	F40BX/SP63A
11	INCAND. FIXT. - CLG. MT	HIGHTECH	28401	15W A15
6	INCAND. FIXT. - WALL MT	WIEGHTOLIER	7052	(1)100WT4 CLR LMP

⊡	2X2 Standard Fluorescent Fixture	⊚	Junction Box - Ceiling Mount
⊙	2X4 Standard Fluorescent Fixture	⊏	Panelboard Flush Mount
⊏⊙⊐	1X4 Standard Fluorescent Fixture	‖	Double Conduit Tick Mark
⊠	2X2 Emergency Fluorescent Fixture	⫯	Single Conduit Tick Mark with Neutral
⊠	2X4 Emergency Fluorescent Fixture	⫲	Double Conduit Tick Mark with Neutral
○	Ceiling Incandescent Fixture	⫲	Double Conduit Tick Mark with Switch Leg
⊢○	Wall Incandescent Fixture		

A light fixture schedule.

Schedules and Attributes

The single most powerful feature of CAD is not its ability to draw lines—but its ability to attach attributes, or specifications, to an object in the drawing. As you work, you are creating both graphic and alphanumeric databases. You are also creating schedules for doors, windows, lighting fixtures, plumbing fixtures, and many other building components. These alphanumeric data can be extracted from the drawing and collected into a database or a text file or even diffused back into the drawing and plotted out on the drawing sheet.

In the coming years, the database aspect of CAD will flex more and more muscle. Some ASG products already let you modify the database and redraw automatically with the database changes now incorporated into the drawing.

With ASG Architectural, several symbols have preassigned attributes that you may elect to have prompted. You can insert a symbol and (1)

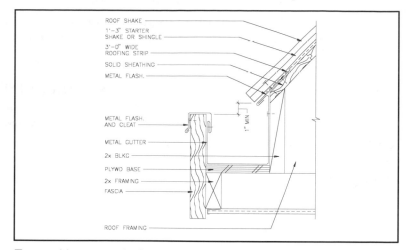

Eave with concealed gutter, and wood shakes.

not be prompted for attributes, (2) be prompted for some attributes, or (3) be prompted for all the preassigned attributes.

You may also modify the attribute prompts and add your own. For example, you can insert a door by indicating only the width and the height, if the 3D toggle is turned on. You can also have the software prompt you for the door number or designation, or you can switch on all the attributes and be prompted for the door type, finish, fire rating, glass type, frame type, frame finish, hardware group, and cost. By making your selection from the settings menu, you control which prompts are requested.

With ASG Architectural, you can choose to be prompted for specification information when you insert doors, windows, plumbing fixtures, structural elements, lighting fixtures, appliances, and furnishings. This information can be automatically arranged into a schedule by ASG Architectural and printed on notebook paper or plotted onto the drawing.

Details

ASG Architectural is primarily designed to create plans, elevations, and sections. Other ASG applications may be used to create complete sets of details. ASG Structural® contains hundreds of components for structural and architectural detailing, including the complete AISC database, wood members, reinforcing steel, and other components.

ASG Detailer™ is designed to create architectural details by selecting and arranging components; it contains more than 20,000 components. Attached to each are CSI numbers, standard notes, and information about the component. ASG Dynamic Details™ are complete predrawn details for hundreds of conditions, such as window, door, roof, and wall details, in both wood and metal construction. The user is able to modify details and create his or her own detail libraries.

Cover Sheet

ASG Architectural offers several features that help you compose and fill in the information that is found on a cover sheet. The software includes box makers that can be used to include location maps, city information, or consultant names. One box is designed to automate your creation of the list of drawings.

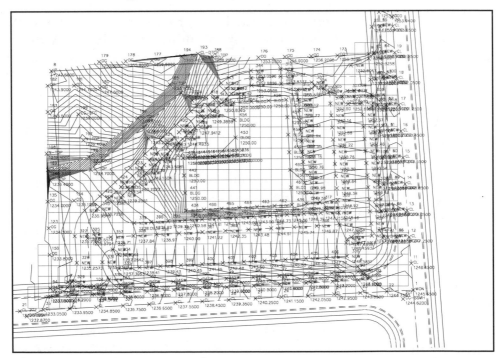

Topographic drawing done with ASG TOPO.

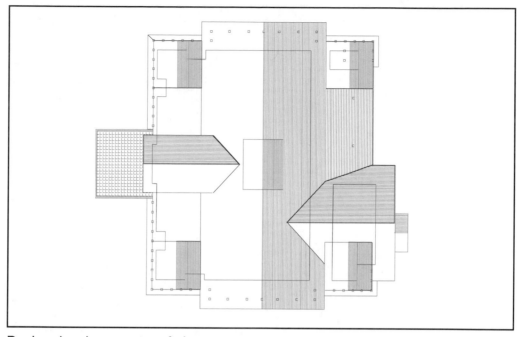

Design developement roof plan.

Site Plans

The site plan is brought into the contract document phase full of information from the previous phases. Now you add notes on slopes for
drainage, utility information, construction phasing information, and
references to details. ASG COGO, TOPO, ASG Roads®, and ASG Site®
planning are available for professionals doing this type of work.

Roof Plans

If you have used the roof-generating feature of the software, the roof
plan is now graphically complete. In the contract document phase, you
add notes on material, slopes, and detail designations. You also indicate
the location for penetrations and any mechanical equipment mounted
on the rooftop.

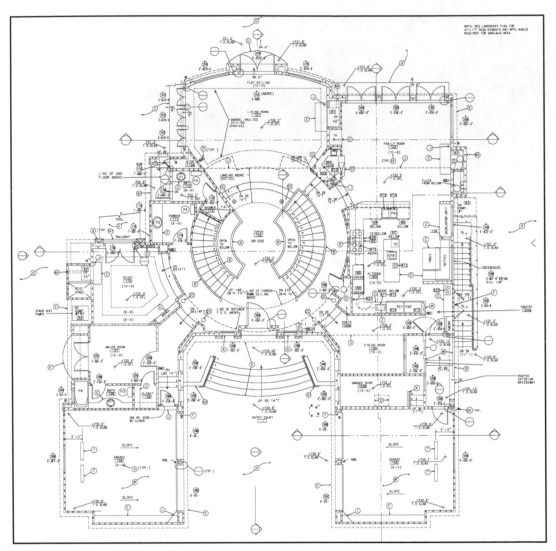

The drawing progresses from the preliminary design to design development to contract documents.

Floor Plans

In addition to notes, detail designations, and dimensions, you can add hatching to the walls to differentiate wall types in the contract phase. The wall-hatching function included with the software is quite simple to use.

Exterior elevation.

Sometimes one section of the plan has considerable detail but the draw-ing scale doesn't let you clearly indicate this detail. In this case, you need to "draw" the particular area at a larger scale. With CAD, the process is easy because all you do is copy the designated area and then plot it out at a larger scale. If you are using AutoCAD Release 10 or lower, it is best to copy the area on a different sheet and let the scale of the entire sheet be of the larger scale. With the AutoCAD Release 11 and 12, you now can easily mix drawings of different scales in the same drawing file or drawing sheet.

Exterior and Interior Elevations

ASG Architectural can create the layout lines for elevations based on the plans when you have drawn the 3D wall, doors, and windows. First, you must put a window around the part of the drawing to be transferred to the elevation, and then indicate if the elevation is to be drawn on the drawing you are working on or on another sheet. Next, indicate the location the drawing is to occupy. The drawing is then automatically created. You can have door and window details added by selections from the software.

Sections

Just as you could designate the information to be included in the exterior and interior elevations, so can you also indicate a section line through the drawing. AutoCAD software then creates a section of your design. As with the elevation routines, you indicate where the section is to be drawn and the direction of the cut; the section is then drawn automatically.

Reflected Ceiling Plans

ASG Architectural has a complete set of functions to automate the creation of reflected ceiling plans. Use the floor plan to create the background drawing. The ceiling grid function can insert a grid ceiling into a room. The software also provides symbols for light fixtures, air supplies, and returns.

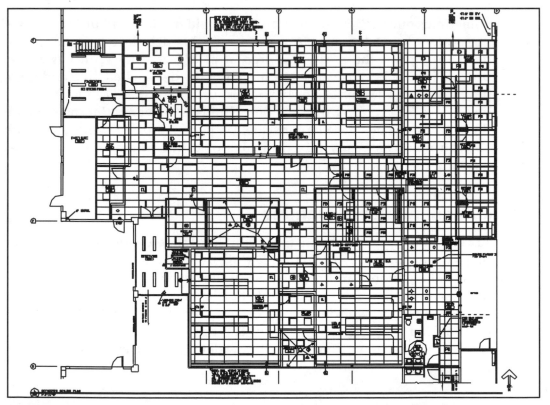

The floor plan drawing is the background for the reflected ceiling drawing.

Chapter 6
Facilities Management

Combining CAD and the database created from the CAD drawings with facilities management software is one of the best and most intensive uses of automation that will flourish in the coming years.

Background

The cost of the building design and construction — that cost about which all designers and owners spend so much time worrying — is less than 10% of the cost of operating the building over a 40 year life span. Facilities management is, in fact, one of the major operations of "big business."

Most companies have much of their capital tied up in buildings they own or rent. Equipment and furnishings add another major investment to their balance sheets, yet most companies today do not know how much space they rent or own, where the people sit, how much equipment they own, where it is, or when it must be maintained. They should know this information.

The term *facilities management* is a catchall phrase that has as many definitions as there are facilities. To the architect, it means area calculations, department layouts, employee locations, and equipment inventories. To the electrical engineer, it means dealing with energy use and equipment maintenance. To the mechanical engineer, the operation of the facility, energy usage, repairs, and preventive maintenance. To the owner of the building it means repainting, leasing information, taxes, and depreciation. To the tenant, it means employees, equipment and furnishings, growth and shrinkage, telecommunications systems, and everything connected with the tenant's operations

Facilities management is the collection, storage, and manipulation of data about the physical facilities, the existing conditions, and changes expected in the future. The quantity of data needed is staggering— and it must be coordinated well among the various players. Surprisingly, at the end of construction, everything about the structure is known by only a relatively few people. For example, the architect and the contractors truly "know" the facility, but in traditional practice, they now roll up the drawings and move on to their next projects.

At this point, the facilities manager unrolls the drawing and opens the specifications and equipment manuals and sets out to manage the facility, hoping that he or she doesn't miss anything "big." The tenant moves in and adds walls, requiring modifications to the electrical and mechanical systems. Sometimes these changes are noted; sometimes not. Over time, remodeling changes even the changes— and often all knowledge of what is owned and how it works is lost.

The area requirements, furnishings, and equipment of the tenant often follow much the same twisty path. Departments overflow beyond their original boundaries, others shrink, and soon the original areas devoted to specific departments become a mystery. Equipment and furnishings are bought, need maintenance, or break; equipment is hauled off; new equipment is leased or purchased; and soon accurate information is no longer available.

Accurate knowledge of what is owned, however, is crucial for management decisions and the economic operation of the company. I know of several firms that purchased vast quantities of furnishings only to later find out that they already had warehouses full of furnishings stashed away; others have rented space only to find out that they already had space or that another department was being reduced and a month later the space would have been available.

Not only are there many definitions of facilities management, but there are equally as many different approaches as to whom should be in charge of the department. In some companies, it is managed by the accounting firm; in others, it is managed by the database expert; in still others, it is managed by someone familiar with construction or architecture.

No matter what the background of the manager, each one is looking for a better way to perform his or her responsibilities. Here CAD is proving to be very helpful indeed.

Facilities Management and CAD

The one thread that ties the entire facilities management process together is the need to collect, store, and manipulate data. The computer is good at storing and manipulating data, while CAD is good at collecting graphic data. Before CAD, graphic information belonged to the world of the draftsperson, but with CAD, this is no longer true. CAD is easy to use when set up properly, and graphic information is often easier to understand than textual information.

Adjacency Requirements

The first step in facility design is to list the required spaces and to then organize them with the optimum adjacency relationships. CAD can help in this process in a number of ways. Several software products available allow you to create an adjacency matrix and then sort the spaces into an optimum layout. An adjacency matrix is a layout or map of what must or must not be adjacent to something else — for example, some codes require that kitchens and bathrooms be separated by halls. Use the basic CIRCLE command to create bubbles and label them. Colors can be assigned to represent different uses. You can use the SPACE to WALL commands of the ASG Architectural application to accurately create bubbles of the correct size.

Stacking and Blocking

The term stacking refers to the layout of the spaces on several floors of a multifloor building. The optimum layout uses each floor to maximum efficiency while putting the uses or departments in the best places. Most designers do this by hand, although several software applications can automate the process. Interviews with designers and facilities managers make clear that the optimum product has not yet reached the market. A desirable one would put the departments on the appropriate floor based on adjacency needs, the projected growth of the use or department, and its relationship to the elevators.

The term blocking refers to the layout of spaces on a given floor based on adjacency requirements. Most designers still do this process manually. However, several software programs automate the process. The better programs take into account the layout of the building and the core

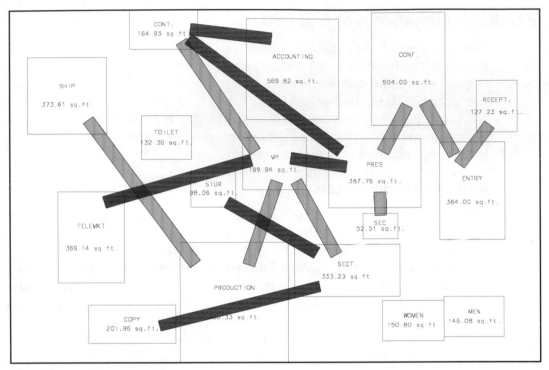

Stacking and blocking diagram.

space. In the coming years, great advances in blocking programs will decrease the time necessary for blocking design.

Attributes

Today, thousands of ASG users are entering facilities information into the CAD system. This ability to add attributes to items in the CAD drawing is the basis of CAD facilities management. As a symbol is inserted into the system, you may also add textual information to the symbol either automatically or manually. If the system has been programmed to add information automatically, the attributes or specifications are added to the database. For instance, if the symbol is a specific chair and the attributes are already attached to the symbol, every time you put the chair into the drawing the database adds the chair information automatically.

You can also insert a generic chair and then preset the software to prompt you for information about it. For example, when you insert a chair and have turned on the attribute prompting, ASG Architectural asks you to enter information on the manufacturer, model, size, color, and several other items about the chair. You have the option of answering all the questions or only those that interest you or you can modify the prompts to ask only the questions of interest.

You can search either the database or the drawing. With our chair example, you can either search the database or you can select the chair in the drawing and display the attributes on the monitor screen.

Users can insert any imaginable object into drawings and attach attributes to these symbols. On walls, you can indicate the assembly, finishes, and even paint colors or mixing formulas. Ceilings can carry information about the mounting height, assembly, and finishes. Floors can include information about the area of the space and finishes. Symbols for structural, plumbing, lighting, furnishings, equipment, electrical, and mechanical elements are all included in ASG applications, and you can easily add additional unique symbols.

Area Calculations

One of the major reasons for using CAD to manage facilities is its ability to accurately calculate areas. Throughout my architectural career before CAD, we used to have several employees each calculate the area of the project building and then average the results to get the information we put on the drawings. To make matters even worse, areas must be calculated differently for (1) the building department, (2) the planning department, (3) the contractor, and (4) leasing.

Each calculation must be accurate because errors can have terrible results. I've talked to several landlords who have been startled to learn that they have been undercharging on rent for years because of inaccurate area calculations; it's even worse when the tenant discovers that he or she has overpaid for years. In large buildings, area errors have amounted to tens of thousands of square feet.

Standard Facilities

Many facilities managers and designers work on projects that have a well-defined scope. These users often create standard facilities documents for plans, details, and equipment. Many projects can be modified slightly to meet site-specific details without making major changes.

In such cases, the AutoCAD's STRETCH and TRIM commands may be all that's needed. Companies that have standardized retail stores are logical users of CAD and realize substantial savings. Standardized kitchen and laboratory designs are also logical CAD projects. With attributes attached to equipment, it is easy to make equipment changes; related schedules are automatically created from the drawings.

AutoCAD also allows sophisticated programming that can create drawings with minimal or no drawing input. This approach is ideal for an employee who is not trained in drafting. Software has also been written that automatically creates plans and elevations and even assembles details based on a question-and-answer sheet.

Facilities managers who work with repetitive projects can now get graphic information without needing a draftsperson to enter and modify the information. With automated applications, the attributes attached to symbols in the drawing can be modified by changing the database table, with the resulting changes made in the drawings.

In the area of facilities management, spectacular applications are about to step over the threshold. These software applications are already providing new opportunities for professional designers. By creating your drawings, schedules, and specifications electronically, you will have the foundation of information that will allow you to be involved with the management of your creations.

Chapter 7
Zooming In on the Future of CAD

We have just begun to see the changes that are being brought into our lives by the PC workstation and CAD. The designing, building, and management process has traditionally been a fragmented process filled with hundreds of players working with bits of information. Sometimes the information is correctly passed from one player to the next, but, more often, it has to be rediscovered by each person as he or she needs it.

For example, a client may ask for a certain size window in a room and the architect draws that window. The mechanical engineer later measures the window and looks up the type of glass to determine the heat gain. An electrical engineer measures the window and looks up the type of glass to determine the contribution from natural lighting and the artificial lighting necessary in the room. The structural engineer repeats the process to calculate the weight of the window on the building frame and the wind load on the window. The contractor measures the window and looks up the type of frame and the type of glass to estimate the cost for the bid.

Later, the fabricator repeats the process to manufacture the window and to cut the glass. At the job, the carpenter looks for the window schedule for the size of the rough opening and—because he or she has had past bad experiences with schedule accuracy—also checks the window size with the manufacturer. Finally, after the window is installed, the blind installer visits the site and measures the window before making the blinds. If the window ever breaks, the glass installer drives out to measure the window to cut the new glass.

Repeat this process — or a similar one — for each and every item in a building and you have an accurate picture of the inefficiencies associated with traditional non-CAD design, construction, and facilities management. Imagine the cost savings of a reliable storage location for the accurate information about the window and all the rest of the building parts. That's what CAD offers.

Before CAD, these cost savings were unattainable because the data storage contained only alphanumeric information and not graphic information, which is necessary to indicate location, exposure, geometry, and relationships to other elements. Today, we are just at the beginning of database developments. The bad news is stepping-stones are still being placed on the path. The good news is that we can use parts of the path as soon as they are completed.

In the near future, a master database will be ready to be filled in as statistical or graphical information is added. There is a proper location for every bit of information, just as if the CAD program were an electronic file cabinet. Once that information is put in, you will be able to access and update it throughout the entire design, construction, and management process. The amount of control you will gain will be enormous; the quantitative gains will be so great that we will truly be moving into a new era.

Into the Time Machine

When I entered the University of California in 1962 to begin my education in architecture, the computer and the automation of the architectural design and drafting process were not even remote concerns. Architecture had been practiced virtually unchanged for thousands of years. I knew I had much to learn about design, color, textures, materials, manufacturers' products, engineering, drawing and drafting, and the profession of architecture. Clearly, it was a profession of both creative ability and experience.

Around 1965, several of my classmates started taking computer classes. I saw them writing routines and transferring their work to cardboard punch cards that they would take to the computer center; they would hand their cards through a window so that the operator could run their programs. In 1965, however, computers still had no place in my study of architecture.

Less then 25 years later, the PC has changed the practice of architecture forever. The profession will never be the same. Architectural education will change in the near future, and your practice, if it has not already started to change, will certainly be altered in the next few years. The changes will be for the better and the changes will be dramatic.

While writing this chapter, the main question I asked myself was, "How far into the future should I look?" Obviously, 25 years from now, the computer will have caused changes so revolutionary that they are impossible to predict. Twenty-five years is thus too far forward to have any real meaning today. Also, who will remember then if I was right or wrong? As recently as 1992, a ten-year projection would have been my choice, but some events that I thought would not occur for several more years have already touched down! The future is flying toward us even faster than I had ever imagined, so this chapter looks only six to eight years into the future.

As noted, architecture is a profession that requires creative ability, knowledge, and experience. The PC gives you tools to improve in these areas. So far, this book has followed the design process and the uses of PCs and PC software available today. This chapter now looks at the hardware and software that will be available by the year 2000 and at the changes they will make in the education and practice of the architect.

Hardware

From 1987 to 1993, PC hardware has advanced in processing speed several times over. Graphic operations that took 20 to 30 seconds in 1987 now take one to two seconds; in five years, they will take only two to three-tenths of a second. Processing speed has always been one of the main weak links in using a PC for CAD. Ideally, you want the computer to keep pace with your mind. Although PCs may not get *that* fast in the next few years, they will be close enough that I don't think anyone will pass up the computer because of its lack of processing speed.

The computer is a warehouse for information. The more information that may be stored and accessed easily, the more useful the computing tool. In the mid-eighties we had just moved from storage on 360 Kb, or 0.36 Mb floppy disks to hard-disk storage in the 20 to 40 Mb range. Today, 100 Mb to 300 Mb hard disks are common, 1000 is available, and 650 Mb CD-ROM disks are available. Five years from now, you will have access to thousands of megabytes (gigabytes) of information on your PC.

Such speed, combined with new storage and access capabilities, will give you the most powerful productivity tool you have ever had.

Software

The advances in software will be even more remarkable than the advances in hardware. CAD software will continue to fall into two main categories: the graphic engine software — AutoCAD — and the applications software — ASG.

The next generations of graphic engine software will continue to get faster and faster. The software will give you multiple views on the screen, created from the 3D geometry of the drawing. Changes you make to one drawing in a set will be reflected throughout the entire set of drawings. You'll be able to work on drawings of multiple scales side by side on one sheet. Mass, volume, areas, and other geometric information will be instantly available.

Fantastic advances will also occur in applications software. ASG's goal is to weave together the information and drawings that make up the design, construction, and management process. The first step of the process involves gathering and indexing information. Today, with hand drawing throughout the entire process, information is kept in hundreds of files and on thousands of slips of paper. The current process is a constant modification and regathering of information that has been gathered time and time again by other members of the designing and building team. In the future, you'll have a master database for the storing and retrieving of information.

As the process moves along, information will be added and modified but will continue to be found in a consistent location. The master database will include all the information about the project, including the program, code information, architectural and engineering drawings, and all the statistics contained within the drawings, analysis results, manufacturers' data, specifications, and estimates. Moreover, the master database will be interactive so that as you change one bit of information, either graphically or alphanumerically, the software will adjust accordingly throughout the database. This interactive database will organize the entire process.

The Architectural Phases in the Future

Programming

In the future, you will build both an alphanumeric database as well as a graphic database for the program requirements. Sophisticated adjacency programs will help you lay out the spaces. Stacking programs will look at the vertical layout within buildings. Research papers will be available to you on the subject of your project. You will be able to gather information about equipment graphically so that you will be able to begin the design process graphically.

Preliminary Design Phase

During the design process, you will no longer draw double lines for walls. You won't need to draw in all the detail for doors and windows. You'll create diagrams and the software will create the graphically correct drawing. During this phase, you'll be able to automatically generate cost estimates and construction schedules. You'll be able to study the massing of the design through renderings and animation created automatically by the software, and you'll be able to mold the design and to continue to make studies to refine the design ideas.

Software will provide libraries of buildings to call on for elements and ideas. If you want to experience the spatial feeling of an existing significant building, just call up the geometry and animate it to stroll through the building. Even if you have actually physically visited the building, with electronic graphics, you'll be able to view the building from many more vantage points. You'll be able to walk around and even fly around and through the building! In one afternoon, you'll be able to visit scores of buildings electronically.

Codes and ordinances will be stored and searched electronically. You'll be able to enter the location of a site and the applicable codes and planning requirements will be provided. Once you have indicated the type of building and occupancy you are designing, the fire, planning, and other applicable codes will be searched and the pertinent information provided.

Converting the codes to electronic format will dramatically point out the inconsistencies and conflicts in today's codes, which will lead to necessary corrections.

Presentations

In the future, architectural presentations will be truly breathtaking. They will jump alive with animation, titles, spectacular renderings, and even digital sound. These presentations will be created by all members of the design team, not just by a highly trained specialist. Prior to design review meetings, you'll be able to give the members of the board the full presentation for the project. You'll have access to databases that will allow accurate information to be provided on environmental issues, similar projects, and traffic studies. Both shadow studies and wind studies will be created electronically.

Design Development and Contract Documents Phases

I believe that these two phases — design development and contract documents — will merge into one phase because in the preliminary design phase, you will automatically move well beyond the traditional preliminary design information. By the time the preliminary design phase is finished, you will be ready to move into contract documents.

In the future, as you draw you will find displayed in the lower left-hand corner of the monitor the cost of the project; in the bottom right-hand corner will be displayed the time to build the project; in the upper right-hand corner will be the energy requirements for the project. Manufacturers' data, drawings, photographs, details, specifications, costs, and availability will all be part of the drawing session.

When you select a window, you will see the cost implications and its effect on the schedule based on the manufacturers' information and the construction process. You'll be able to call up photographs of the elements being considered and to study your selections in photorealistic perspective views. You will be able to animate your designs for design studies. Changes to the architectural drawings will be reflected in changes to the engineering drawings. Real-time flythroughs will be possible so that you'll be free to set your path as you move through the design.

Bidirectional changes will be possible. Change the CFM of the air diffuser in the database and the ducts will be redrawn correctly or add a diffuser to the drawings and the analysis will be rerun and the drawings then redrawn to reflect the changes. Modifying the drawings from the database is the most powerful feature of CAD and alphanumeric data processing. You'll do less drawing, and the drawings will be created faster and more accurately.

Specifications will be tied to the drawing. As you add elements, the specifications will be created and tied directly to the products you've used in the project. You'll be able to automatically create either generic or manufacturer-specific specifications. In addition, the specifications software will check for conflicts and inconsistencies.

Most details will be created automatically given the design of the building and the materials specified. You'll have the option of drawing with generic or with manufacturer-specific details. Manufacturers will provide the details for their products.

Electronic code checks will be performed before you submit the drawings and calculations for permits. The code-checking software will review your drawings and point out code violations so that they may be addressed before the permit process or before construction. Using CAD and alphanumeric processing on the PC workstation will greatly reduce errors and omissions and will thus result in lower insurance costs for design professionals.

Bidding and Negotiation

The contractor and the subcontractors will receive the contract documents both in electronic format and in traditional drawing and specification formats. Working with the electronic information, they will be able to accurately determine all the physical characteristics of the project. Square footage, area of walls and ceiling, cubic yards of concrete, and materials takeoff for all materials in the project will be available and accurate. The time required for estimation will shrink as the accuracy sharpens. Direct ties to estimation data services will read your information into their databases. The construction cost will fall because the contractor will estimate more accurately and will spend less time estimating.

Construction

The computer, which will soon be as common a sight on the job as the contractor's pickup truck, will be used to track the building schedule and material deliveries. CAD will be used to record the "as built" conditions; progress photographs will be taken and stored digitally for review and transfer. The workers will be able to study any condition electronically before the actual construction; 3D displays and animation will be used to study complicated intersections and details.

CAD will provide exact information on the parts of an assembly so that the individual pieces will fit together. Modifications that used to delay projects will be made at the job site, while cost adjustments will be determined and approvals received after electronic review at the home office. In fact, the entire project database will be available at the construction site.

Facilities Management

After the project is completed, the most important phase in the life of the structure begins — the management of the facilities. As noted earlier, facilities management is a broad-spectrum concept that includes interior space layout, furniture and equipment inventories, management of the leased areas, maintenance and operations, cable and communications, and renovation.

Today, when the project is completed, the design and construction teams turn over to the owner or facilities manager piles of manuals, specifications, manufacturer literature, and drawings. The facilities manager must then wade through the information and assume responsibility for the building. In the future, this information will be better organized and will be passed on electronically, enabling the facilities manager to search the information electronically and make modifications to the electronic information to keep the database current.

Maintenance manuals will not take the form of paper books but will be animated instructions on the operation, maintenance, and repair of the equipment, with instructions given by experts in the field.

Managing the growth or shrinkage of a company will be based on the integration of the various databases. For example, growth within a department will be indexed to the available space for expansion and the cost of various possibilities. Tying together the various databases for the building will give the facilities manager tremendous power.

Conclusion

I am not writing science fiction. Everything discussed in this chapter is possible today. Several of these features are already working in developmental software. The only element separating the future from today is time. New technology will only make the future arrive earlier and with more power.

In the past, the architect sat and drew the same window over and over again by hand, realizing that all of his or her training and knowledge was not being put to good use. The lack of automation and the waste of valuable time were frustrating. Today we know the path to the future (but we're still frustrated— we can only run down that path so fast). As we proceed, we will discover and develop more and more of the fantastic tools that you will have to perform your work at peak efficiency.

In fifteen years, from 1985 to 2000, the practice of architecture will have undergone a complete transformation. In 1985, the PC arrived in the AEC professions; by the year 2000, it will have changed these professions forever. The PC, with graphic engine software and applications software, will make the work of the design professional more accurate, will make the designs better, and will make the construction process more cost-effective and complete.

The PC and the software of the year 2000 will see a new design professional in the driver's seat. You, as new professional, will be more like a master builder: You'll be responsible for the complete design of the structure; you'll have the power of the best minds in structure, design, electrical, mechanical, plumbing, color, and program information; you won't be distracted by calculations; and you'll be able to imagine an idea and test the idea for every conceivable concern.

If you are a student, you need to start thinking now about this "new architectural practice" and about what you will need to know to take on the master builder role. If you are already an architect, these predictions may seem farfetched; they aren't. They may even seem somewhat frightening; in many ways, they are. How do we license the architect of the future? How do we educate the students of the future and the architects of today so that they can move into the future?

Actually, these are simple questions, so they will be answered. You need to stay in touch with the technology in the coming years, for it will come quickly. You also need to become involved in helping to mold the future by reviewing products, providing feedback to the designers of the software, and keeping in touch with the licensing boards and the educational institutions.

Architecture is a wonderful profession, a mixture of art and sculpture balanced against the complexity of construction and the realities of business. CAD and alphanumeric data processing will make this profession even better and more enjoyable in the near future.

We are entering the most exciting age ever for architects and engineers. I look forward to seeing what you will do with this fantastic new CAD tool.

Part 2

The ASG Architectural 6.0 Tutorial

Bob Callori

Dedication

To the memory of Tamara, a close and loving companion.

Acknowledgement

I would like to express my appreciation to Dennis Neeley for supporting this project, to Stewart Sabadell, who provided technical support for ASG Core, and to Jan Yoder, who furnished assistance for ASG Architectural.

I am extremely grateful for the expertise of Laura Sanchez, who served as technical editor, and of Kris Kuipers, who assisted with the desktop publishing.

A special thanks to Edith Thacher, who organized the original documentation and continually supplied me with current software.

Preface

I wrote this tutorial to apply the features offered by ASG software as an architectural application. It demonstrates how ASG software manages the design process from inception to final presentation.

As architects, we start a project by writing a program and assigning sizes and locations to individual spaces or rooms. Then a building plan is created by arranging spaces, as a series of single-line diagrams, into a *space diagram.* Proceeding to the next step, we convert the spaces into double lines, representing *walls* with thickness. Eventually *doors and windows* are added to our design. As the building takes on a volume, we create a *roof* appropriate to the structure.

To further explore the volume, we define faces for the structure by drawing *draft elevations.* Later, *annotations and tags* are assigned to describe our design and identify its details. *Symbols* are added to form a core with plumbing fixtures and stairs, and to designate furniture locations.

As we explore the capabilities of CAD, we learn to make drawings intelligent by creating attributes to extract information from the drawing, and exporting the drawings into a *database.* We are then able to import the database back into the drawing as a *schedule,* or to external programs such as dBASE®or R:BASE® symbol.

Then we decide to expand the design into a *multi-story* building, learning how to manipulate layers an™d floor levels. Finally, we are able to communicate the design to clients by a *walk through and around* the computer-generated building.

This tutorial takes us through all of these steps. Although this tutorial is designed specifically for AutoCAD users, people who are unfamiliar with AutoCAD should be able to complete it with occasional assistance. I have installed the ASG software on drive C: with the path set to ASG6, using AutoCAD Release 12. You must have ASG Core and Architectural previously installed and fully operational. You can refer to the ASG Core reference manual for installation procedures. This tutorial is designed for ASG's latest release as of May 1993; if you are running ASG release 6.0, some prompts may vary.

I have divided the tutorial into ten sessions, each of which can potentially be completed in one to two hours. The sessions are meant to advance you naturally through the design process.

You should start at Session 1 and advance through each session of the tutorial. Be careful to save your drawing at the end of each session, because you will edit it in later sessions. After completing the tutorial you will be able to edit a drawing from a specific session to practice a routine. The user's disk includes the final drawing from each session.

Procedures in the tutorial are intentionally repeated to reinforce the learning process. Alternate routes and methods are explained for many operations so that users can take advantage of ASG's shortcuts as they gain experience.

Each operation begins with a series of steps that explain what you will be doing. Following this overview, the menu path to the specific command is shown in white type on a black background, with greater-than symbols (>) separating the menu names. Dialog boxes are shown enclosed in braces ({ }).

Following the menu path, full, unedited command prompts are shown to help you understand the ASG program. Notes are inserted at intervals to provide comments or tips concerning the current command. This should be especially helpful if you want to customize a specific feature of that command.

Responses to the prompts appear in **bold** typeface and are provided regardless of the default values, which may differ from those on your system. When a command is automatic (based on previous selections) or when the selection set is complete, the response is shown as **[Enter]**. Although most responses to commands are typed, you can select commands from the side menu if preferred. Some responses to prompts must be selected from the side menu; additional instructions appear in boldface and enclosed in brackets ([ ]) to explain a specific screen pick location or to provide detailed instructions.

I have also included illustrations of icon symbol menus and the corresponding pull-down tree structure to access them.

Although this tutorial applies only to the ASG Architectural module, any ASG or AutoCAD user should find references to the ASG Core module very helpful.

Bob Callori
April, 1993

Session 1
Space Diagram

The first session of this tutorial will show you how to set up your drawing environment, and then show how an architect begins the design process with a space diagram—a single-line representation of spaces or rooms.

This exercise designs a single story office building consisting of 14,750 square feet (SF). The program space and area requirements are:

Office-1	60' x 45'
Entry	30' x 30'
Office-2	2,700 SF, minimum width of 60'
Corridor	10' wide
Office-3	approximately 5,550 SF
Service	approximately 2,000 SF

Setting Up Directories

1. This tutorial assumes that you previously have ASG installed on your hard drive. The ASG program is installed in a directory named ASG6. Creating a directory named ASG6TUT with separate subdirectories for each session will help you to organize your work. Create separate drawing files for each session by using the completed drawing as a prototype for the next session. An example of a partial directory tree appears as follows:

   C:\ASG6TUT
       |—SESSION1
       | Session1.dwg
       |—SESSION2
       | Session2.dwg
       |—SESSION3
       | Session3.dwg

2. The ASG program creates a file named RUNASG.BAT to start AutoCAD and ASG. Refer to the Core manual to set up the drawing environment and start the ASG program.

3. This tutorial will acquaint you with some of the basic features of ASG Core and Architectural. Most commands direct you to use the Pull-down menu or specific dialog boxes.

Set Up Drawing Environment

1. Display the pull-down cascading menu by moving the cursor up to the menu bar to view the following seven menu bar items: File, Display, Dim, Draw, Modify, Modes, and Assist as shown in Figure 1.

2. Highlight the File menu bar with your pointing device, then pick Re-Map as shown in Figure 1 to display additional commands. Pick Menu Style... to open the Menu Style dialog box. Activate the radio button adjacent to ASG New by picking the rectangular box with your pointing device, then select OK as shown in Figure 2.

   > Command: MStyle

   > Mapping menu style...

   Note: This tutorial uses the ASG New menu style, which was designed specifically to correspond with the AutoCAD Release 12 pull-down menu options.

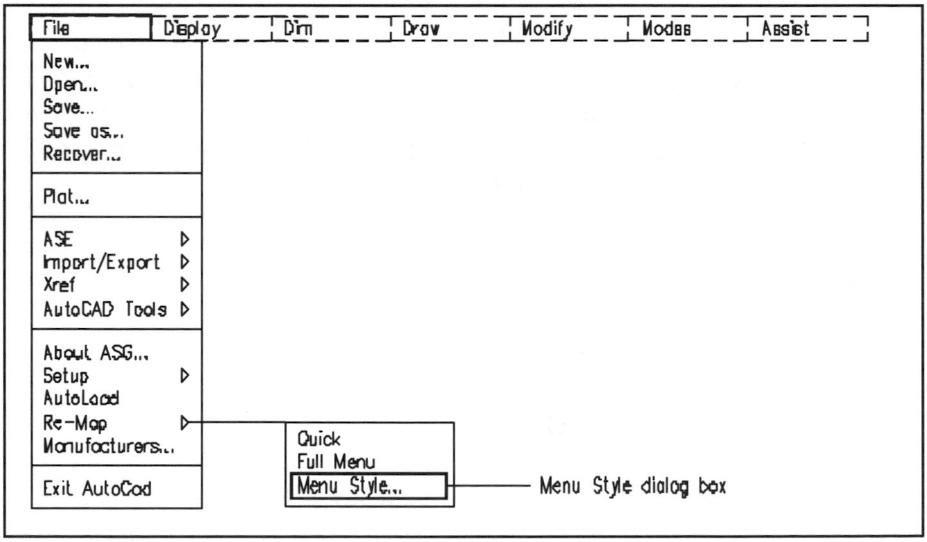

Figure 1.

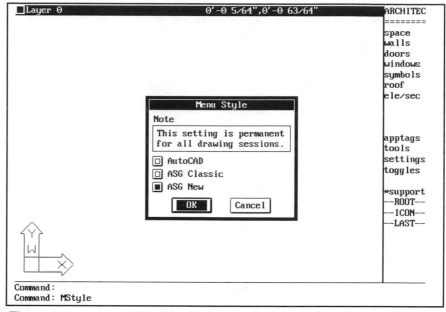

Figure 2.

Note: The Quick option enables you to quickly remap the ARCHITEC application menu after plotting.

3. Set up the new drawing environment from the Drawing Setup dialog box .

4. Highlight the File pull-down menu again, then select the Setup option to open a cascading submenu.

5. Select Setup... as shown in Figure 3 to open the Drawing Setup dialog box displaying drawing setup parameters in section and pick boxes.

6. Section boxes for Scale and Sheet contain subdialog pick boxes, edit boxes, or popup lists as shown in Figure 4. Additional pick boxes can be selected to set the drawing Units, create a Border, insert Title blocks, and so on.

7. New entries can be typed or default options chosen from Scale and Sheet section boxes to set the drawing scale and sheet size. Picking the down arrow in each section box opens a popup list to display available options. Setup parameters, such as the drawing scale, can also be typed in the Drawing: edit box.

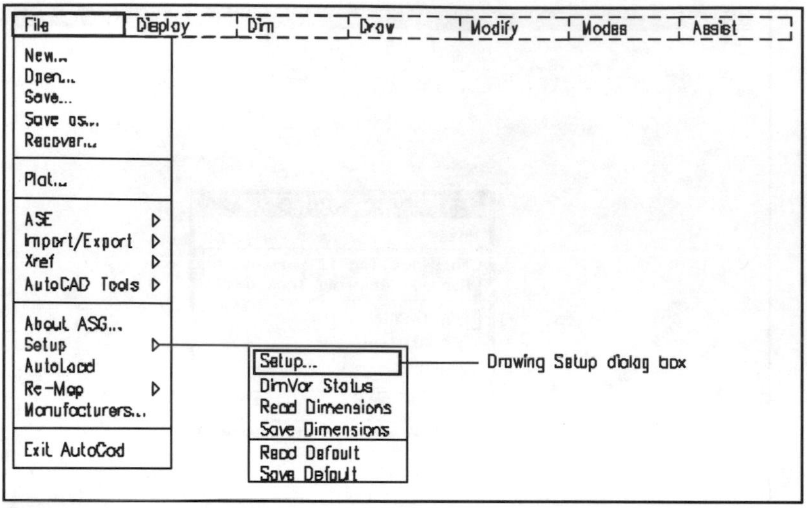

Figure 3.

8. The Units... pick box opens the Units subdialog box to display Section boxes for Drawing Units, Unit Notation, and Angular Notation. The Precision popup lists default units of measure, and the Direction... box controls the angular direction. Each Section box contains radio buttons to assign specific criteria. Only one button in each group can be active at a time.

9. Select the Units... pick box as shown in Figure 4 to open the Units subdialog box. Pick the radio buttons with your pointing device, toggling both Inches and Architectural to establish Drawing Units and Unit Notation, as shown in Figure 5.

10. Expand the Precision: popup list by pressing on the down arrow and choose the default value of 0'-0' 1/64" for the smallest fractional denominator as shown in Figure 6, then pick OK.

11. Set the drawing scale at 1/8"=1'-0" by entering 96 in the Drawing: edit box, or expanding the popup list as shown in Figure 7. (The value 96 = 1 foot divided by 1/8".)

12. Enter specifications for an E-sheet size with length 44.00 and width 34.00 in the Length X: and Width Y: Sheet section boxes as shown in Figure 8.

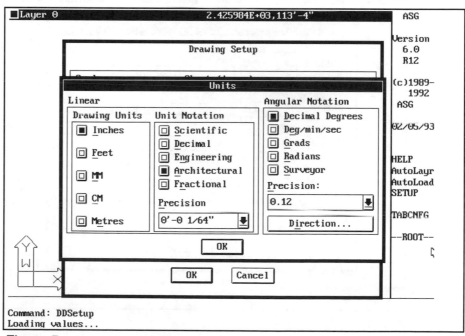

Figure 4.

Figure 5.

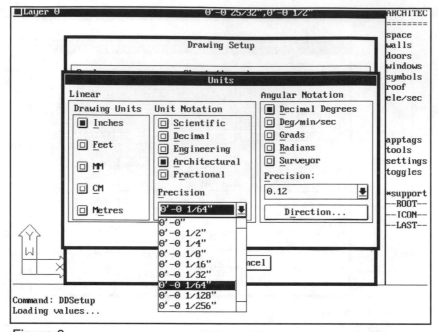

Figure 6.

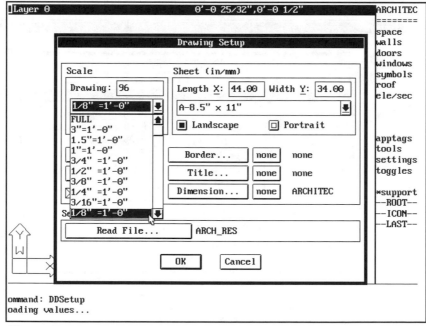

Figure 7.

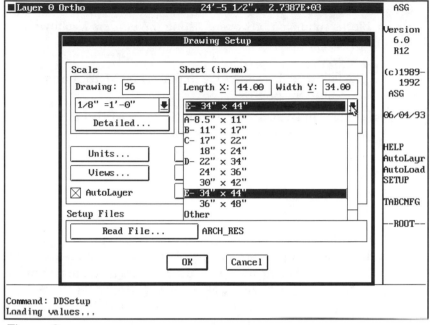

Figure 8.

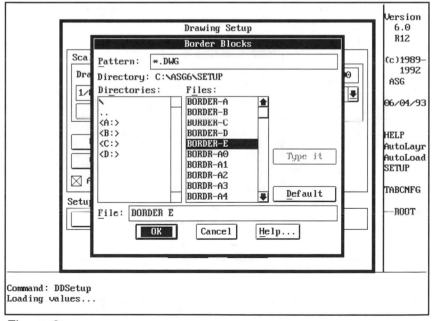

Figure 9.

13. Choose the Border...pick box to insert an E size border into the drawing. The Border Blocks subdialog box opens listing the borders as shown in Figure 9. Pick OK to close the dialog box.

Note: The following list shows the Imperial and Metric border default sizes that will appear in the popup list box:

Imperial Sizes in Inches:		Metric Sizes in Millimeters:	
BORDER-A	(11x8.5)	BORDER-A4	(297x210)
BORDER-B	(17x11)	BORDER-A3	(420x297)
BORDER-C	(22x17)	BORDER-A2	(594x420)
BORDER-D	(34x22)	BORDER-A1	(841x594)
BORDER-E	(44x34)	BORDER-A0	(1189x841)

14. Select the Detailed... pick box to open the Detailed Scales subdialog box as shown in Figure 10. Set the final plotted text height by typing 0.5 in the Height: edit box. Notice the drawing scale is automatically set at 96 for both the Dimension scale and Linetype scale. These values change each time the drawing scale is revised. Pick OK to close the subdialog box.

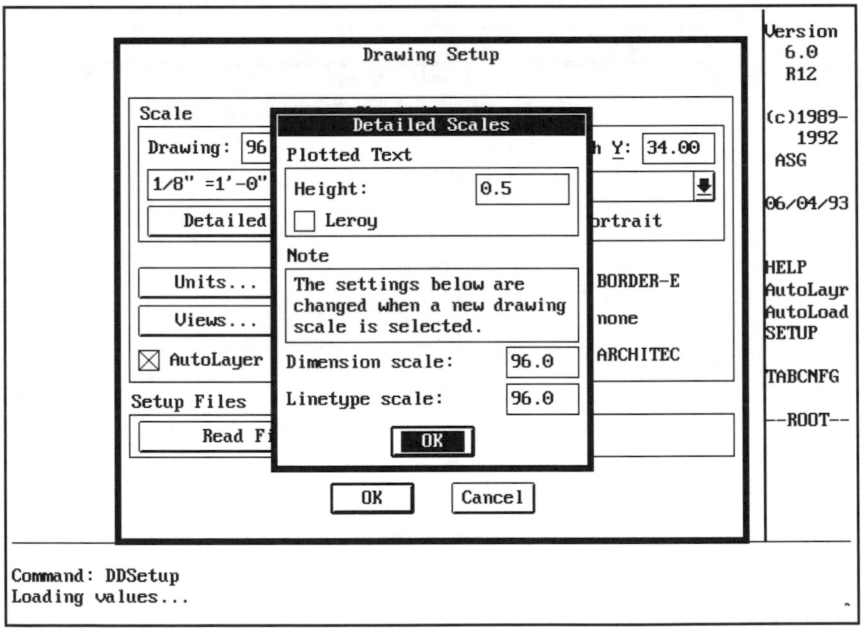

Figure 10.

```
■Layer 0 Ortho                24'-5 1/2",  2.7387E+03          ASG

                                                              Version
                    ┌──────────── Drawing Setup ────────────┐  6.0
                    │                                        │  R12
                    │  ┌Scale────────┐ ┌Sheet (in/mm)──────┐ │
                    │  │Drawing: [96]│ │Length X: [44.00] Width Y: [34.00]│(c)1989-
                    │  │             │ │                   │ │  1992
                    │  │[1/8" =1'-0" ▼]│[E- 34" x 44"      ▼]│  ASG
                    │  │[ Detailed... ]│ [■ Landscape  □ Portrait]│06/04/93
                    │  │             │                       │
                    │  │  [ Units... ]  [ Border... ][none] BORDER-E│HELP
                    │  │  [ Views... ]  [ Title... ][none]  none    │AutoLayr
                    │  │ ⊠ AutoLayer   [Dimension...][none] ARCHITEC│AutoLoad
                    │  └─────────────┘                       │  SETUP
                    │  Setup Files                           │
                    │  [      Read File...   ][ ARCH_RES   ] │  TABCNFG
                    │                                        │
                    │            [ OK ]    [ Cancel ]        │  --ROOT--
                    └────────────────────────────────────────┘

Command: DDSetup
Loading values...
```

Figure 11.

Note: A value of 0.5 makes the absolute size of text height for the room names and area appear larger.

15. The Drawing Setup dialog box should appear with the values for a 1/8"=1'-0" scale drawing, an E-size sheet, and an X in the AutoLayer pick box on as shown in Figure 11. If not already activated, toggle the pick box with your pointing device to place an X in the AutoLayer check box.

***Tip – AutoLayer

1. AutoLayer manages and places all lines, entities, and symbols on preassigned layers when selected from the pull-down menu, side screen, or digitizing tablet.

2. This command can be set from the Drawing Setup dialog box under the File pull-down menu, or from the Layering Tools cascading submenu under the Modes pull-down menu.

Drawing Setup Dialog Box

1. After setting up the drawing environment from the Drawing Setup dialog box, pick OK.

2. Prompts to enter a new layering template for adding layer prefix names appear when you save and exit the Drawing Setup dialog box settings.

    Note: Throughout this tutorial, the menu path you will use to perform operations is shown in white lettering on a black bar. The names of the dialog boxes are enclosed in braces. Following the menu path, the command line prompts are given in full with your responses in bold type.

    `File>    Setup>Setup...{Drawing Setup}`

    > DDSetup

    > Loading values...

    > Setting values...set.

    > Entering layering template <MAIN>: **[Enter]**

    > Enter MAJOR name or . for none <.>: **[Enter]**

    > Processing completed.

ASG Core Setup - Save Default/Read Default

1. You can save the current setup values by selecting the Save Default option on the Setup cascading pull-down submenu as shown previously in Figure 3.

2. ASG's original default CORE.SET filename can be overridden to accept the new values. However, assigning a name that will identify the saved setup is recommended. For example, the name SET96E provides the following association: set = setup; 96 = drawing scale; e = e size sheet].

3. All setup files are stored in the C:\ASG6\SETUP directory.

    `File>    Setup>Save Default`

    > Enter SETUP (SET) file to write, or Dir/Help/eXit<CORE>: Type **Set96e**

    > Processing completed.

4. To recall the saved default for a new drawing with the same setup values, open the Drawing Setup subdialog box and select READ FILE in the Setup Files Section box as previously shown in Figure 11. The Setup Default Files subdialog box opens, as shown in Figure 12, to view saved default files. Double clicking the file name closes the subdialog box to re-display the Drawing Setup dialog box with the Read Default name as shown in Figure 13. Pick OK again to save the new values.

> Enter SETUP (SET) file to read, or Dir/Help/eXit : **D**

> Select .SET name from screen menu<CORE>: **[select the file Set96e from the side menu]**

> Reading default values... Default values read.

> Enter layering template <MAIN>: **[Enter]**

> Enter MAJOR name or . for none <.>: **[Enter]**

> Enter BASIC name or . for none <.>: **[Enter]**

> Processing completed.

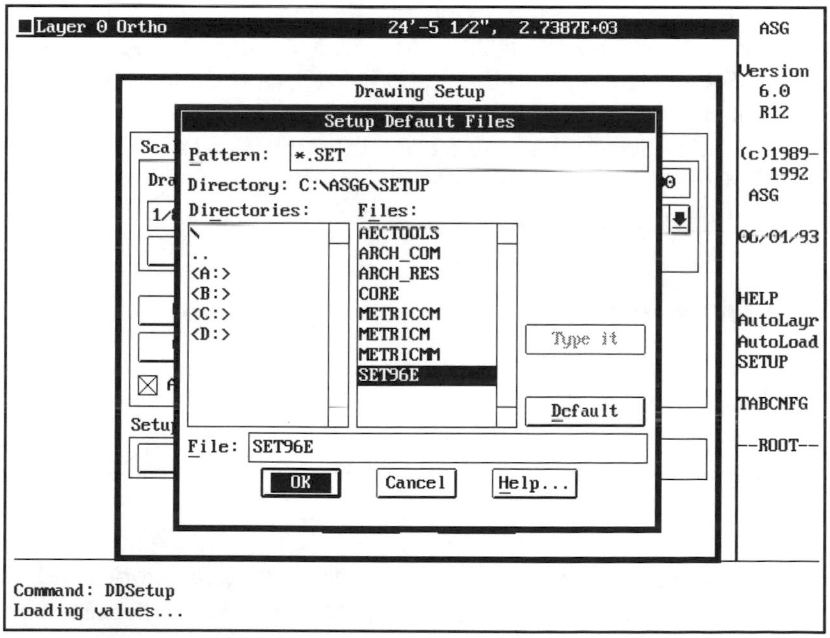

Figure 12.

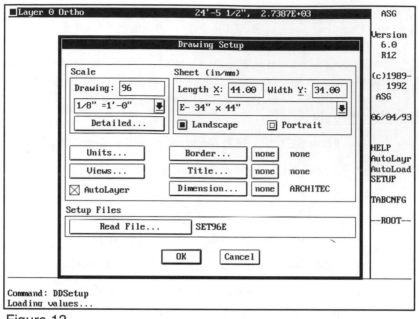

Figure 13.

Note: ASG offers the option of assigning prefixes to layer names. The MAIN layer name for walls is ARWALL. A MAJOR prefix named FL01, as well as BASIC prefixes named EXST and DEMO, can be added before the layer name. ASG then has the ability to create separate layers for existing and demolition walls, which will appear on either the FL01-EXST-ARWALL or FL01-DEMO-ARWALL layer. (We will use this feature in Session 9 to create a multi-story building.)

Save the Drawing

1. As discussed earlier, I made a directory named ASG6TUT with subdirectories for each session.

2. Select Save or Save As... from the File pull-down menu to save the current drawing.

3. The Save Drawing As dialog box opens listing Directories and Files as shown in Figure 14. Enter the name SESSION1 in the File: edit box, then pick OK.

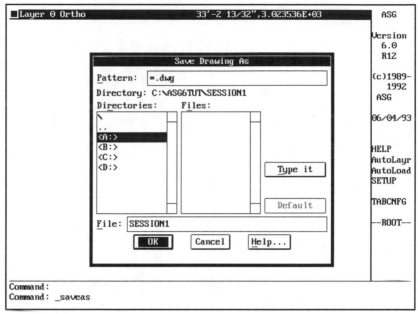

Figure 14.

AutoLoad

1. The original seven pull-down menus expand to ten when specific application menus, such as Architectural, Structural, or 3D Piping are loaded. We will use the ASG Architectural application for this tutorial. The File menu item retains its location while the remaining items Display, Dim, Draw, Modify, Modes, and Assist are repositioned. Each of the seven original pull-down menus contains basic AutoCAD commands, as well as specific ASG Core routines with additional cascading levels. An overview of ASG Core commands (with the AutoCAD commands) is shown in Figure 15.

2. Select and load the ASG Architectural module by picking AutoLoad from the File pull-down menu and then picking ARCHITEC from the side screen menu list at the "Select Application..." prompt as shown in Figure 16. This expands the menu items, inserting menu headings for Architec, Settings, and Tools. An overview of the ASG Architectural pull-down menus is shown in Figure 17.

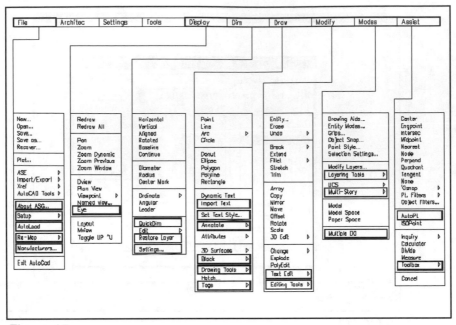

Figure 15.

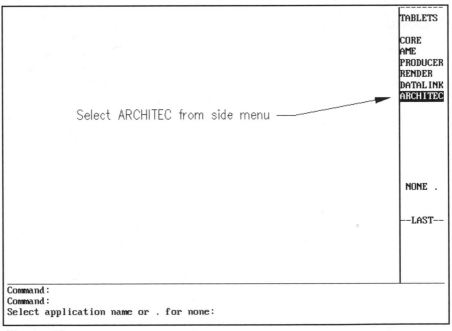

Figure 16.

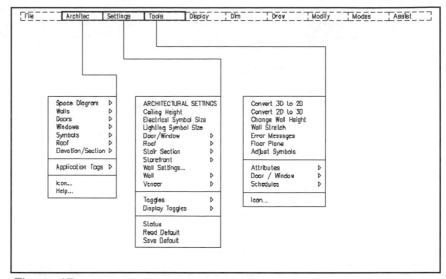

Figure 17.

> Select application name or . for none: C:\ASG6\ ARCHITEC\ ARCHITEC **[select ARCHITEC from side screen menu]**

> Processing — please wait.

Overview – Space Diagram

1. When AutoLayer is set to ON, lines and entities are automatically assigned to specific layers when selected from the pull-down, side screen, or tablet menus.

2. Lines for the space diagram are drawn automatically on layer ARWALL1LINE.

3. The room name and area are inserted into the middle of the space diagram as attributes and automatically placed on layer ARWALL1LINE.

4. The Space Diagram commands first prompt for the room name with default values appearing on the side menu.

5. Room names may appear with a hyphen, for example, OFFICE-. A second menu follows to add a number to the name.

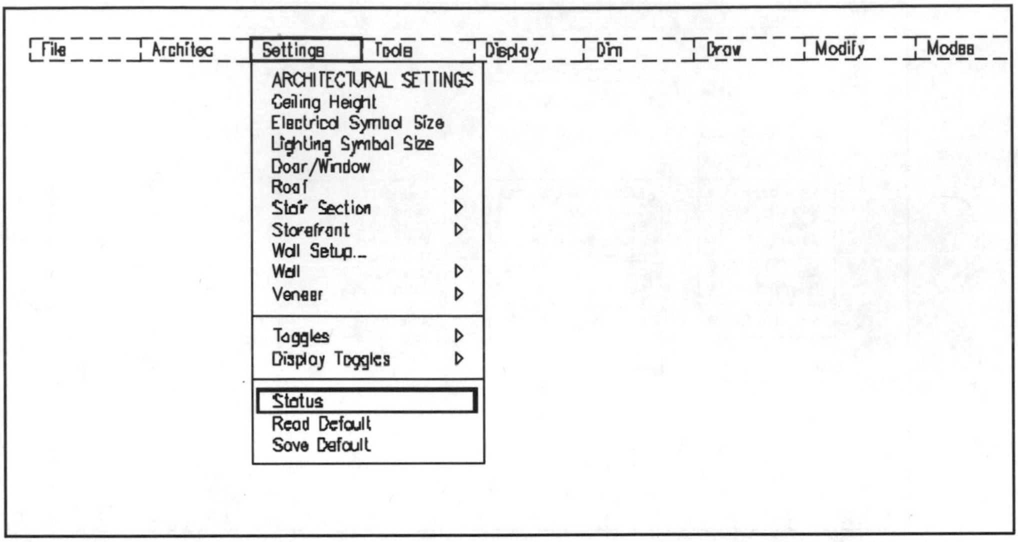

Figure 18.

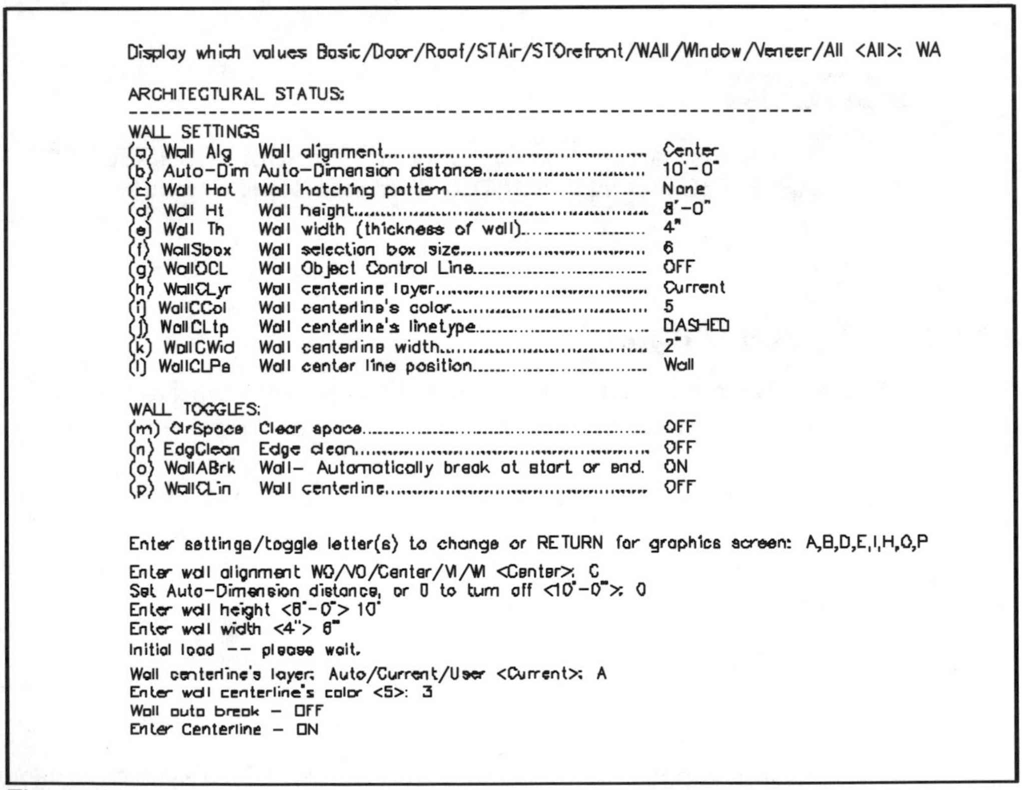

```
Display which values Basic/Door/Roof/STAir/STOrefront/WAll/Window/Veneer/All <All>: WA

ARCHITECTURAL STATUS:
------------------------------------------------------------
WALL SETTINGS
(a) Wall Alg     Wall alignment................................ Center
(b) Auto-Dim     Auto-Dimension distance....................... 10'-0"
(c) Wall Hat     Wall hatching pattern......................... None
(d) Wall Ht      Wall height................................... 8'-0"
(e) Wall Th      Wall width (thickness of wall)................ 4"
(f) WallSbox     Wall selection box size....................... 6
(g) WallOCL      Wall Object Control Line...................... OFF
(h) WallCLyr     Wall centerline layer......................... Current
(i) WallCCol     Wall centerline's color....................... 5
(j) WallCLtp     Wall centerline's linetype.................... DASHED
(k) WallCWid     Wall centerline width......................... 2"
(l) WallCLPs     Wall center line position..................... Wall

WALL TOGGLES:
(m) ClrSpace     Clear space................................... OFF
(n) EdgClean     Edge clean.................................... OFF
(o) WallABrk     Wall- Automatically break at start or end.     ON
(p) WallCLin     Wall centerline............................... OFF

Enter settings/toggle letter(s) to change or RETURN for graphics screen: A,B,D,E,I,H,O,P

Enter wall alignment WO/VO/Center/VI/WI <Center>: C
Set Auto-Dimension distance, or 0 to turn off <10'-0">: 0
Enter wall height <8'-0"> 10'
Enter wall width <4"> 6"
Initial load -- please wait.
Wall centerline's layer: Auto/Current/User <Current>: A
Enter wall centerline's color <5>: 3
Wall auto break - OFF
Enter Centerline - ON
```

Figure 19.

6. The space diagram is inserted into the drawing ghosted and then you are prompted for a new location point.

7. As you are completing the last point, type "C" or select "CLOSE" from the side menu. The Custom command requires that you also select <DONE> to complete the process.

8. Using AutoCAD's point filters, which ASG calls the Autopoint command, can make referencing selection points easier. (Point filters allow you to align points in an X-, Y-, or Z-axis. If you are not familiar with point filters, this exercise will demonstrate their application.)

9. The single lines on the diagram are used as centerlines when converted to double line walls. If your exterior wall has outer or inner veneers of different thicknesses, they are defined by the space diagram based on a formula (described on pages 4 to 5 in the Architectural Manual) and may need to be adjusted.

10. Open spaces or courtyards should be defined as enclosed spaces.

Settings and Toggles

1. Set up the wall variables for the Space Diagram by selecting Status from the Settings pull-down menu as shown in Figure 18.

2. To use the Settings and Toggles Status menus, pick Status, and enter the appropriate uppercase letter(s) at the prompt, typing the appropriate letter(s) and separating each with a comma. When the Status menu appears, enter the appropriate letters for the values you wish to change. The screen will scroll to view the selected changes as shown in Figure 19.

    `Settings>    Status>WA`

    > Initial load — please wait.

    > Display which values Basic/Door/Roof/STAir/STOrefront/ WAll/WIndow/Veneer/All <All>: WA

    Note: The Architectural Status screen will display the default Wall settings and Toggles values.

3. Settings and toggles should be set to display lines as follows:

Wall Alignment	Center
Wall Height	10'-0"
Wall Width	6"
Wall Centerline Layer	ON
Wall Centerline Color	green
Wall Centerline	ON

Note: Check your values, as some defaults may have already been set.

> Enter settings/toggle letter(s) to change or RETURN for graphics screen:**A,D,E,H,I,P**

> Enter wall alignment WO/VO/Center/VI/WI <Center>: **Center**

Note: This value is already set to center but you should notice the other options available.

> Enter wall height <8'-0">: **10'**

> Enter wall width <4">: **6**

> Wall centerline's layer: Auto/Current/User : **A**

Note: The Auto option automatically places the centerline on layer ARWALLCEN

> Enter wall centerline's color <5>: **3**

> Enter Centerline – ON

Note: This is a toggle and will change to ON; no prompt will appear.

4. The Architectural Status screen will then scroll to display the new settings.

ARCHITECTURAL STATUS:

WALL SETTINGS:

(a) Wall Alg	Wall alignment	Center
(b) Auto-Dim	Auto-Dimension distance	OFF
(c) Wall Hat	Wall hatching pattern	None
(d) Wall Ht	Wall Height	10'-0"
(e) Wall Th	Wall width (thickness of wall)	6"
(f) WallSbox	Wall selection box size	6"
(g) WallOCL	Wall Object Control Line	OFF

(h) WallCLyr	Wall centerline layer	AUTO
(i) WallCCol	Wall centerline color	3
(j) WallCLtp	Wall centerline linetype	HIDDEN
(k) WallCWid	Wall centerline width	2″
(l) WallCLPs	Wall centerline position	Wall

WALL TOGGLES:

(m) ClrSpace	Clear space	OFF
(n) EdgClean	Edge clean	OFF
(o) WallABrk	Wall - Automatically break at start or end	ON
(p) WallCLin	Wall centerline	OFF

> Enter settings/toggle letter(s) to change, or RETURN for graphics screen: **[Enter]**

5. Setting and Toggle selections are available from other pull-down menus. (Session 2 discusses all the Setting and Toggle pull-down menu locations.)

***TIP:ASG Architectural - Save Default/Read Default

1. Save the Architectural Status settings and Toggles values as you did for Core Setup.

2. Select Save Default from the Settings pull-down menu as previously shown in Figure 18, assigning the name Session1.

> Enter ARCHITECTURAL (CFG) file to write, or Dir/Help/eXit <ARCHITEC>: **SESSION1**

> Processing completed.

3. The file that stores the Wall Status values is saved separately from the drawing to the C:\ASG6\ARCHITEC directory as SESSION1.CFG. Select Read Default from the Settings pull-down menu to retrieve the saved values for the tutorial exercises.

> Enter ARCHITECTURAL (CFG) file to read, or Dir/Help/eXit <ARCHITEC>: **D [enter the Dir option to display the saved files on the side screen menu]**

> Select .CFG name from screen menu:
> **[pick SESSION1 from the side screen menu]**
> C:\ASG6\ARCHITEC\SESSION1.CFG

> Processing completed.

4. You must remember to read the Wall Status default value SESSION1 if you end this drawing. Accepting the ARCHITEC.CFG file will restore ASG's original default values unless you have replaced this file with the new settings.

5. It may be helpful to record your saved default file settings as a print screen. Pressing the F1 function key for the text screen, then the Print Scrn key should send the current STATUS image to the printer.

***TIP: DO

1. Some commands will appear with the word DO at the prompt line.

2. DO means that the previous command remains active and can be repeated when you type DO.

3. Type DO, then press Enter or the space bar to repeat the last command.

Office-1 – Width x Depth

1. The Space Diagram commands are located under the Architec pull-down menu. Selecting the command opens a submenu listing several methods for drawing spaces.

2. Draw the first space by selecting Space Diagram from the Architec pull-down menu as shown in Figure 20, or the icon Space Diagram menu as shown in Figure 21.

3. Select the Width x Depth option, specifying the width as 60' and the depth as 45', from the Space Diagram submenu or from the icon menu.

4. The bottom left corner of the space will be attached to your crosshairs for insertion into the drawing.

   Note: The room name and area attributes size can be adjusted by using the AutoCAD command ATTEDIT, or by reselecting Scale from the Setup pull-down menu and editing the final plotted text height value.

Architec>   Space Diagram>Width X Depth

File	Architec	Settings	Tools	Display	Dim	Draw	Modify

ARCHITECTURAL
Space Diagram   ▷
Walls   ▷
Doors   ▷
Windows   ▷
Symbols   ▷
Roof   ▷
Elevation/Section ▷

Application Tags   ▷

Icon...

Area and Width
Width x Depth
Dynamic
Custom

Space to Wall

Display Space
Display Wall
Display Both

Icon...

Figure 20.

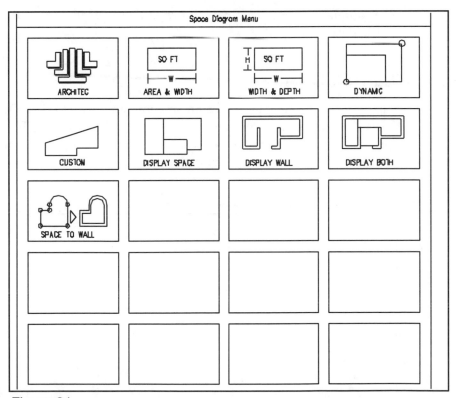

Figure 21.

> DO

> Enter room name: **OFFICE-1**

Note: Name the space OFFICE-1. Select a suggested name from the side screen menu or type it.

> Enter room width: **60'**

> Enter room depth: **45'**

> Pick insertion point: **[pick a location as shown in Figure 22]**

> Would you like to move the diagram Yes/No <No>: **No**

> Processing completed.

Note: Use the AutoCAD REDRAW command to refresh the screen and restore lines as necessary.

4. The completed space diagram is shown in Figure 23 to help you visualize the finished exercise.

Entry – Width X Depth

1. Since this is a repeat of the last command you can activate Width Depth several ways. You can type Do, or press Enter, or press the Space bar. If you used the cascading submenu, highlight Architec on the pull-down menu and then double click to reactivate the command.

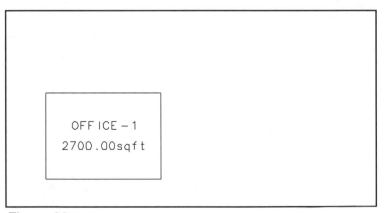

OFF ICE – 1
2700 .00sqf t

Figure 22.

2. Respond to the prompts with the space name, using 30' for both room width and depth.

3. Place the area at the intersection of the upper right corner of OFFICE-1, shown in Figure 24, and relocate the area when prompted as shown in Figure 25.

> DO

> Enter room name: **ENTRY [select ENTRY from side screen menu]**

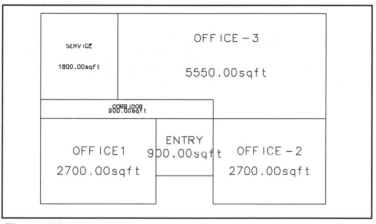

Figure 23.

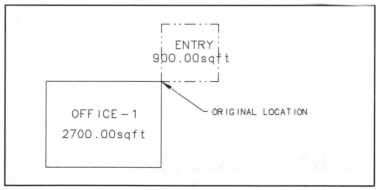

Figure 24.

> Enter room width: **30'**

> Enter room depth: **30'**

> Pick insertion point: **[pick a point or locate the area as shown in Figure 24]**

> Would you like to move the diagram Yes/No <No>: **Yes**

> Pick base point: **INT** of **[intersection at upper left corner of ENTRY]**

> Pick second point: **INT** of **[intersection at upper right corner of OFFICE-1 as shown in Figure 25]**

> Processing completed.

Office–2 – Area and Width

1. Use the Area and Width command from the Space pull-down menu to place OFFICE-2 as shown in Figure 26.

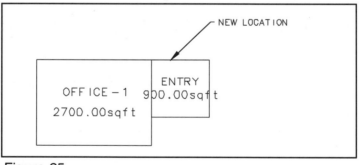

Figure 25.

2. Specify area as 2700 and width as 60'.

| Architec>   Space Diagram>Area and Width |

> DO

> Enter room name: **OFFICE-2**

> Enter room area in square FEET: **2700**

> Enter room width: **60'**

> Pick insertion point: **[select any point on the screen]**

> Would you like to move the diagram Yes/No <No>: **Yes**

> Pick base point: **INT** of **[upper left corner of OFFICE-2]**

> Pick second point: **INT** of **[upper right corner of ENTRY as shown in Figure 26]**

> Processing completed.

***TIP: Status – Final Plotted Text Height

1. Since the corridor is a narrow space, change the text height to fit the CORRIDOR space by resetting the final plotted text height from 1/2" to 1/4".

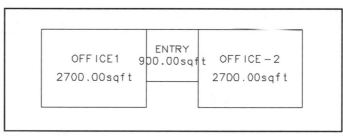

Figure 26.

2. Select Setup under the File pull-down menu then choose Setup... to open the Drawing Setup dialog box. Pick the Detailed... pick box to open the Detailed Scales subdialog box and enter 0.25 in the Height: edit box as shown in Figure 27. Pick OK to close each dialog box.

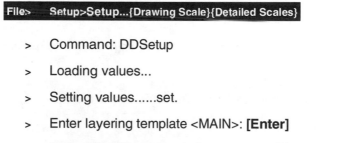

> Command: DDSetup

> Loading values...

> Setting values......set.

> Enter layering template <MAIN>: **[Enter]**

> Enter MAJOR name or . for none <.>: **[Enter]**

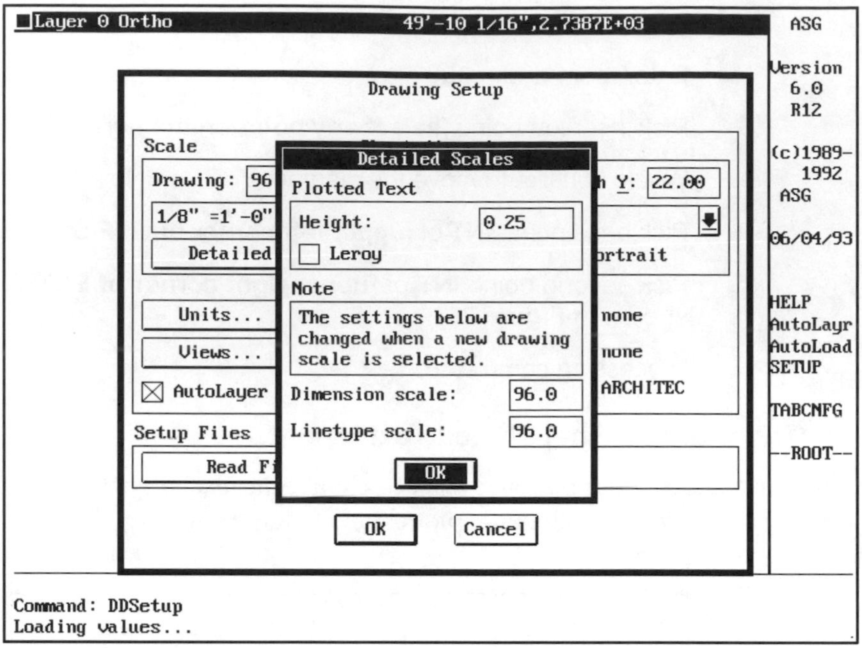

Figure 27.

> Enter BASIC name or . for none <.>: **[Enter]**

> Processing completed.

Note: Using the scale option of the setup command will make all subsequent text appear at this new height. Keep in mind that the height of the actual text defined as 1/2″ (or 0.5) is 4′ based on the scale of this 1/8″=1′-0″ drawing.

Corridor – Dynamic

1. Use the Dynamic command from the Space pull-down menu to draw a 10′ wide CORRIDOR.

2. Specify the intersection osnap at the lower right corner to indicate one end of the corridor.

3. Apply the point filters to extract the X value for the upper left corner of the corridor.

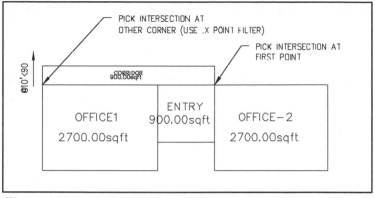

Figure 28.

4.   The Y value of the upper left corner end of the corridor can be assigned by typing @10'<90.

5.   The completed Corridor space is shown in Figure 28.

Architec>   Space Diagram>Dynamic

> DO

> Enter room name: **CORRIDOR**

> Pick first corner: **INT 3[pick upper right corner of ENTRY]**

Note: When a rubberband box appears, use the .X point filter.

> Pick other corner: **.X [point filter]**

> of **INT [when rubberbanding box appears with osnap, pick upper left corner of OFFICE-1]** (need YZ): **@10'<90**

> Would you like to move the diagram Yes/No <No>: **No**

> Processing completed.

Office-3 – Custom

1.   Use the Custom command from the Space pull-down menu to draw the space for OFFICE-3.

2. The Custom routine uses the Pline command with the linetype DASH2L to draw an initial outline. The pline temporarily created by this routine is shown in Figure 29.

3. First select the upper right corner of the Entry space, then the upper right corner of the Corridor.

4. Continue a distance @50'<180 along the top of the corridor, then @45'<90 upward, and a horizontal length of 110'<0 toward right side of the building.

5. Select the upper right corner of OFFICE-2 and CLOSE by picking from the side menu or using the C option of the command.

6. The room name and area appear attached to the crosshairs automatically after selecting CLOSE, or manually when selecting <Done> from the side menu. The completed space is shown in Figure 30.

Architec>   Space Diagram>Custom

>   DO

>   Enter room name:**OFFICE-3**

>   Draw a space- Enter DONE when finished

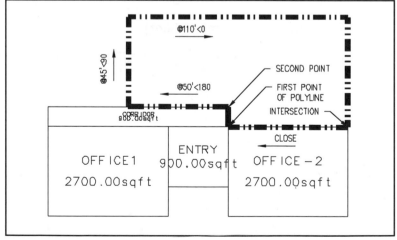

Figure 29.

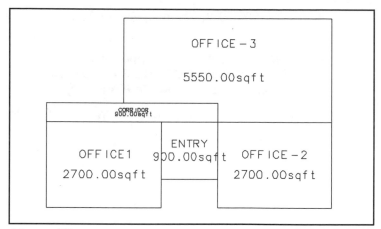

Figure 30.

> From point: **INT** of [**pick upper right corner of the ENTRY area as the first point; a rubberband will appear connected to the crosshairs**]

> Arc/Close/Halfwidth/Length/Undo/Width/<Endpoint of line>: **INT** of [**pick upper right corner of the CORRIDOR area as the second point; a wide polyline begins to appear as shown in Figure 29**]

> Arc/Close/Halfwidth/Length/Undo/Width/<Endpoint of line>: **@50'<180**

> Arc/Close/Halfwidth/Length/Undo/Width/<Endpoint of line>: **@45'<90**

> Arc/Close/Halfwidth/Length/Undo/Width/<Endpoint of line>: **@110' <0**

> Arc/Close/Halfwidth/Length/Undo/Width/<Endpoint of line>: **INT** of [**pick upper right corner of OFFICE-2**]

> Arc/Close/Halfwidth/Length/Undo/Width/<Endpoint of line>: **CLOSE [pick CLOSE from side menu]**

Note: If you type C to close the space, you must pick <DONE> from the side menu to complete the routine. Otherwise, select the CLOSE option on the side menu to automatically execute <DONE>.

> Command: **DONE**

> Area = 799200.00 square in. (5550.0000 square ft.), Perimeter = 330'-0"

> Pick insertion point: [**a box appears temporarily; select a point in the center of OFFICE-3 and the box will change into text and area as shown in Figure 30**]

> Would you like to move the diagram Yes/No <No>: **No**

> Processing completed.

***TIP: Change Attribute

1. The attribute size may be too small, based on changing the height from 1/2" to 1/4". Use the Change Attribute option of the Editing Tools menu after the space is completed and the attribute appears.

2. Select Editing Tools under the Modify pull-down menu to display the cascading menu; then pick Change Attribute, as shown in Figure 31.

    `Modify> Editing Tools>Change Attribute`

> CHATTR

> Select block(s) to change <none>: [**pick the Office-3 text block**]

> Select objects: **1 found**

> Select objects: [**Enter**]

> Angle/Height/Layer/Position/Style/Text/ON/OFF/<Text>: **H**

> Globally change attributes? Yes/No <No>: **Yes**

> Enter Height for all attributes<2'>: **4'**

> Processing completed.

Note: Selecting the OFFICE-3 block changes both the size of "OFFICE-3" and "5550.00sqft" for that block. Accepting the default <No> will change attributes separately.

Service – Dynamic

1. Use the Dynamic command from the Space Diagram menu to create a space that will complete the plan as shown in Figure 32.

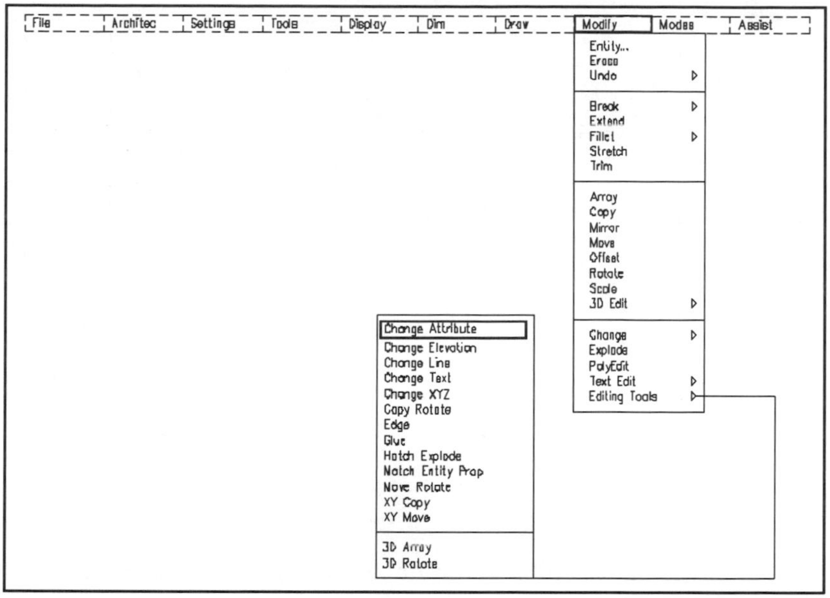

Figure 31.

2. Specify the points with the osnap ENDpoint to define the room.

3. Accept the area of 1800 sqft created automatically by picking the other corner.

Architec   Space DiagramDynamic

> DO

> Enter room name: **SERVICE**

> Pick first corner: **INT** of **[upper left corner of CORRIDOR]**

Note: A rubberband box appears after selecting the first point.

> Pick other corner: **INT** of **[upper left corner of OFFICE-3]**

> Would you like to move the diagram Yes/No <No>: **No**

> Processing completed.

***TIP:Save Drawing

1. You have now completed the Space Diagram.

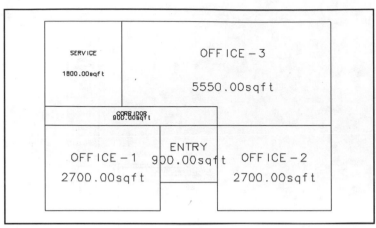

Figure 32.

2.   Enter the AutoCAD END command to save and exit Session 1, or SAVE and
     continue to Session 2.

3.   Entering SAVE opens the Save Drawing As dialog box similar to Figure 14. Pick
     OK.

4.   Save your drawing at the end of each session to the session name. Copy the
     completed drawing to a floppy disk for future retrieval, or for editing in later
     sessions.

5.   Name each completed saved drawing as SESSION1, SESSION2, etc. as a
     reminder of that session.

6.   In the next session we will use a copy of the SESSION1 drawing as a prototype,
     assigning the new filename SESSION2 to create double line walls from our
     Space Diagram.

Session 2
Walls

In this lesson, you will convert the single line space diagram from Session 1 to double line walls, using the Space to Wall command. Then you will add interior walls to create spaces in the SERVICE area and OFFICE-2 for restrooms, small offices, and a stairway.

Begin a New Drawing

1. Begin a new drawing to display the AutoCAD screen.

2. Create a copy or prototype of the completed drawing called SESSION1 from SESSION ONE with the filename SESSION2.

3. Select New from the File pull-down menu to display the Drawing Modification dialog box.

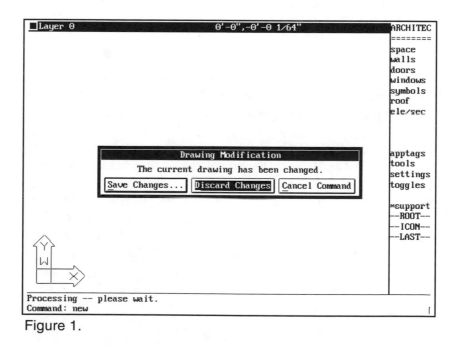

Figure 1.

4. Pick Discard Changes as shown in Figure 1 to open the Create New Drawing dialog box. Select Prototype... as shown in Figure 2 with your pointing device.

5. The Prototype Drawing File subdialog box opens to display Directories: and Files: list boxes

```
■Layer 0                          0'-0",-0'-0 1/64"            ARCHITEC
                                                              ========
                                                              space
                                                              walls
                                                              doors
                                                              windows
                                                              symbols
                                                              roof
                 ┌──────────────────────────────────┐        ele/sec
                 │        Create New Drawing         │
                 │                                   │
                 │  ┌───────────┐ ┌───────────────┐  │        apptags
                 │  │ Prototype...│ │ acad          │  │        tools
                 │  □ No Prototype                   │        settings
                 │  □ Retain as Default              │        toggles
                 │                                   │
                 │  ┌─────────────┐ ┌─────────────┐  │        *support
                 │  │New Drawing Name...│ │           │  │        --ROOT--
                 │        ┌────┐  ┌────────┐         │        --ICON--
                 │        │ OK │  │ Cancel │         │        --LAST--
                 │        └────┘  └────────┘         │
                 └──────────────────────────────────┘

 ↑Y
 │W
 └──►X

Processing -- please wait.
Command: new
```

Figure 2.

6. Locate the drawing SESSION1 by picking the appropriate directory in the Directories: list box, then double click the SESSION1 drawing filename when it appears in the Files: list box as shown in Figure 3.

7. After the SESSION1 drawing appears in the Prototype... edit box, enter SESSION2 in the New Drawing Name... edit box, then pick OK.

8. The AutoCAD drawing screen opens a new drawing named SESSION2, which is a copy of the SESSION1 drawing file with the architectural module loaded as shown in Figure 4. We will use the Space to Wall command to change the single lines to double line walls as shown in Figure 5.

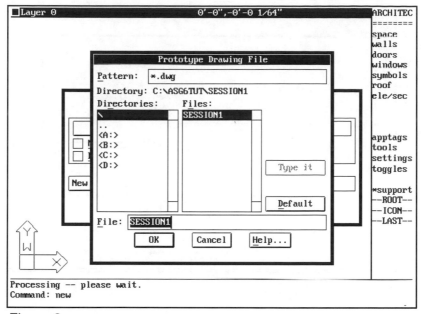

Figure 3.

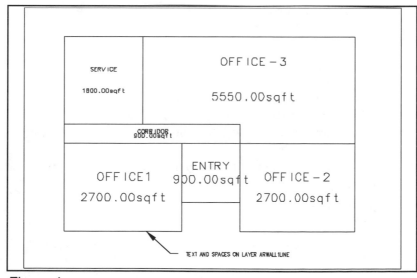

Figure 4.

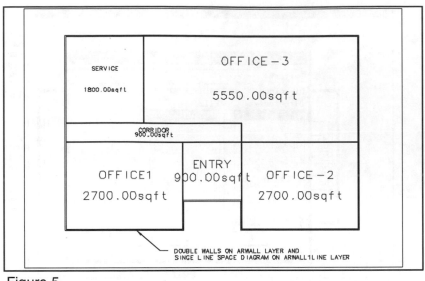

Figure 5.

***TIP - AutoLoad

1. The architectural module remains active in the main menu and is saved with the drawing. Move your pointing device to the the top of the screen to verify and display the Architec, Settings, and Tools menu items.

2. Whenever you wish to deactivate the Architectural module, select AutoLoad from the File menu, then pick Core or NONE from the side menu. Type a period (.) if you are responding to the prompt at the command line as shown below. Next time you open up this drawing file, the Architec, Settings, and Tools menu items will not appear in the status line for the pull-down menu.

3. In most cases, you will want to keep the Architectural module loaded for your drawing sessions.

    `File>AutoLoad`

    > Select application name or . for none: **. [type a period]**

Architectural Module - Read Default

1. Restore the default values saved from SESSION 1.

2. Select Read Default from the Settings pull-down menu as shown in Figure 6.

3. Enter the Dir option at the Enter ARCHITECTURAL (CFG) file to read, or Dir/Help/eXit ARCHITEC: prompt. The side menu will display several saved defaults.

4. Pick SESSION1 to recall saved settings from the last session, including the 10′ wall height, wall thickness, and so forth.

> Enter ARCHITECTURAL (CFG) file to read, or Dir/Help/eXit ARCHITEC: **D [select from side menu]**

> Select .CFG name from side screen menu : **C:\ASG6\ARCHITEC\SESSION1.CFG**

> Processing completed.

File	Architec	Settings	Tools	Display	Dim	Draw	Modify

ARCHITECTURAL SETTINGS
Ceiling Height
Electrical Symbol Size
Lighting Symbol Size
Door/Window   ▷
Roof   ▷
Stair Section   ▷
Storefront   ▷
Wall Setup...
Wall   ▷
Veneer   ▷

Toggles   ▷
Display Toggles   ▷

Status
Read Default
Save Default

Figure 6.

Convert Spaces to Walls

1. Select Space Diagram from the Architec pull-down menu to display the cascading submenu command to convert spaces to walls.

2. Pick Space to Wall from the Space Diagram pull-down menu as shown in Figure 7 to convert the single line space diagram to double wall lines.

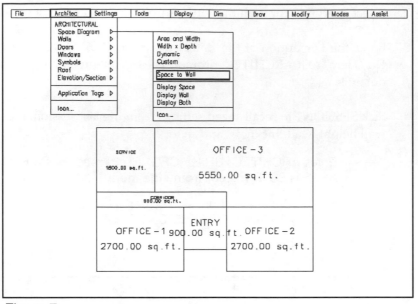

Figure 7.

3. The routine will prompt to draw a line around the building. Pick exterior corner endpoints outlining the building.

4. Specify an interior wall thickness of 3.5″ and an exterior wall thickness of 8″.

ArchitecSpace Diagram>Space to Wall

> DO

> Draw a line around the building. Enter DONE when finished.

> From point (ENDpoint): **[pick any exterior corner and proceed picking points around the building as shown in Figure 8]**

Note: An aperture box will appear automatically to indicate a running endpoint/intersection osnap mode. You may begin at the upper left corner of Service and continue selecting endpoints clockwise or counterclockwise around the exterior building wall line.

> Arc/Close/Halfwidth/Length/Undo/Width/<Endpoint of line>:
> **[pick endpoint]**

Continue selecting each exterior corner of the building in response to the Endpoint of line.

> Arc/Close/Halfwidth/Length/Undo/Width/<Endpoint of line>:
> **[pick endpoint]**

> Arc/Close/Halfwidth/Length/Undo/Width/<Endpoint of line>:
> **[pick endpoint]**

> Arc/Close/Halfwidth/Length/Undo/Width/<Endpoint of line>:
> **[pick endpoint]**

> Arc/Close/Halfwidth/Length/Undo/Width/<Endpoint of line>:
> **[pick endpoint]**

> Arc/Close/Halfwidth/Length/Undo/Width/<Endpoint of line>:
> **[pick endpoint]**

> Arc/Close/Halfwidth/Length/Undo/Width/<Endpoint of line>:
> **[pick endpoint]**

> Arc/Close/Halfwidth/Length/Undo/Width/<Endpoint of line>:
> **CLOSE [select CLOSE from the side screen menu]**

The routine draws a pline around the exterior walls as shown in Figure 8.

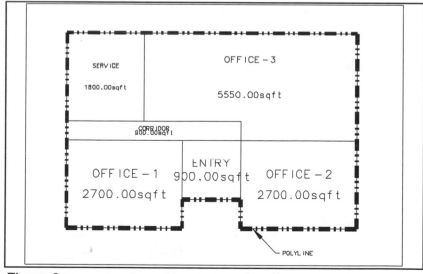

Figure 8.

> Command: DONE

> Processing — please wait

> Select space diagrams to convert or **{Enter}**

> Select objects: **W [use Window selection set]**

> First corner: **[pick point at lower left corner of drawing]** Other corner: **[pick point at upper right corner of drawing]** 6 found

> Select objects: **[Enter]**

> Enter interior wall thickness <5">: **3.5**

> Enter exterior wall thickness <8">: **8**

> Enter exterior inner veneer thickness or 0 for none <0">: **[Enter]**

> Enter exterior outer veneer thickness or 0 for none <0">: **[Enter]**

> Processing — please wait

> Indicate inside the space: **[select a point inside the building as shown in Figure 9]**

> Processing completed.

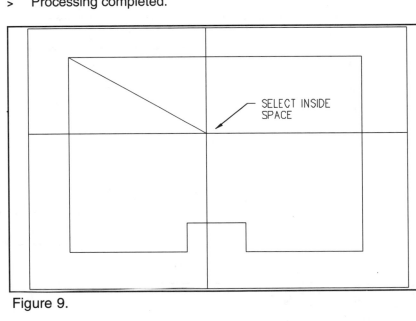

Figure 9.

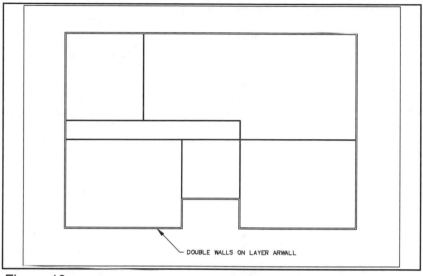

Figure 10.

5. The plan will appear as double line walls, with the single line walls, room names, and areas on layer ARWALL1LINE turned off, as shown in Figure 10.

Display Walls

1. The Display Walls command offers three display options shown in Figures 10, 11 and 12 to view walls only, spaces only, or both walls and spaces.

2. The ASG Architectural Manual discusses guidelines for creating space diagrams on page 4-2.

3. Select each of the Display Walls options described below. (The isometric view created by the Vpoint command in Figure 13 shows that work is being drawn as both two- and three-dimensional lines.)

Architec>Space Diagram>Display Wall

Display Wall — freezes the space diagram layer ARWALL1LINE and turns on the layer ARWALL as shown previously in Figure 10.

Prompt response: Walls and Veneers displayed...

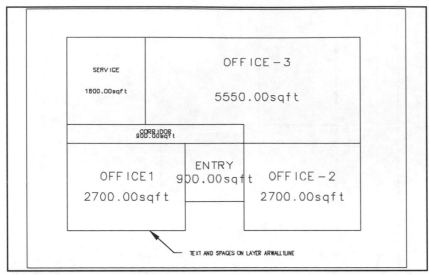

Figure 11.

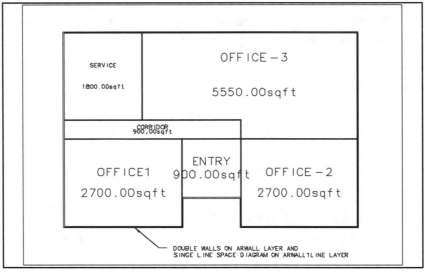

Figure 12.

Display Space — thaws the display diagram layer ARWALL1LINE and turns off the layer ARWALL as shown in Figure 11. Prompt response: Spaces displayed...

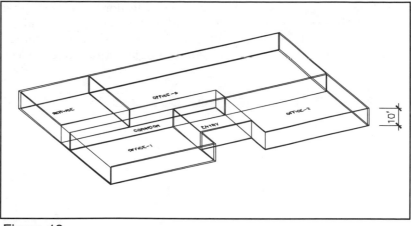

Figure 13.

Architec>Space Diagram>Display Both

Display Both — turns on all layers ARWALLLINE, ARWALL, and ARWALLV as shown in Figure 12.

Prompt response: Spaces, Walls and Veneers displayed...

Walls – Settings and Toggles

1. Now that you have created double exterior and interior walls for major spaces, add additional interior spaces.

2. Use the Wall Settings dialog box to change the value for wall thickness from 6″ to 4″.

3. Wall alignment and height should be set to Center and 10′ from Session 1.

4. Toggle Wall Auto Break OFF so that you can use the intersection commands to clean up intersecting walls. Auto Break automatically breaks the double wall lines created with the Continuous Wall command, cleaning intersections at each osnap pick.

5. Toggle Auto Dimension distance OFF to prevent wall dimensioning as continuous walls are drawn.

Note: Wall Settings and Toggles menu selections can also be made by picking (a) Wall Settings... in the Architec pull-down menu, or (b) Wall, Wall Settings... or Status in the Settings pull-down menu as shown in Figure 14. The Wall cascading submenu is convenient for single setting/toggle selections.

Figure 14.

```
Display which values Basic/Door/Roof/STAir/STOrefront/WAll/Window/Veneer/All <All>: WA


ARCHITECTURAL STATUS:
------------------------------------------------------------
WALL SETTINGS
(a) Wall Alg    Wall alignment.................................. Center
(b) Auto-Dim    Auto-Dimension distance......................... OFF
(c) Wall Hat    Wall hatching pattern........................... None
(d) Wall Ht     Wall height..................................... 10'
(e) Wall Th     Wall width (thickness of wall).................. 6"
(f) WallCCol    Wall centerline's color......................... 5
(g) WallCLtp    Wall centerline's linetype...................... HIDDEN
(h) WallCWid    Wall centerline width........................... 2"
(i) WallSbox    Wall selection box size......................... 6
(j) WallCLyr    Wall centerline layer........................... ARWALLCEN
(k) WallCLPs    Wall center line position....................... Wall

WALL TOGGLES:
(l) ClrSpace    Clear space..................................... OFF
(m) EdgClean    Edge clean...................................... OFF
(n) WallCLin    Wall centerline................................. ON
(o) WallABrk    Wall- Automatically break at start or end.       OFF
(p) WallOCL     Wall Object Control Line........................ OFF


Enter settings/toggle letter(s) to change or RETURN for graphics screen: E,N
Enter wall width <6">: 4
Set Auto-Dimension distance, or 0 to turn off <10'>: 0
```

Figure 15.

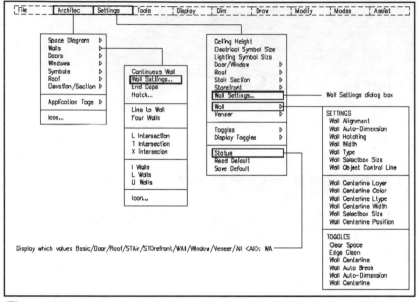

Note: Opening a dialog box or activating the Status display is useful when multiple Setting/toggle changes are required. The status display prompts to change Basic, Door, Roof, Stair, Storefront, Wall, Window, Veneer, or All settings and toggle values.

The Wall value display choices are shown in Figure 15.

Continuous Wall – Wall 1

1. Use the Continuous wall command to draw double line walls of specified thickness and height with hatch patterns, polyline centerlines, and associated automatic dimensioning.

2. The Continuous Walls command can be activated from a pull-down menu or an Icon Menu. (Other options to invoke commands from the tablet menu and the side screen menu are not discussed in this tutorial.)

3. Pick the Walls cascading submenu under the Architec pull-down menu as shown in Figure 16 and select the Continuous Wall command to draw double line walls. Press Return to accept the AutoPT default placing the wall start point at a location relative to a base point.

4. The drawing should be set to Display Walls and look similar to Figure 10.

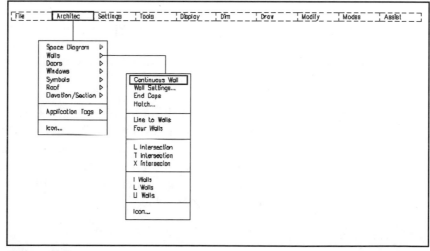

Figure 16.

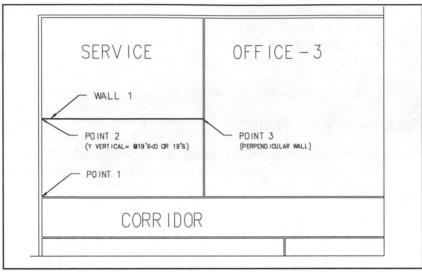

Figure 17.

5. In general, to place a continuous wall, start the command by selecting a start point using an intersection, endpoint, or midpoint osnap option. Then specify the distance of the wall. Complete the process by picking the wall that the new wall is perpendicular to with the perpendicular osnap option. The command offers options to revise Wall settings by opening a dialog box.

6. Begin at the lower left interior corner of the Service area as shown in Figure 17.

7. When prompted to Enter Y Vertical change, type the offset distance of 19'-6".

8. Before proceeding to the next point, open the Wall Settings dialog box to change values as described previously in Walls - Settings and Toggles.

9. Select the D option to display the Wall Settings dialog box as shown in Figure 18. Set the toggle for Auto-Dimension distance OFF by picking the check box adjacent to Auto Break so no X mark is displayed. Enter 4" in the Width: edit box or pick the down arrow from adjacent popup list to change the wall width as shown in Figure 18. Peruse wall alignment and height settings for center and 10', then pick OK as shown in Figure 19.

10. As the Next point,

   > Select the wall to which the new wall will be perpendicular.

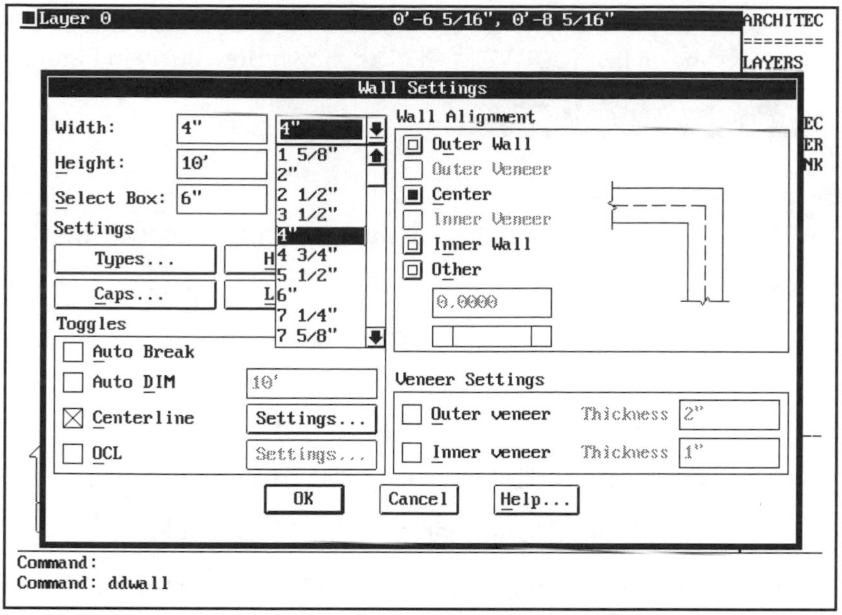

Figure 18.

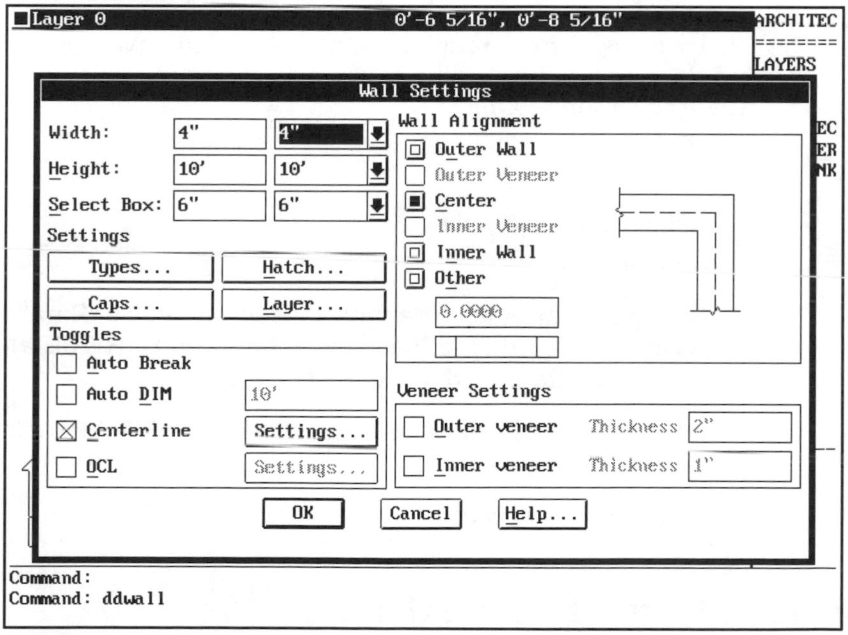

Figure 19.

11. Press Return to complete the command for a double wall line of 4" thick with a centerline on layer ARWALLCEN as shown previously in Figure 17.

> **Architec>Walls>Continuous Wall**

> DO

> Pick start point for the first wall segment <Autopt>:**[Enter]**

AutoPt will recall the start point of your last line segment.

> Pick base point <last>: **INT of [point 1 as shown in Figure 17]**

> Enter distance <x,y,z change>:**[Enter]**

> Enter X HORIZONTAL change <0">:**[Enter]**

> Enter Y VERTICAL change <0">: **19'6 [point 2]**

The distance can be entered as 19'6 or @19'6<90. Negative numbers can also be entered for –X and –Y directions.

> Enter Z change <0">:**[Enter]**
  Autopt/Bearing/Close/Dialog/Fillet/Parallel/Relative/ Undo:D

The Wall Settings dialog box opens. Settings to assign or verify are:

Auto-Dimension	OFF
Auto Break	OFF
Width	4"
Wall alignment	Center
Wall height	10'

> Next point or Autopt/Bearing/Close/Dialog/Fillet/Parallel/ Relative/Undo: **PER to [select wall between SERVICE and OFFICE-3 referenced in Figure 17 as point 3]**

> Next point or Autopt/Bearing/Close/Dialog/Fillet/Parallel/ Relative/Undo:**[Enter]**

> Processing completed.

Architectural Settings - Save Default

1. Save the changes by selecting Save Default from the Settings pull-down menu to save default values. The Enter ARCHITECTURAL (CFG) file to write, or

Dir/Help/eXit: prompt appears with the default filename ARCHITEC. Instead of accepting the default filename, assign a name suggesting values that are saved. For example, the filename T6W10CL2.CFG may represent a 6" thick wall height (T6) 10' high (W10) with a centerline width of 2" (CL2). If you use a particular setting/toggle for most projects, replacing the original ARCHITEC file with your own values is recommended.

Settings>Save Default

> The Enter ARCHITECTURAL (CFG) file to write, or Dir/Help/
> eXit/ARCHITEC: **T6W10CL2**

Clean up Intersections

1. Zoom into the Service area and use the T intersection from the Walls submenu as previously shown in Figure 16 or the Wall Menu icon as shown in Figure 20 to clean up intersections at the start and endpoints of the continuous wall.

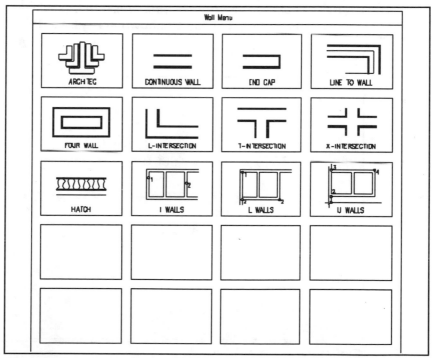

Figure 20.

2. Select Walls under the Architec pull-down menu, then Icon, to open the Wall Menu icon. To activate the command, double click the T-intersection icon.

3. Pick a point at the intersection of the wall lines. When the aperture box appears, select one of the wall lines as indicated by Figure 21.

3. The ARWALLCEN centerline layer does not affect the cleanup and can remain on while executing the command.

4. Invoke the command again to clean up the intersection at the opposite end of WALL 1. Use the Do command discussed in Chapter 1 by typing DO, pressing the Enter key or space bar to repeat the T-intersection command.

Architec>Walls>Icon...>T Intersection Intersection

> DO

> Pick intersection <select>: **[pick near the intersection with your crosshairs]**

> Pick leg of the T (NEArest)>: **[the aperture box will appear; pick one of the wall lines as shown in Figure 21]**

> Processing completed.

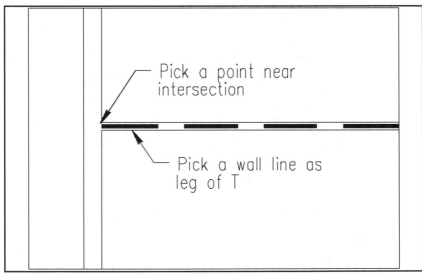

Figure 21.

Wall – Automatically Break at Start or End

1. Change the Wall setting "Wall - Automatically break at start or end" to ON to draw WALL 2. Wall lines will automatically clean up at start and endpoints as each new wall is drawn.

2. Since only one value needs to be changed, select the Wall Auto Break command from the Wall cascading submenu under the Settings pull-down menu as shown in Figure 22.

   The Wall Auto Break command can also be changed from within the Continuous Wall command using the dialog box.

   Settings>Wall>Wall Auto Break

   > Wall auto break- ON

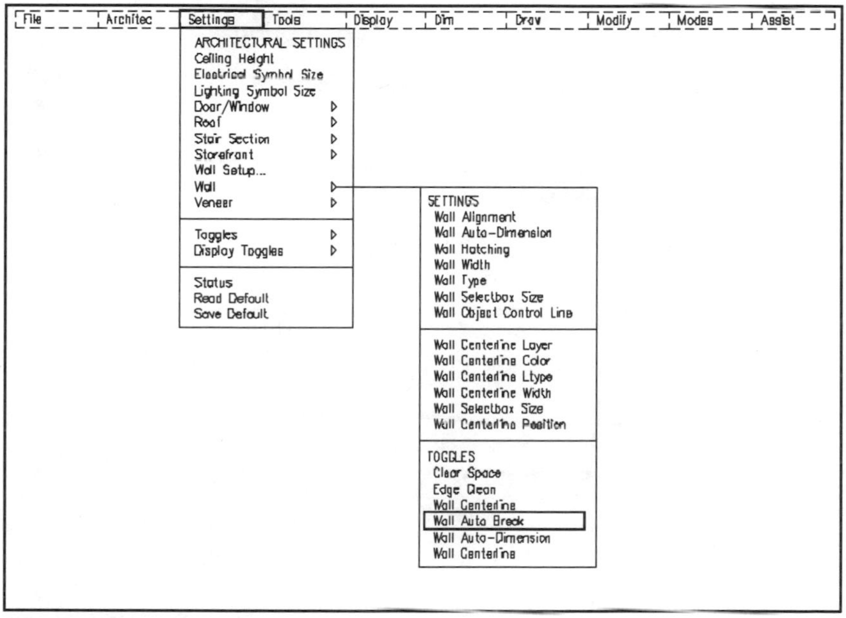

Figure 22.

Continuous Wall – Wall 2

1. Select the Continuous Wall again from the Walls pull-down menu.

2. This next wall is parallel to the exterior wall of the Service Room and offset 21'6 to the right. Select the intersection at POINT 2 as shown in Figure 23.

3. As you execute the command, override the line rubberbanding at a point and select your first point.

4. After WALL 2 is completed, you may wish to zoom into the start and endpoints to examine the cleaned up intersections.

Architec>Walls>Continuous Wall

> DO

> Pick start point for the first wall segment <Autopt>:**[Enter]**

> Pick base point <last>: **INT of [point 2 as shown in Figure 23]**

You may also choose to accept the <last> option.

> Enter distance <x,y,z change>:**[Enter]**

> Enter X HORIZONTAL change <0">: **21'6**

> Enter Y VERTICAL change <0">: **[Enter]**

> Enter Z change <0">:**[Enter]**

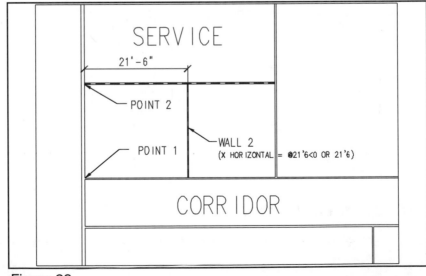

Figure 23.

> Next point or Autopt/Bearing/Close/Dialog/Fillet/Parallel/ Relative/Undo: **PER to [top wall of Corridor]**

> Next point or Autopt/Bearing/Close/Dialog/Fillet/Parallel/ Relative/Undo: **[Enter]**

> Processing completed.

The last menu item pick on pull-down menus remains active and can be retrieved by double clicking at the status line. For example, if you highlight the Architec menu item to reopen the Walls cascading menu, the Continuous Wall command will appear also highlighted. Double click Architec and the Continuous Wall command will automatically execute at the command line.

Architec>Walls>Continuous Wall

> **[Double click Architect]**

Continuous Wall – Wall 3

1. Press return or select Continuous Wall again from the Walls pull-down menu to draw WALL 3 as shown in Figure 24.

   Highlighting the Architec pull-down menu, then double clicking repeats the previous Walls pull-down menu command.

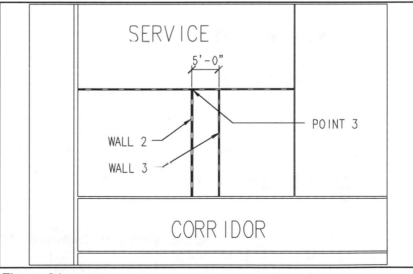

Figure 24.

2.   WALL 3 is parallel to WALL 2 at a distance of 5'.

> **Architec>Wall>Continuous Wall**

> > DO

> > Pick start point for the first wall segment <Autopt>:**[Enter]**

> > Pick base point <last>: **INT of [point 3 as shown in Figure 24]**

The rubberbanding line appears at the last beginning point of the previously drawn line, which you can accept by pressing return.

> > Enter distance <x,y,z change>:**[Enter]**

> > Enter X HORIZONTAL change <0">: **5'**

> > Enter Y VERTICAL change <0">: **[Enter]**

> > Enter Z change <0">:**[Enter]**

> > Next point or Autopt/Bearing/Close/Dialog/Fillet/Parallel/Relative/Undo: **PER to [select opposite wall]**

> > Next point or Autopt/Bearing/Close/Dialog/Fillet/Parallel/Relative/Undo: **[Enter]**

> > Processing completed.

Continuous Wall – Wall 4 (Plumbing Wall)

1.   Press Enter to reselect Continuous Wall without AutoPT. Start WALL 4 at the midpoint of WALL 2.

2.   Reset Wall Thickness from 4" to 6" from the Wall Settings dialog box.

3.   Drag across perpendicular to the opposite wall as shown in Figure 25.

> **Architec>Walls>Continuous Wall**

> > DO

> > Pick start point for the first wall segment <Autopt>: **MID of [WALL 2 as shown in Figure 25]**

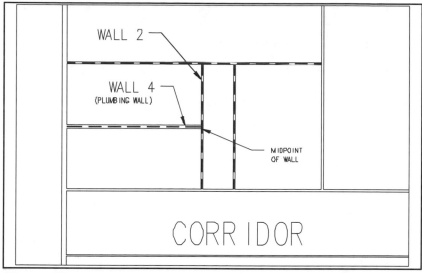

Figure 25.

> Next point or Autopt/Bearing/Close/Dialog/Fillet/Parallel/
Relative/Undo: **D**

Wall Settings dialog box opens. Enter 6" in Width: edit box, then pick OK.

> Next point or Autopt/Bearing/Close/Dialog/Fillet/Parallel/
Relative/Undo: **PER to [opposite wall]**

> Next point or Autopt/Bearing/Close/Dialog/Fillet/Parallel/
Relative/Undo: **[Enter]**

> Processing completed.

Continuous Wall – Wall 5

1. Press Enter again to select the Continuous Wall command and begin at the inside lower left corner of OFFICE-2 as shown in Figure 26.

2. Change the Wall Alignment to Wall Outer (WO) and Wall Width to 3.5" from the Wall Settings dialog box as shown in Figure 27.

3. Wall Outer will align WALL 5 with the interior face of the front Entry wall.

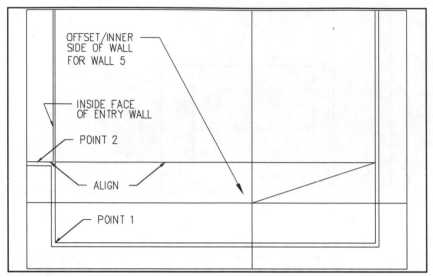

Figure 26.

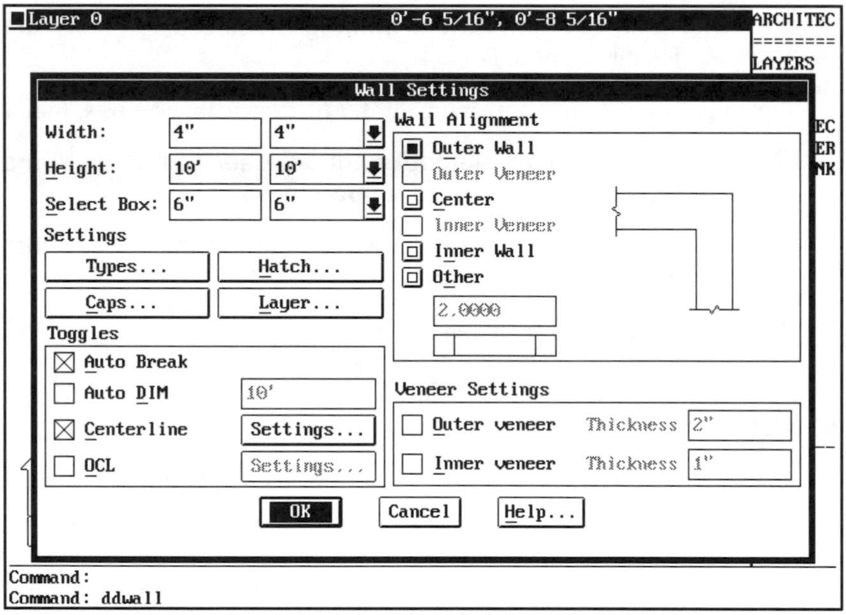

Figure 27.

4. Proceed perpendicular to the inside face of the Entry wall, dragging across to the OFFICE-2 right exterior wall.

5. A green line first appears defining the face of the outer wall, then as you are prompted to pick offset/inner side of wall, pick a point below the line.

6. The completed double wall with the centerline is shown in Figure 28.

Architec>Wall>Continuous Wall

> DO

> Pick start point for the first wall segment <Autopt>: **[Enter]**

> Pick base point <last>: **INT of [POINT 1, inside lower left corner of OFFICE-2 as shown in Figure 26]**

> Enter distance <x,y,z change>: **[Enter]**

> Enter X HORIZONTAL change <0">: **[Enter]**

> Enter Y VERTICAL change <0>: **PER to [POINT 2, inside face of front entry wall as shown in Figure 26]**

> Enter Z change <0">: **[Enter]**

> Next point or Autopt/Bearing/Close/Dialog/Fillet/Parallel/Relative/Undo: **D [dialog box opens, change wall thickness and alignment]**

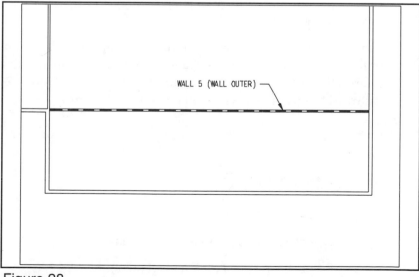

WALL 5 (WALL OUTER)

Figure 28.

> Next point or Autopt/Bearing/Close/Dialog/Fillet/ Parallel/ Relative/Undo: **PER to [opposite wall]**

> Pick offset/inner side of wall: **[pick below the wall line as shown in Figure 26]**

> Incorrect number of wall lines found, intersection break is terminated!

Since wall widths vary at POINT 1 the Auto Break command does not recognize this intersection.

> Next point or Autopt/Bearing/Close/Dialog/Fillet/Parallel/ Relative/Undo: **[Enter]**

> Processing completed.

AutoCAD Commands – Clean Up Intersections

1. The L, T, or X intersection clean up commands do not apply to the wall conditions with different intersecting widths. The wall intersection command may display one of the following messages:

   > 7 wall lines found matching pattern ARWALL, looking for 3... ;
   > 7 wall lines found matching pattern ARWALL, looking for 3

   > Incorrect number of wall lines found, intersection break is terminated!

2. Use AutoCAD's Trim or Break command from the AutoCAD/ASG Modify pull-down menu to trim the intersection adjacent to the Entry area. The intersection condition before cleanup is shown in Figure 29. The entire AutoCAD/ASG pull-down menu is shown in Figure 30.

3. If you select Break, pick the Select Object, Two Points command as shown in Figure 29.

   `AutoCAD/ASG    Modify>Break`

   > Command: BREAK

   > Select object: **[select vertical wall line]**

   > Enter second point (or F for first point): **F**

> Enter first point: **INT** of **[first intersection as shown in Figure 29]**

> Enter second point: **INT** of **[second intersection]**

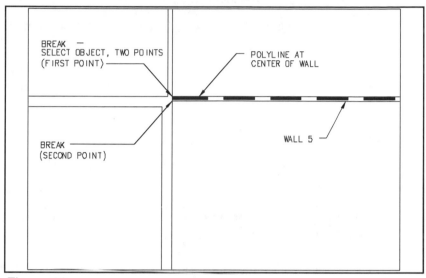

Figure 29.

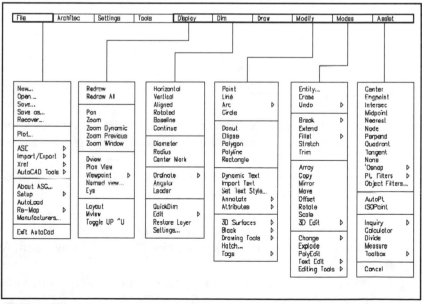

Figure 30.

Error Messages

1. A frequent wall error message occurring when inserting doors or windows into walls is:

    No wall line found matching pattern

    The line may be a polyline. Explode the line and try the command again.

2. If you cancel a command, it may cause lines to be on different Z coordinates. Use the Vpoint command with the coordinates -1,-1,1 to view the condition in isometric view. Redrawing the wall lines may be the easiest solution.

Edge Clean and Clear Space

1. Toggle Clear Space and Edge Clean on from the Wall Status display under the Settings pull-down menu.

2. When Edge Clean is on, the wall intersections will clean up automatically as each wall is drawn, as shown in Figure 31.

3. Clear Space will create a clear space of 20' from face of wall to face of wall.

> `Settings>Status>WA>M,N`

Walls 6 and 7

1. Select the I Walls command from Walls under the Architec pull-down menu to divide the space enclosed by WALL 5 into three small offices.

2. Specify a point along the inside face of the exterior wall of this new space in OFFICE-2 as the referenced wall, as shown in Figure 31.

3. A rubberbanding line appears, prompting the user to select a direction from POINT 1 to POINT 2. Pick a point inside the building, as shown in Figure 31.

4. As second and third prompts appear, respond with a wall width of 20' and wall height of 10' to create WALLS 6 and 7.

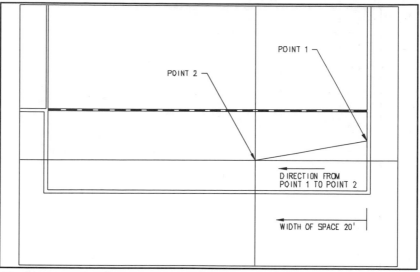

Figure 31.

5. The I wall command creates two smaller offices at 20′ apart (without centerlines), cleaning up the intersection during the process as shown in Figure 32.

    Architec>Walls>I Walls

    > DO

    > Width does not include wall thickness...

    > Pick wall line - POINT 1 (NEAREST): **[using the default osnap option, pick POINT 1 inside the building as shown in Figure 30]**

    > Indicate direction from POINT 1 to POINT 2: **[pick POINT 2 to your left as shown in Figure 31]**

    > Enter width of the space (point 1 to Point 2): **20′**

    > Enter height of the new walls <10′-0">: **[Enter]**

Continue on to the second space for Wall 7.

    > Enter width of the space: **20′**

    > Enter width of the space: **[Enter]**

    > Processing completed.

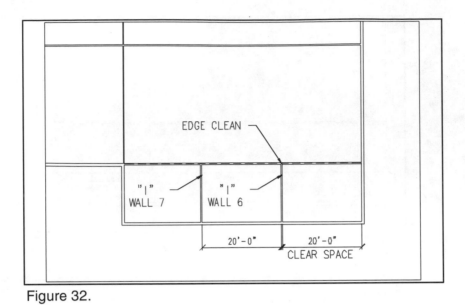

Figure 32.

Custom Wall (Curved Wall)

1. Create a curved custom wall within the Entry area with point filters by selecting AutoPt from the Assist pull-down menu.

2. Use the AutoCAD ARC command with filters (which ASG calls Autopoint or Autopt) as described below at points A, B, and C and shown in Figure 33.

   Point A — To specify your first point, select the Start, Cen, End option of the ARC command from the Draw pull-down menu. Use the AutoPt command from the Assist pull-down menu. Then while the Assist menu is active, pick INTersection for the base point at point A. Select xyz change and specify the horizontal distance as 6' from the left wall of the Entry and the vertical distance as -7' from the back wall of the Entry.

   Point B — Continuing with the arc command, select AutoPt, then MIDpoint on the Assist menu to specify point B as the base point. Point B is the midpoint of the back wall of the Entry. Specify the distance as 5' and the direction as straight down at the "Enter distance <x,y,z> change:" prompt.

   Point C — To complete the arc, select AutoPt, then INTersection again from the Assist pull-down menu. The base point is point C. Select xyz change and specify the horizontal distance as -6' from the right wall of the Entry. The vertical distance is -7' from the back wall.

Draw>Arc>Start,Center,End

> Command: ARC

> Center/<Start point>: **[select AutoPt from Assist menu]**

> Pick base point <last>: **INT of [select intersection at point A as shown in Figure 33 from Assist pull-down menu]**

> Enter distance <x,y,z change>: **[Enter]**

> Enter X HORIZONTAL change <0">: **6'**

> Enter Y VERTICAL change <0">: **-7'**

> Enter Z change <0">: **[Enter]**

> Center/End/Second point: **[select AutoPt from the pull-down Assist menu]**

> Pick base point <last>: **MID of [select midpoint at point B as shown in Figure 33 from Assist pull-down menu]**

> Enter distance <x,y,z change>: **5'**

> Enter direction: **[select a point downward or below]**

> End point: **[select AutoPt from Assist pull-down menu]**

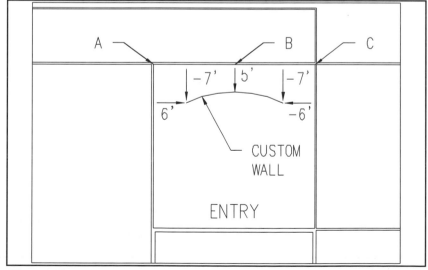

Figure 33.

> Pick base point <last>: **INT of [select intersection at point C as shown in Figure 33 from Assist pull-down menu]**

> Enter distance <x,y,z change>: **[Enter]**

> Enter X HORIZONTAL change <0">: **-6'**

> Enter Y VERTICAL change <0">: **-7'**

> Enter Z change <0">: **[Enter]**

3. Change the arc to the ARWALL layer using the Match Entity Prop command from the Modify menu as shown in Figure 34. Select the arcs and respond to the LA option to match by layer.

Modify>Editing Tools>Match Entity Prop

> Command: MATCHENT

> Change properties of selected objects...

> Select objects: **[select the arc]** 1 found

> Select objects: **[Enter]**

> Match by Color/Height/LAyer/LType/Reset/Thickness/ Ins.Pt. <none>: **LA**

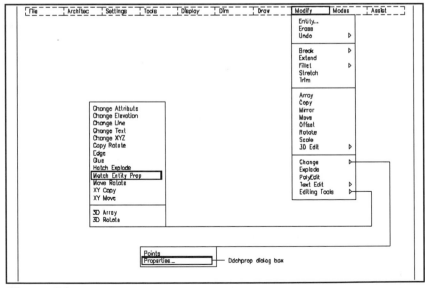

Figure 34.

> Select object with the LAyer to match <none>: **[select any wall line (All walls are on the ARWALL layer)]**

> Match by Color/Height/LAyer/LType/Reset/Thickness/ Ins.Pt. <none>: **[Enter]**

> Processing completed.

4. Use the Properties... option of the Change command from the Modify pull-down menu as shown in Figure 34 and change the wall thickness to 8'. When the Ddchprop dialog box opens, enter 8' in the Thickness: edit box as shown in Figure 35, then pick OK. The arc will be on the layer ARWALL and 8' high.

Modify>Change>Properties...{Change Properties}

> Command: DDCHPROP

> Select objects: **[select arc]** 1 found

> Select objects: **[Enter]**

> **[Change Properties dialog box opens]**

> **[Enter 8' in Thickness: edit box as shown in Figure 35]**

> **[Pick OK]**

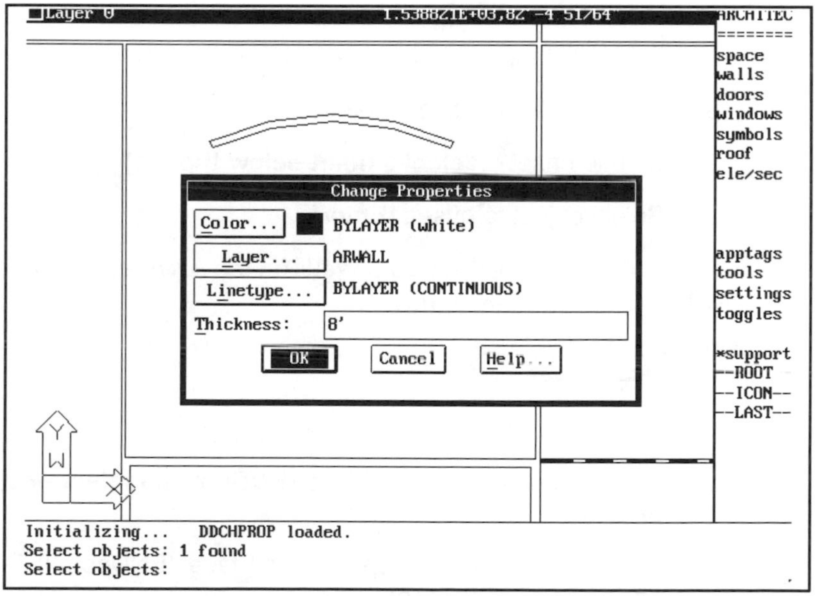

Figure 35.

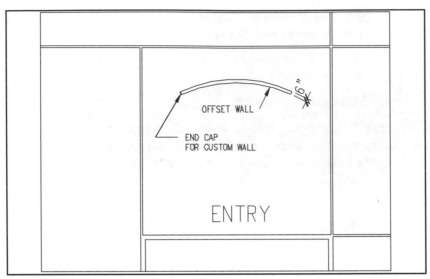

OFFSET WALL

END CAP
FOR CUSTOM WALL

6"

ENTRY

Figure 36.

5.   Select OFFSET from the Modify pull-down menu as shown in Figure 34. Specify a distance of 6″ for the offset shown in Figure 36.

Modes>Offset

> Command: OFFSET

> Offset distance or Through <Through>: **6**

> Select object to offset: **[select arc]**

> Side to offset? **[select a point below the arc]**

> Select object to offset: **[Enter]**

6.   Use the End Caps command from Walls on the Architec menu to cap the walls at each end as shown in Figure 36.

Architec>Walls>End Caps

> Command: DO

> Pick endpoint of one wall face (ENDpoint): **[select endpoint of arc]**

> Pick endpoint of the opposite wall face (ENDpoint): **[select endpoint of other arc]**

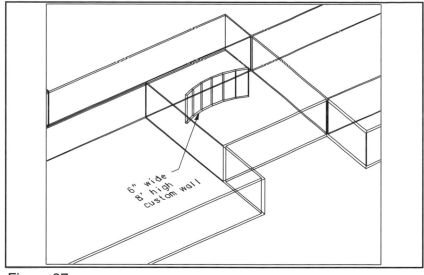

Figure 37.

> Processing completed.

7. Double click on the Architec pull-down menu to repeat the End Caps command or press the space bar to cap the other end of the custom wall.

8. An isometric view of the custom wall is shown in Figure 37.

Session 3
Doors and Windows

The basic floor plan layout is now complete. In this session, we will add doors and windows using ASG's Architectural module to produce the drawing shown in Figure 1.

Set Up Drawing

1. Pick Save from the File pull-down menu to save the drawing from SESSION2.

2. Use the Save As... command to make a copy of the SESSION2 drawing, renaming it to SESSION3.

3. Select Save As... from the File pull-down menu to display the Save Drawing As dialog box.

4. Locate the drawing SESSION2 by picking the appropriate directory in the Directories: list box. Then double click the SESSION2 drawing filename when it appears in the Files: list box.

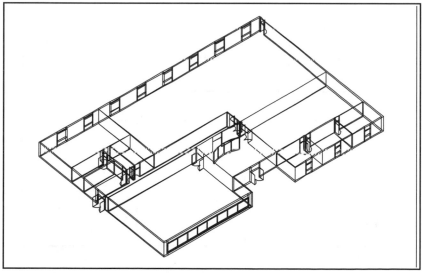

Figure 1.

5. When the SESSION2 drawing appears in the List box, enter the new path and drawing name in the File: box.

6. Enter C:\ASG6TUT\SESSION3\SESSION3 as shown in Figure 2, then pick OK.

7. The AutoCAD drawing screen displays the plan with the prompt: Current drawing name set to C:\ASG6TUT\SESSION3\SESSION3.

8. The ASG Architectural module remains loaded as we continue this next drawing session, learning how to insert doors and windows.

    >   Select application name or . for none: .

    >   Processing completed.

    If you set the AutoLoad default to None as described in the beginning of Session 2, the Architectural menu items do not appear the next time you open the drawing. In this case, you need to select AutoLoad and pick Architec.

9. Select Modify Layers from the Modes pull-down menu and turn off the dashed centerline layer ARWALLCEN.

Modes>Modify Layers>[ARWALLCEN off]

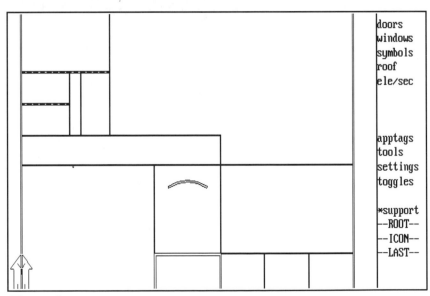

Figure 2.

Setting – 3D

1. The ASG Architectural Settings pull-down menu controls the parameters for inserting symbols.

2. Before proceeding with door and window insertions, verify that the 2D-3D Symbol toggle from the Basic Status display screen is on, so that you can insert all doors as 3D symbols (shown in Figure 3).

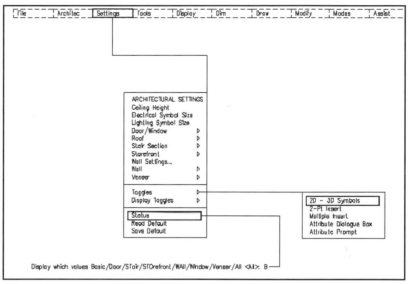

Figure 3.

3. Select Status or Toggles under the Settings pull-down menu to toggle 3D on as shown in Figure 3.

4. Enter letter D from the Basic Status screen toggles 2D - 3D Symbols ON as shown in Figure 4.

> Display which values Basic/Door/STair/STOrefront/WAll/ WIndow/Veneer/All <All>: **B, D**

```
      Display which values Basic/Door/Roof/STAir/STOrefront/WAll/Window/Veneer/All <All>: B


      ARCHITECTURAL STATUS:
      ------------------------------------------------------------------
      SETTINGS
      (a) Cell Ht    Ceiling height...........................................  96.0
      (b) ElSymSiz   Electrical symbols size..........................  0.1875
      (c) LiSymSiz   Lighting symbols size.............................  0.1875
      TOGGLES:
      (d) 2D - 3D    2D - 3D Symbols.....................................  2D
      (e) 2-Pt Ins   2-Pt Insert...............................................  OFF
      (f) AttDioBx   Attribute dialogue box...........................  OFF
      (g) AttPrmpt   Attribute prompt....................................  OFF
      (h) Icon       Automatically display icon menu..............  off
      DISPLAY TOGGLES:
      (i) Door       Door headers..........................................  None
      (j) Window     Window headers......................................  None
      (k) Walls      Walls.......................................................  None
      (l) Hatching   Wall hatching.........................................  None
      (m)Veneers     Wall veneers..........................................  None
      (n) Info       Roof information.....................................  None
      (o) Outline    Roof outline............................................  None

      Enter settings/toggle letter(s) to change or RETURN for graphics screen:D

      3D Symbol Insert - ON
```

Figure 4.

Toggle – Fastdoor

1. Verify that the setting for Fastdoor is off. When Fastdoor is off, each door is immediately inserted, breaking the wall line and creating door headers, when selected from the menu.

    If Fastdoor is on, each door can be placed into position without actually inserting it. The first door can be inserted into position at the wall, then copied to other locations. After the doors are positioned in the wall, the Install command inserts all doors and breaks walls in a "batch mode." Working with Fastdoor on can be very helpful if most of the doors are the same size.

2. Select Fastdoor from Status or Door/Window under the Settings pull-down menu as shown in Figure 5.

3. The Door Status display options are shown in Figure 6. The Door and Window Status boxes both display the same setting and toggle options.

    Settings>StatusD>G

    Settings>StatusWI>G

    > Display which values Basic/Door/Roof/STAir/STOrefront/WAll/WIndow/Veneer/All <All>: **D**

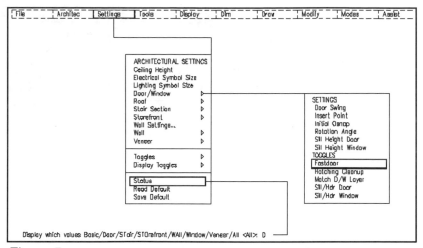

Figure 5.

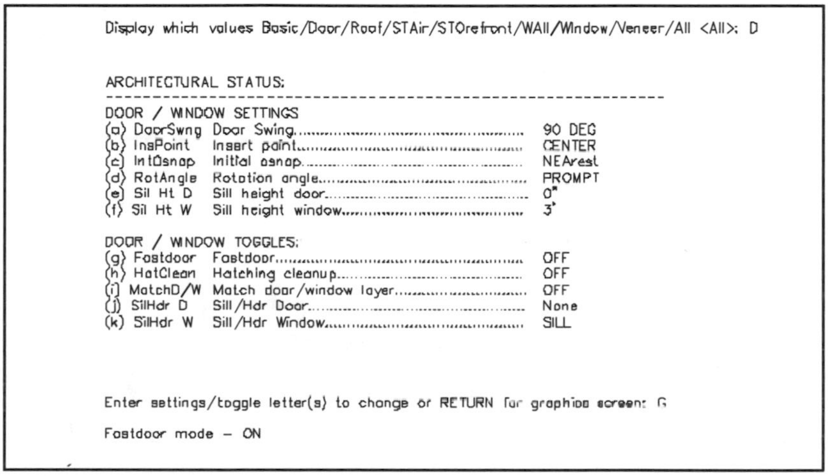

Figure 6.

> Enter settings/toggle letter(s) to change or RETURN for graphics screen: [**Enter**] [**Fastdoor is already set to OFF**]

Settings and Toggles

1. The Settings pull-down menu offers several methods for adjusting door settings and toggles.

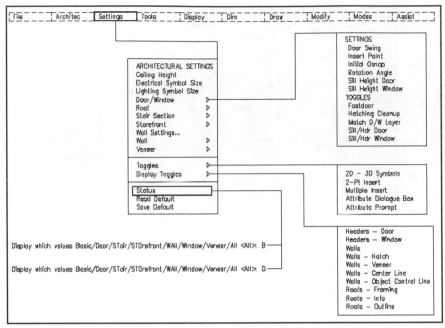

Figure 7.

2.   The full range of setting and toggle selections for either the cascading menus or the Status display screens is shown in Figure 7.

3.   Door settings and toggles are located in both the Basic and Door Status display screens as previously shown in Figures 4 and 6.

The Door Prompts

1.   Choose Door types by picking Doors from the Architec pull-down menu to open a cascading submenu of abbreviated door types as shown in Figure 8, or by picking Icon... to display the Door Menu as shown in Figure 9.

Architec>Doors>[pick a door from the list]

or

Architec>Doors>Icon... >[pick a door from box adjacent to icon slide]

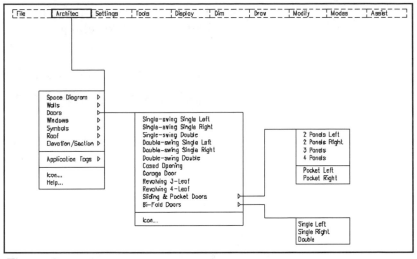

Figure 8.

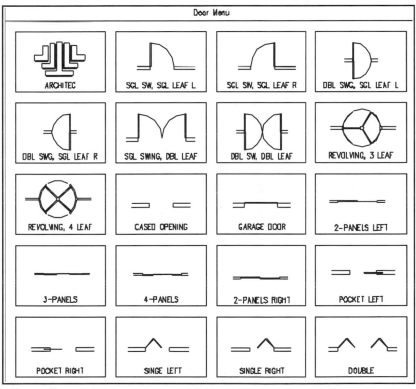

Figure 9.

2.   When the Door command is chosen, the command line offers several opportunities to change options before actually inserting the door. The prompt options are explained below in detail.

> Sill height: 0'-0".Width: 6'-0". Height: 7'-0". Insert: CENTER.

> Pick insertion point or Size/Ins.Pt./Osnap/Rotation (NEArest) <drag>:

S: Size - The door width and height can be changed by typing S or by picking Size from the side menu. (If 3D is off, you won't be prompted for height.) Picking Size calls up the following prompts:

> Enter door width <3'-0">:

> Enter door height <7'-0">:

Note: To change the Door Sill Height, open the Door/Window submenu under the Settings pull-down menu, or Door Status display screen.

Settings>StatusD>E

I: Insertion Point – The insertion point options on doors are strike, center, hinge side, left, and right.

Note: The side menu for Single-swing Single Left, Single-swing Single Right, Double-swing Single Left, and Double-swing Single Right use the options Strike, Center, and Hinge. All other doors use insertion point options Left, Center, and Right. (You can't type H for Hinge or S for Strike.)

The insertion point will move from Left (Strike) to Center to Right (Hinge) side of door as the I option is continuously selected for the prompt.

> Enter new insertion point location Strike/Center/Hinge <Hinge>:

O: Osnap – The door default osnap modes for placing openings can only be reset by making a selection from the side screen menu. For example, typing "Mid" at the options prompt displays the error message "Requires a positive integer." However, you can type the corresponding Osnap value:

Value	Mode
1	Endpoint
2	Midpoint
4	Center
8	Node

16	Quadrant
32	Intersection
64	Insert
128	Perpendicular
256	Nearest
512	Quick

In addition to the standard Osnap options, combination osnaps are also on the side screen menu.

> Enter initial osnap mode for the door insertion <MIDpoint>:

(MIDpoint): If you want to accept the default osnap mode, pick the appropriate wall line to insert the door, otherwise, type or select the a new osnap mode from the side screen.

<drag>: Pressing enter will allow you to see the door dragging from its insertion point at the crosshairs; otherwise accept the MIDpoint osnap to insert the door.

> Pick insertion point <NEArest>:

If any of the above settings are changed, the routine returns you to the initial insertion prompt.

R: Rotation – The rotation angle can be manipulated with the cursor. Use ortho (F8) for cursor control. Selecting an angle from the side menu will keep it as the default. PROMPT determines rotation on a case-by-case basis.

> Enter initial rotation angle <PROMPT>:

Selecting a default rotation angle inserts the opening at that angle, otherwise you are prompted for the rotation angle.

D: Distance – This is the distance the opening is offset from its insertion point. The following prompt appears after you have inserted the door.

> Enter offset distance <0'-4">:

<no offset>: If you don't want to offset the door, press enter to accept the default and the opening will be placed at that exact location.

M: Mirror – Mirror will only reverse the door swing. (Use the AutoCAD mirror command to mirror the door swing to the opposite side of the wall.)

P: Position – Position can be used to relocate the door in the same wall or to another wall.

> Pick new insertion point: **INT** of

Note: The default values for these prompts may differ depending upon your current settings.

Doors

1. A door schedule indicating the door number, size, and room name for all doors to be placed into the plan is shown in Figure 10. Figure 11 shows the same door sizes, using enlarged door tag symbols. (Door tags will be discussed in Chapter 8 – Schedules and Two-way Databases.)

No	Width	Height	Room Name	Typ	Hdw	FireR	Cons	Glas	Fin	Thick	FrC	FrF	Head	Jamb	Sill	Notes	Cost
01	6'-0"	6'-8"	ENTRY														0.00
02	6'-0"	6'-8"	ENTRY														0.00
03	3'-0"	6'-8"	OFFICE-2A														0.00
04	3'-0"	6'-8"	OFFICE-2B														0.00
05	3'-0"	6'-8"	OFFICE-2C														0.00
06	3'-0"	6'-8"	OFFICE-2														0.00
07	3'-0"	6'-8"	OFFICE-3														0.00
08	6'-0"	6'-8"	OFFICE-1														0.00
09	3'-0"	6'-8"	SERVICE														0.00
10	3'-0"	6'-8"	MEN														0.00
11	3'-0"	6'-8"	WOMEN														0.00
12	3'-0"	6'-8"	OFFICE-1														0.00
13	3'-0"	6'-8"	CORRIDOR														0.00
14	3'-0"	6'-8"	OFFICE-3														0.00
15	3'-0"	6'-8"	STAIRS														0.00
16	3'-0"	6'-8"	CORRIDOR														0.00

Figure 10.

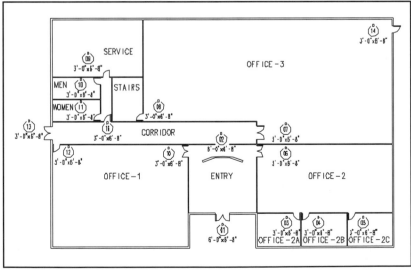

Figure 11.

2. Insert each door into the plan using the icons from the Door Menu under the Doors cascading submenu in the Architec pull-down menu. After you become familiar with the door insertion routine, you may decide to select the door commands from the abbreviated door names listed on the pull-down menu.

Door 01

1. Zoom into the Entry area shown in Figure 12.

2. Insert Door 01, a 6'-0" wide x 6'-8" high Single-swing, double door at the midpoint of the front Entry wall using the Icon menu.

Architec>Doors>Icon...SGL SWING, DBL LEAF

> DO

> Sill height: 0'-0".Width: 6'-0". Height: 7'-0". Insert: CENTER.

> Pick insertion point or Size/Ins.Pt./Osnap/Rotation (NEArest) <drag>:**S**

> Enter door width '-0": [**Enter**]

> Enter door height '-0": **6'8**

> Sill height: 0'-0".Width: 6'-0". Height: 6'-8". Insert: CENTER.

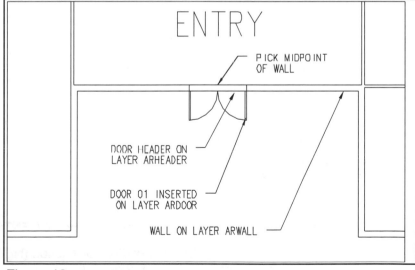

Figure 12.

> Pick insertion point or Size/Ins.Pt./Osnap/Rotation (NEArest) <drag>: [Enter] [**the door is now visible attached to the cursor crosshairs**]

> Pick insertion point (NEArest): **MID** of [**select midpoint of wall as shown in Figure 12**]

> Enter rotation angle <0>: [**use puck and Ortho (F8) to rotate door into correct orientation and pick the screen**]

> The current offset distance is 4".

> Indicate direction of offset or Distance /Ins.pt. /Mirror /Position <no offset>: [**Enter**] [**door is in correct position and no offset is required**]

> Processing completed.

Note: The wall line for the ARWALL layer will break to insert the door on layer ARDOOR, automatically creating the door header on layer ARHEADER. If you want to see the door without the door header, turn ARHEADER layer off by selecting the Display command from the Toggles portion of the Set/Tog pull-down menu.

Warning: If door headers are erased, related door commands will not work properly. Doors cannot be inserted into walls that are polylines.

Door 02 (Cased Opening)

1. Zoom into the area shown in Figure 13 and select Cased Opening from the Doors menu to create a wall opening at the midpoint of the lower wall line behind the custom wall in the Entry.

2. Specify a width and height as listed in the Door Schedule, Figure 10 and shown on the Plan in Figure 11.

3. Try using Cased Opening from the cascading submenu under Doors, instead of the icon menu, to change the values.

Architec>Doors>Cased Opening

> DO

> Sill height: 0'-0".Width: 3'-0". Height: 6'-8". Insert: CENTER.

> Pick insertion point or Size/Ins.Pt./Osnap/Rotation (NEArest) <drag>: [**S**] [**select S to change door width**]

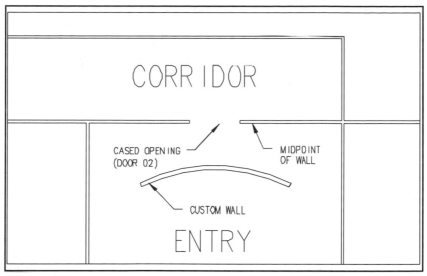

Figure 13.

> Enter cased opening width <3'-0">: **6'**

> Enter cased opening height <6'-8">: [**Enter**]

> Sill height: 0".Width: 6'-0". Height: 6'-8". Insert: CENTER.

> Pick insertion point or Size/Ins.Pt./Osnap/Rotation (NEArest) <drag>: **MID** of [**midpoint of lower wall line**]

> Enter rotation angle <0>: [**use puck to orient the cased opening**]

> The current offset distance is 4".

> Indicate direction of offset or Distance/Ins.Pt/Mirror/Position <no offset>: [**Enter**]

> Processing completed.

Note: The door will insert automatically into a wall drawn at any angle. The door does not have to accurately align with the wall; it will locate the nearest ARWALL layer and reposition itself.

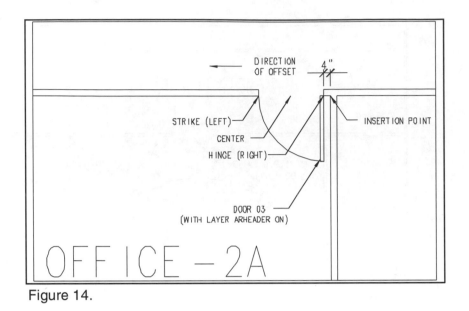

Figure 14.

Door 03

1. Use Figure 11 to locate OFFICE-2A and zoom into this area (adjacent to the ENTRY) as shown in Figure 14. Select a 3'-0" x 6'-8" Single-swing, Single left door from the Icon or Pull-down menu and insert into the plan.

2. All Single-swing doors are inserted 4" from the edge of the wall.

> **Icon menu: Architec>Doors>Icon...SGL SW, SGL LEAF L**

> **Pull-down menu: Architec>Doors>Single-swing Single left**

> >   DO

> >   Sill height:0'-0".Width: 3'-0". Height: 6'-8". Insert: HINGE.

> >   Pick insertion point or Size/Ins.pt./Osnap/Rotation (NEArest) <drag>: **[enter]** [**the door will appear in a dragging mode connected to the cursor crosshairs**]

> >   Pick insertion point (NEArest): **INT** of [**intersection of wall as shown in Figure 14**]

> >   Enter rotation angle <0>: [**use puck to orient the door**]

> >   The current offset distance is 4".

> Indicate direction of offset or Distance/Ins.Pt./Mirror/ Position
  <no offset>: [**pick a point toward left or strike side of door**]

> Processing completed.

Doors 04 – 16

1. Insert the remaining doors listed in Figure 10 and shown in Figure 11.

Icon menu: Architec>Doors>Icon... [select from available options]

Pull-down menu:Architec>Doors>[select from available options]

Overview - Door Tools Menu

1. Use the door Tools menu shown in Figure 16 to make changes to your doors
   and windows. The options and applications are discussed below.

Install

When the Fastdoor mode is on, all the doors are positioned, but not yet inserted
into the walls. This command allows you to insert all the doors and windows
in "batch mode."

> All selected doors and windows will be inserted in 3-D...

> Enter wall thickness <0'-4">: (**See Note below**)

> Select doors and windows to install <all>:

> Select objects:[**press Enter or pick door(s)**]

> Processing — please wait.

Note: If the wall thickness is significant, this prompt to locate the opposite
wall will appear. Don't cancel the prompt if you are not sure of the wall
thickness, as the following prompt will appear:

> Pick opposite wall line (PERpendicular):

Offset

Relocates any door or window from one wall to another by removing the door
or window and restoring the original wall lines.

> Window the door or window to offset...

> Pick first corner:

> Pick second corner:

> Pick insertion point (NEArest):

> Enter rotation angle:

> Processing — please wait.

Reflect

Mirrors the door swing from the strike to hinge side and vice versa. However, you must use the AutoCAD MIRROR command to mirror the door to the opposite side of the wall.

> Select doors to reflect:

> Select objects: 1 found

> Select objects:

> Processing completed.

Remove

Completely removes the door or window and mends the wall. This command will turn ARHEADER layer on during processing. When the ARHEADER layer is frozen, a prompt appears: "Warning: layer ARHEADER is frozen. Will not display until thawed."

> Select windows and doors to remove:

> Select objects: 1 found

> Select objects:

> Processing completed.

Note: If the wall height is less than 3', you may get the prompt "Wall height too low."

Suggestion: If you are drawing lines for layer ARWALL and are not using the Continuous Wall command, change the wall thickness to 8'.

Note: You may get the message "No appropriate door or window found matching layer ARWALL..." or "No wall line found." The walls must reside in the ARWALL layer.

Suggestion: The wall on layer ARWALL may be a polyline; explode the wall line and try again.

Scale Fastdoor

Rescales selected doors placed with Fastdoor on, but not yet installed. This command allows you to change doors in two ways:

You can pick individual doors to rescale, or you can create a selection set using detailed search information to change only the doors matching the given criteria. The following prompts appear:

> Detailed fastdoor selection process? Yes/No <Yes>:

Respond Yes for <u>detailed</u> selection process.
Detailed selection lets you set up a selection set.

Respond No to use a <u>manual</u> selection process.
Manual selection lets you pick doors to change.

If you select No (manual selection) the following prompts appear:

> Select door to rescale <all>:

> Select objects: [**pick doors you want to change, using the AutoCAD selection set, then press Enter. You are then prompted for the parameters to change.**]

If you select Yes (detailed selection) the following prompts appear:

> Detailed selection lets you pick only doors that match certain criteria.

> Enter selection parameter Drtyp/Wintyp/DHeight/ WHeight/DWidth/WWidth <Drtyp>: [**pick the first search parameter from the side screen menu**]

Drtyp

> Select door type from screen menu <none>: [**pick the door type you want to change from the side screen menu**]

Wintyp

> ➤ Select window type from screen menu <none>:
> **[pick the window type you want to change from the side screen menu]**

DHeight/WHight/DWidth/WWidth

> \> Enter selection parameter Drtyp/Wintyp/DHeight/ WHeight/DWidth/WWidth <done>: **[select DH, WH, DW or WW]**

> ➤ Enter operator Equal/Less/LE/Grtr/GE <GE>: **[pick an operator from the screen menu]**

Equal	Equal to (=)
Less	Less than (<)
LE	Less than or equal to (<=)
Grtr	Greater than (>)
GE	Greater than or equal to (=>)

Note: After selecting the operator, you can specify a value for the operation. Separate prompts appear similar to the following to change door or window height and width:

> ➤ Enter door height: **[type a value]**

After the doors are rescaled, use the Install command from the Tools Door/ Window pull-down menu.

Swing

Allows you to change the degree of the door swing. You can type or select only those options listed on the side screen menu: closed, 45 degrees, 90 degrees, or 180 degrees.

> \> Enter door swing (Closed,/45/90/180) <90>:

> \> Select doors to change swing:

> \> Select objects: 1 found

> \> Select objects:

> \> Processing completed.

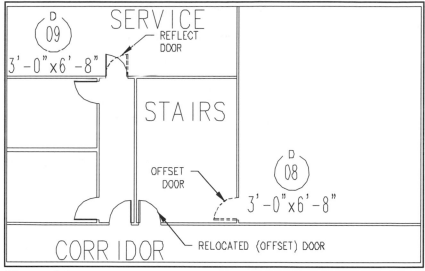

Figure 15.

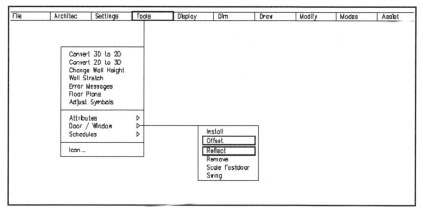

Figure 16.

Offset Door

1. Offset door 08 in the Stairs area from Office-3 to the Corridor as shown in Figure 15.

2. Select Offset from the Door/Window submenu under the Tools pull-down menu as shown in Figure 16.

    Tools>Door/Window>Offset

> Window the door or window to offset...

> Pick first corner: [**select first corner of the crossing window**]

> Pick second corner: [**select second corner of the crossing window**]

> Pick insertion point (NEArest): [**reposition the door to another wall, then use the STRETCH command if an exact location is required**]

> Enter rotation angle: [**use puck to orient the door; use the F8 key to turn OSNAP on**]

> Processing — please wait.

> Processing completed.

Reflect Door

1. Reflect door 09 as shown in Figure 15 by selecting Reflect from the Tools menu.

Tools>Door/Window>Reflect

> Select doors to reflect:[**pick door with puck**]

> Select objects: 1 selected, 1 found

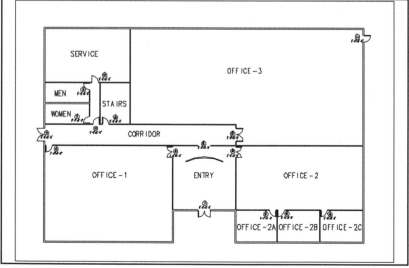

Figure 17.

> Select objects:[**Enter**]

> Processing completed.

2. The revised Floor Plan with all the doors inserted is shown in Figure 17.

Windows

1. Figure 18 is a window schedule indicating the window number, size, and room name for all windows to be placed into the plan. Figure 19 contains enlarged window tag symbols that show the window numbers and sizes for this exercise.

2. Insert all windows as 3D symbols. This Toggle was set to 3D from the previous exercise.

`Settings>Toggles>2D - 3D Symbols`

or

`Settings>StatusB>D`

3. Insert the first three windows with Fastdoor OFF. The Fastdoor toggle applies to both doors and windows. When toggled to OFF, doors and window are inserted immediately. (This toggle was set to OFF earlier in this exercise.)

`Settings>Door/Window>Fastdoor`

or

`Settings>StatusD>G`

or

`Settings>StatusWl>G`

No	Width	Height	Sill Ht	Room Name	Typ	Cons	Glass	Fin	GlsThk	Head	Jamb	Sill	Notes
01	4'-0"	4'-0"	3'-0"	OFFICE-2A									
02	4'-0"	4'-0"	3'-0"	OFFICE-2B									
03	4'-0"	4'-0"	3'-0"	OFFICE-2C									
04	6'-0"	5'-6"	3'-0"	SERVICE									
05	6'-0"	5'-6"	3'-0"	SERVICE									
06	6'-0"	5'-6"	3'-0"	OFFICE-3									
07	6'-0"	5'-6"	3'-0"	OFFICE-3									
08	6'-0"	5'-6"	3'-0"	OFFICE-3									
09	6'-0"	5'-6"	3'-0"	OFFICE-3									
10	6'-0"	5'-6"	3'-0"	OFFICE-3									
11	6'-0"	5'-6"	3'-0"	OFFICE-3									
12	-	10'-0"	4"	OFFICE-2A									

Figure 18.

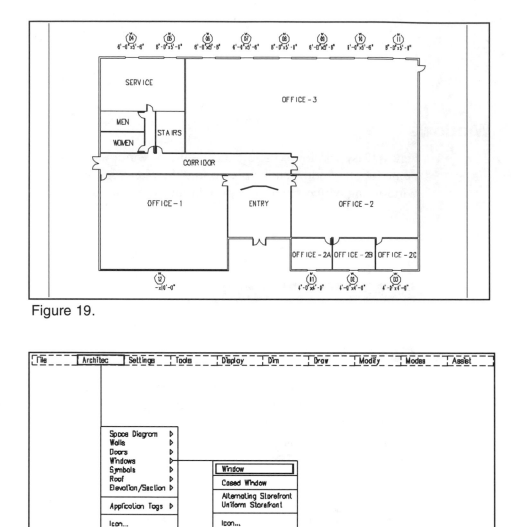

Figure 19.

Figure 20.

Window 01

1. Insert a window from the Architec/Windows pull-down as shown in Figure 20, or icon Window Menu shown in Figure 21, at the midpoint of the interior wall line in OFFICE-2A.

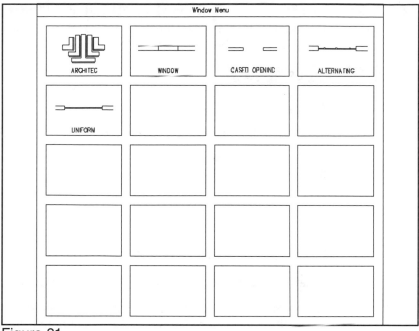

Figure 21.

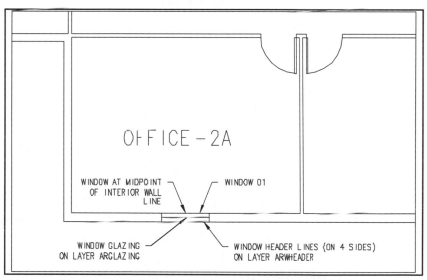

Figure 22.

2. Zoom into OFFICE-2A as shown in Figure 22 and insert Window 01, a 4'-0" wide x 4'-0" high window with a sill height of 3'-0". Unlike the door prompt, you will be prompted for the sill height if 3D symbols is on.

Architec>Windows>Window

> DO

> Sill height: 3'-0".Width: 3'-0".Height: 3'-0". Insert: CENTER.

> Pick insertion point or Size/Osnap/Rotation (NEArest) <drag>: [**S**]

> Enter window width <3'-0">: **4'**

> Enter window height <3'-0">: **4'**

> Enter window sill height <3'-0">: **3'**

> Sill height: 3'-0".Width: 4'-0".Height: 4'-0". Insert: CENTER.

> Pick insertion point or Size/Osnap/Rotation (NEArest) <drag>: [**MID**] of [**interior wall of OFFICE-2A as shown in Figure 22**]

> Enter rotation angle <0>: [**pick with puck to orient window**]

> The current offset distance is 4".

> Indicate direction of offset or Distance/Position <no offset>: [**Enter**]

> Processing completed.

Windows 02 and 03

1. Insert windows 02 and 03 at the midpoint of the interior wall lines in rooms OFFICE-2B and OFFICE-2C as shown in Figure 23.

2. Use the same procedural prompts as Window 01. Press Enter or the space bar to recall the previous windows command. If you used the pull-down menu, highlight Architec along the status bar at the top of the screen then double click this item to repeat the Windows command.

Architec>Windows>Window

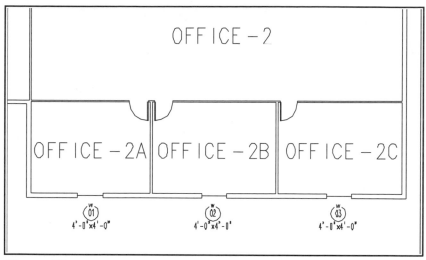

Figure 23.

Window 04

1. Zoom into the upper left corner of the Service room as shown in Figure 24 to insert window 04 with Fastdoor ON. Use the Osnap intersect or endpoint and offset the window 12'-8" to the right with the Distance option.

2. Reset Fastdoor from the Settings pull-down menu under Door/Window or Status as shown previously in Figure 5 to insert a series of windows of the same size.

`Settings>Door/Window>Fastdoor`

or

`Settings>Status>D>G`

or

`Settings>Status>WI>G`

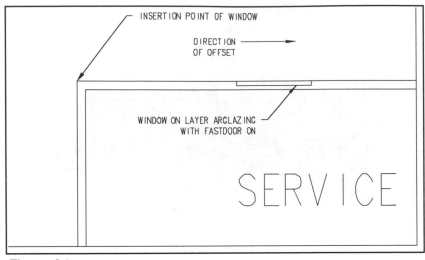

INSERTION POINT OF WINDOW

DIRECTION ⎯⎯⎯⎯⎯⎯→
OF OFFSET

WINDOW ON LAYER ARGLAZING
WITH FASTDOOR ON

SERVICE

Figure 24.

3. The window will remain in position but will not be installed until the Install command is selected from the Tools pull-down menu. Open the Windows submenu and then select Window to install a 6'-0" wide by 5'-6" high window with a 3' sill height.

Architec>Windows>Window

> DO

> Sill height: 3'-0".Width: 3'-0".Height: 3'-0". Insert:CENTER.

> Pick insertion point or Size/Osnap/Rotation (NEArest) <drag>:
  S

> Enter window width <3'-0">: **6'**

> Enter window height <3'-0">: **5'6**

> Enter window sill height <3'-0">:**3'**

> Sill height:3'-0".Width:6'-0".Height: 5'-6". Insert:CENTER

> Pick insertion point or Size/Osnap/Rotation (NEArest) <drag>:
  **[Pick Insert Point from Doors/Windows on the Settings
  pull-down menu]**

> Enter insertion point location Left/Center/Right <Center>: **L** [**type L or pick Left from side menu**]

> Sill height: 3'-0".Width: 6'-0".Height: 5'-6". Insert:LEFT

> Pick insertion point or Size/Osnap/Rotation (NEArest) <drag>: **O**

> Enter initial osnap mode for the window insertion <NEArest>: **ENDP** of [**pick intersection or endpoint at left corner of exterior building wall. (You** *must* **select the INTersec or ENDpoint osnap mode from the side menu, or type 32.)**]

> Enter rotation angle <0>: [**pick with puck to orient window**]

> The current offset distance is 4".

> Indicate direction of offset or Distance /Position <no offset>: **D**

> Enter offset distance <4">: **12'8**

> The current offset distance is 12'-8".

> Indicate direction of offset or Distance/Position <no offset>: [**pick a point to the right of window**]

> Processing completed.

Note: Notice how the window is placed in position, but the wall lines are not broken. The window can be relocated if necessary, using the MOVE command. Only after the Install command is executed, can the Offset option be used to relocate the window and mend the wall lines.

Array Windows 05-11

1. Use the AutoCAD ARRAY command to array window 04 along the exterior building wall line for windows 05-11 before installing them in a "batch mode" as shown in Figure 25 with the Install command.

2. Specify a rectangular array with 1 row and 8 columns and 18' between the columns.

Command: ARRAY

> Select objects: **W**

> First corner: Other corner: 1 found [**include entire window in your window selection set**]

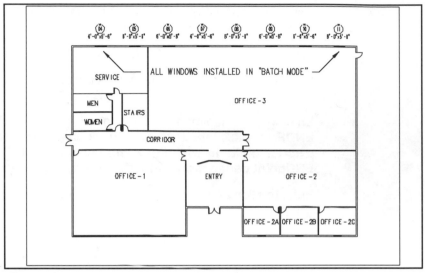

Figure 25.

> Select objects: **[Enter]**

> Rectangular or Polar array (R/P): **R**

> Number of rows (—) <1> **1**

> Number of columns (|||) <1> **8**

> Distance between columns (|||): **18'**

Install Windows

Select the Install command under Door/Window in the Tools menu (see Figure 16) to insert windows 04-11 into the wall. The exterior wall thickness is 8″.

Tools>Door/Window>Install

> DO

> All selected doors and windows will be installed in 3-D...

> Enter Wall thickness <0'-4″>: **[Enter]**

Note: Don't cancel the prompt if you are not sure of the wall thickness. If the wall thickness is significant, the prompt appears "Pick opposite wall line

(PERpendicular):" to locate the opposite wall. An aperture box will appear for selecting the perpendicular wall.

> Select doors and windows to install <all>:

> Select objects: [**Enter**]

> Processing — please wait.

> Processing completed.

Storefront Window 12

1. Installing storefront windows involves an initial preparation and cleanup.

2. Change the Fastdoor toggle mode to OFF from the Settings pull-down menu.

   `Settings>Door/Window>Fastdoor`

or

   `Settings>Status>D>G`

or

   `Settings>Status>WI>G`

3. Select the Storefront option of the Display Status command shown in Figure 26 or open the Storefront submenu as shown in Figure 27 to customize the settings.

4. Storefront terms described in the Status display and cascading submenu are shown in Figure 28.

5. The values to change are described as follows:

(a)	Header depth	8″
(d)	Mullion depth	6″
(f)	Mullion width	2″
(g)	Sill depth	8″
(h)	Sill height	1′-4″
(i)	Storefront height	10′

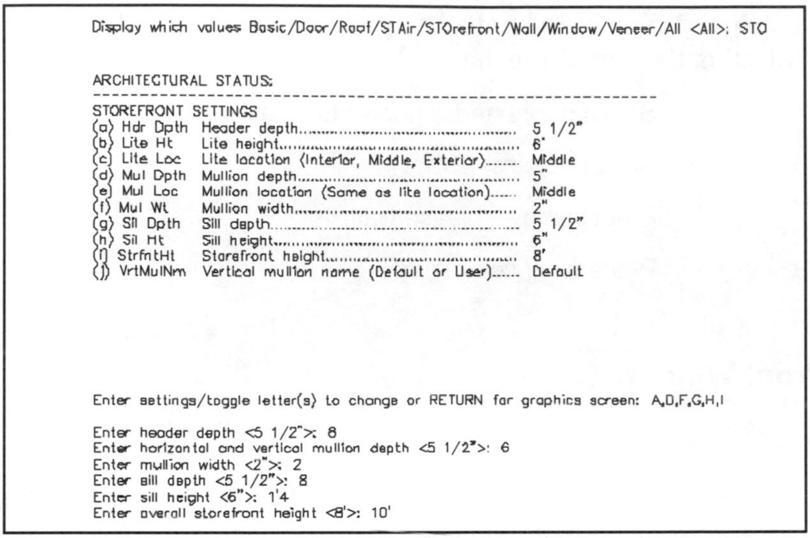

Figure 26.

Figure 27.

or

Settings>Status>STO

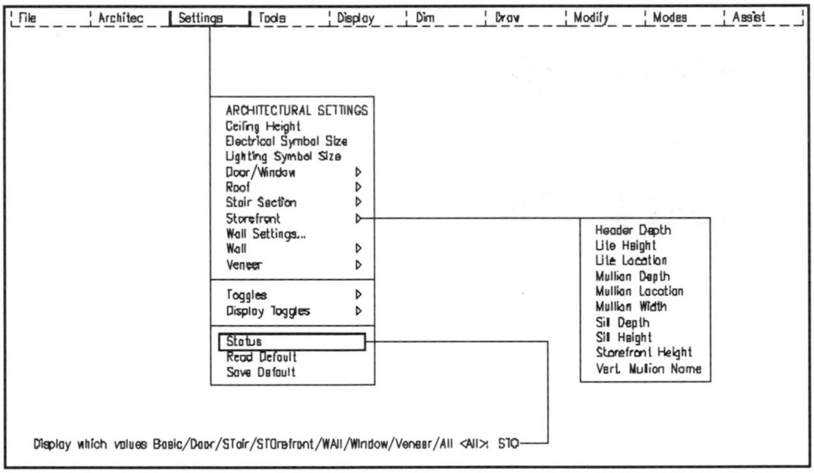

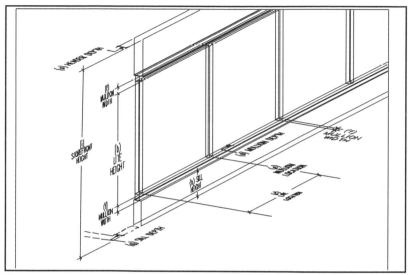

Figure 28.

> Display which values Basic/Door/Roof/STAir/ STOrefront/ WAll/WIndow/All <ALL>:**STO**

> Enter setting/toggle letter(s) to change or RETURN for graphics screen: **A,D,F,G,H,I**

> Enter header depth <5 1/2">: **8**

> Enter horizontal and vertical mullion depth <5">: **6**

> Enter mullion width <2">: **2**

> Enter sill depth <5 1/2">: **8**

> Enter sill height <6>:**1'4**

> Enter overall storefront height <8'>: **10'**

6. Zoom into OFFICE-1 to create two wing walls along the face of the building. Draw a construction line using the AutoPt command that extends 2' from the interior vertical wall line to the left front exterior wall as shown in Figure 29. Do the same for the right side of OFFICE-1. Trim both front horizontal wall lines to your construction lines, then erase the construction line.

`AutoCAD/ASG:Draw>Line [left side]`

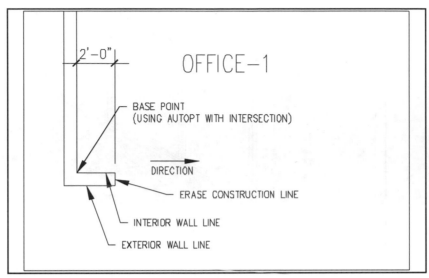

Figure 29.

> Command: LINE

> From point: [**select AutoPt from the Assist pull-down menu**]

> Pick base point (last): **INT** of [**select intersection of interior wall line**]

> Enter distance <x,y,z change>: **2'**

> Enter direction: [**pick a point to the right**]

> To point: **PER** to [**perpendicular to the front exterior wall as shown in Figure 29**]

> To point: [**Enter**]

AutoCAD/ASG:Draw>Line [right side]

> Command: LINE

> From point: [**select AutoPt from the Assist pull-down menu**]

> Pick base point: **INT** of

> Enter distance <x,y,z change>: **2'**

> Enter direction: [**pick a point to the left**]

> To point: **PER** to [**perpendicular to the front exterior wall**]

> To point: [**Enter**]

AutoCAD:Modify>Trim

> Command: TRIM

> Select cutting edge(s)...

> Select objects: **W** [**window the exterior wall including the
left and right side construction lines**]

> First corner: Other corner: 2 found

> Select objects:[**Enter**]

> object to trim/Undo: [**select interior wall line**]

> object to trim/Undo: [**select exterior wall line**]

> object to trim/Undo: [**Enter**]

AutoCAD:Modify>Erase

> Command: ERASE

> Select objects: **W** [**select left and right construction lines**]

> First corner: Other corner: 2 found

> Select objects: [**Enter**]:

7. Select the Uniform storefront command from the Architec Windows pull-down menu as shown in Figure 30. You will draw a storefront with eight windows.

| File | Architec | Settings | Tools | Display | Dim | Draw | Modify | Modes | Assist |

Space Diagram	▷
Walls	▷
Doors	▷
Windows	▷
Symbols	▷
Roof	▷
Elevation/Section	▷
Application Tags	▷
Icon...
Help...

| Window |
| Cased Window |
| Alternating Storefront |
| Uniform Storefront |
| Icon... |

Figure 30.

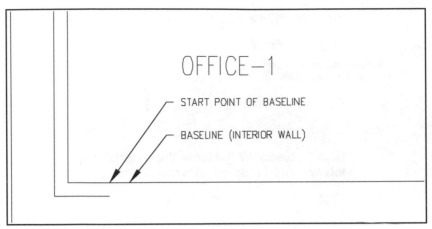

Figure 31.

Architec>Windows>Uniform

> DO

> The storefront INTERIOR wall defines its baseline.

> Pick first baseline endpoint: **ENDP** of [**endpoint of interior wall line as shown in Figure 31**]

Note: Draw a baseline from the endpoint of the left interior wall of OFFICE-1. This line becomes the interior of your storefront.

> Pick second baseline endpoint: **ENDP** of [**opposite interior wall**]

> Indicate EXTERIOR face of the storefront: [**select an area outside of the building below OFFICE-1 as shown in Figure 32**]

> Enter number of windows <1>: **8**

> Processing — please wait.

> Building block...

> New storefront block name: AR_STRF01

> Processing completed.

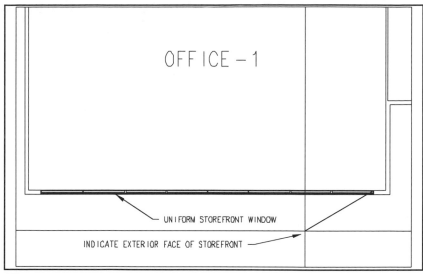

Figure 32.

Note: The storefront becomes a block named sequentially, for example AR_STRF02, AR_STRF03, and so forth, for each window group.

***TIP – Save Drawing

1. You have now completed inserting doors and windows into the Plan drawing.

2. An isometric view of the drawing is shown in Figure 1.

3. Save your drawings at the end of this session and copy the completed drawing to a floppy disk for future retrieval or editing in later sessions.

4. Using this completed SESSION 3 drawing as a prototype, create a new drawing called SESSION 4 to place a roof on the building.

Session 4
Roofs

This lesson will show you how to construct a 3D roof on the building floor plan you created in the first three sessions.

Creating a New Drawing

1. Create a new drawing for Session 4 using the completed drawing from Session 3.

2. Select New from the File pull-down menu and enter SESSION3 in the prototype edit box.

3. Name the new drawing SESSION4 as shown in Figure 1.

4. Edit the SESSION4 drawing to draw a 3D roof on the building.

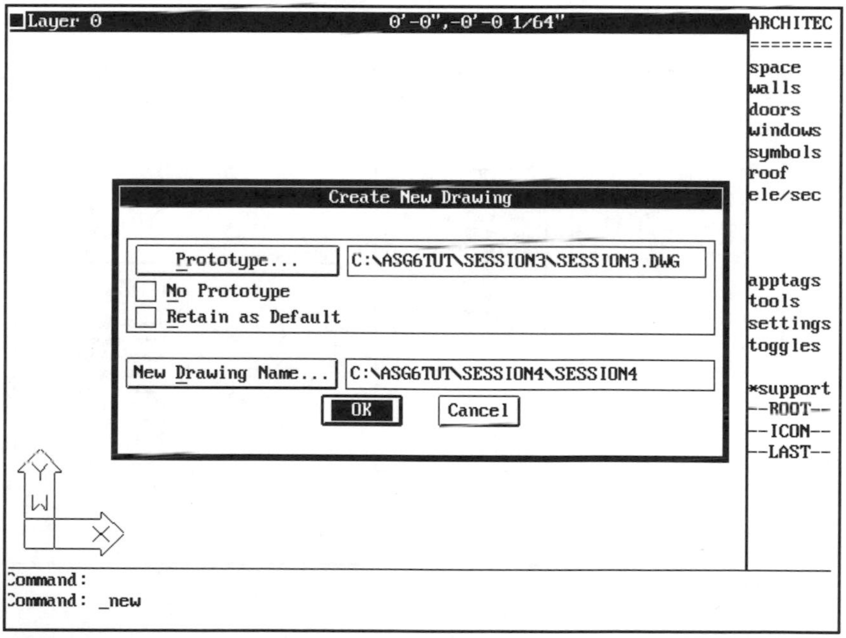

Figure 1.

5. The ASG Architectural program loads automatically when you bring up your drawing.

6. The Roof submenu on the Architec pull-down or icon menu contains three commands that are used in sequence to create a 2D or 3D roof:

(1) Outline the Perimeter

(2) Define Edge-All

(3) Draw Roof

Roof – Settings and Toggles

1. Roof settings and toggles can be changed from the Settings pull-down menu. Selecting Roof opens a submenu as shown in Figure 2 displaying the same commands that are available from the Roof Status display.

2. The settings and toggles of the Settings pull-down menu used for building a 3D roof are described below.

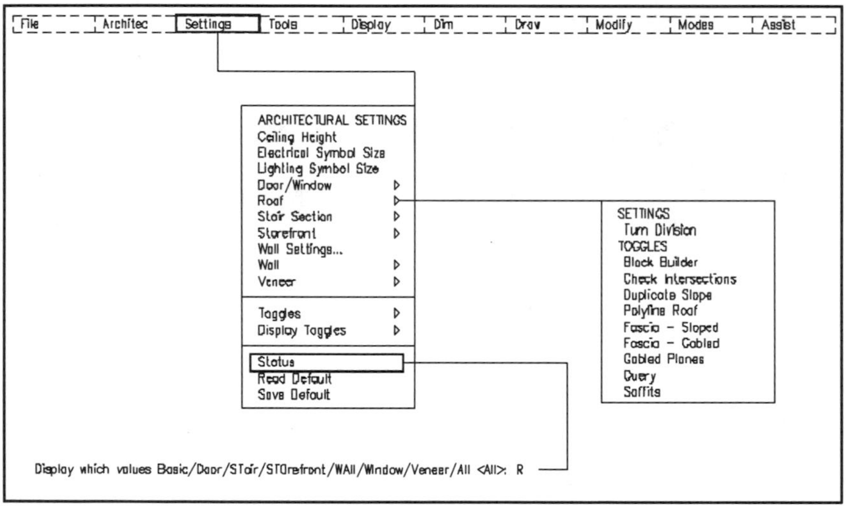

Figure 2.

Turn Division	Controls segment size and number for curved roofs.
Block Builder	Creates a block of the 3D roof.
Check Intersection	Cleans up hip and valley lines for complicated intersecting roof edges.
Duplicate Slope	Offers duplication of slope, elevation, fascia and soffit values for all planes of a roof diagram.
Polyline Roof	Creates roof diagram using polylines instead of lines.
Fascia – Sloped	Controls inclusion of fascias on sloped roof planes.
Fascia – Gabled	Controls inclusion of fascias on gabled roof planes.
Gabled Planes	Creates a plane to fill the space between the top of a wall and the gabled roof planes.
Query	Prompts for changes to roof values during roof slope creation process.
Soffits	Includes option for specifying soffit size during roof prompt.

3. The Roof Status screen shows the following settings:

Block Builder	ON
Check Intersections	ON
Duplicate Slope Values	ON
Polyline Roof	ON
Fascia - Sloped	ON
Fascia - Gabled	ON
Gabled Planes	ON
Soffits	ON

4. Select the Roof status display command from the Settings pull-down menu to verify or change the roof settings shown in Figure 3.

Settings>Status>R,B

> Display which values Basic/Door/Roof/STAir/STOrefront/WAll/WIndow/Veneer/All: **R**

> Enter settings/toggle letter(s) to change or RETURN for graphics screen: **B**

> Build roofs into a block - OFF

```
Display which values Basic/Door/Roof/STAir/STorefront/WAll/Window/Veneer/All <All>; R


ARCHITECTURAL STATUS:
-------------------------------------------------------------
ROOF SETTINGS
(a) TurnDiv    Number of degrees per turn division..........   22.5
               (Specifies how arc'ed roofs are segmented).

ROOF TOGGLES:
(b) BlackBld   Build completed roofs into a block..............   ON
(c) CheckInt   Check for intersections of common roofs...   ON
(d) DupSlope   Duplicate slope values................................   ON
(e) PolyRoof   Polyline outline each roof plane...................   OFF
(f) FasciaSl   Draw edge fascia on sloped roof edges......   ON
(g) FasciaGa   Draw edge fascia on gabled roof edges.......   ON
(h) Gable      Draw gabled planes....................................   ON
(i) Soffits    Draw soffits on roof edges...........................   ON




Enter settings/toggle letter(s) to change or RETURN for graphics screen: B
Build roofs into a block— OFF
```

Figure 3.

Outline Roof Perimeter

1. The first step in drawing the roof is to select Roof, then Outline Perimeter from the Architec pull-down shown in Figure 4, or the icon Roof Menu shown in Figure 5.

2. The Outline Perimeter command will draw a polyline around the building. An endpoint osnap will appear allowing you to snap to the eight exterior corners of the building.

3. A dashed polyline outline is drawn on the layer RFPERIM around the perimeter of your proposed roof as shown in Figure 6.

   Architec>Roof>Outline Perimeter

   > DO

   > Outline the perimeter. Enter DONE when finished.

   > From point (ENDpoint): [**select the first exterior corner of the building**]

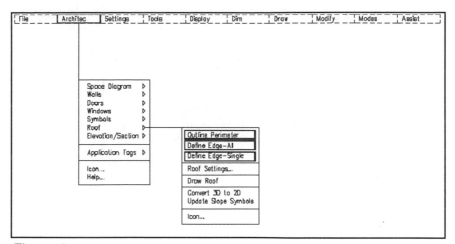

Figure 4.

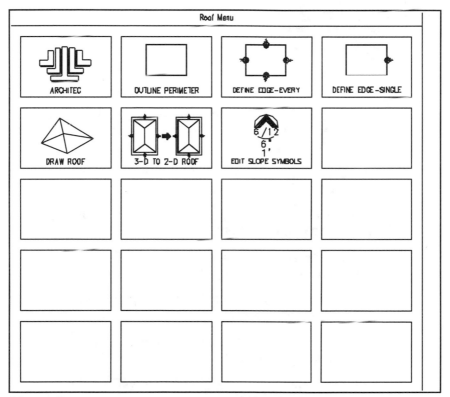

Figure 5.

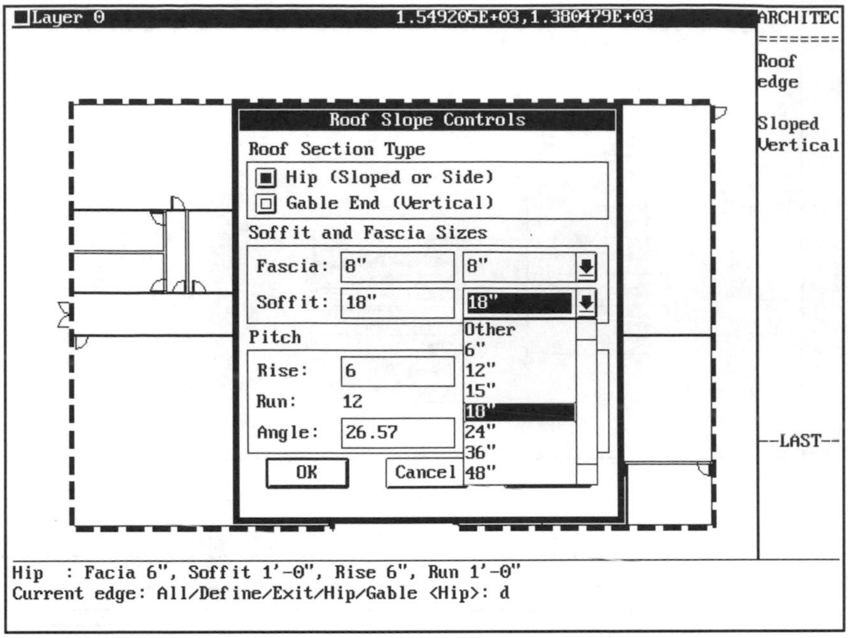

Figure 6.

> Arc/Close/Halfwidth/Length/Undo/Width/<Endpoint of line>:
> [**proceed selecting the remaining building corners as
> shown in figure 5**]

> Arc/Close/Halfwidth/Length/Undo/Width/<Endpoint of line>:
> [**select next intersection**]

> Arc/Close/Halfwidth/Length/Undo/Width/<Endpoint of line>:
> [**select next intersection**]

> Arc/Close/Halfwidth/Length/Undo/Width/<Endpoint of line>:
> [**select next intersection**]

> Arc/Close/Halfwidth/Length/Undo/Width/<Endpoint of line>:
> [**select next intersection**]

> Arc/Close/Halfwidth/Length/Undo/Width/<Endpoint of line>:
> [**select next intersection**]

> Arc/Close/Halfwidth/Length/Undo/Width/<Endpoint of line>:
> [**select next intersection**]

> Arc/Close/Halfwidth/Length/Undo/Width/<Endpoint of line>:
CLOSE

Note: If you type "c" instead of picking CLOSE from the side menu, you must pick DONE from the side menu to complete the process.

Define Roof Edges

1. The second step is to define the roof slope, fascia height, and soffit or roof overhang.

2. The Define Edge – All command enables you to define roof values for each roof plane without actually creating the roof diagram.

3. Pick the Define Edge – All command under the Roof submenu in the Architec pull-down menu and then select the dashed polyline.

4. Select the D option to open the Roof Slope Controls dialog box.

5. Assign a Fascia height of 8" using the popup list as shown in Figure 7, or type it in the Fascia: edit box.

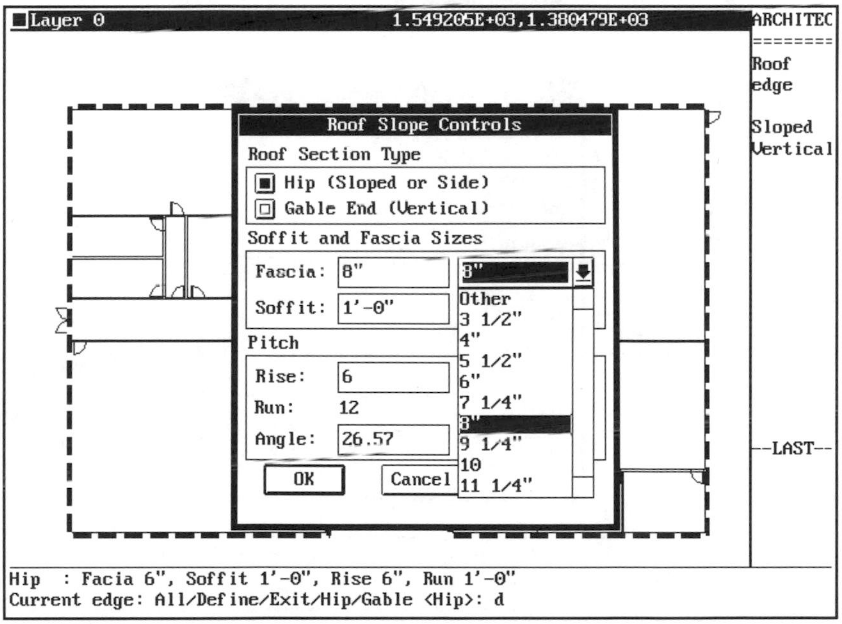

Figure 7.

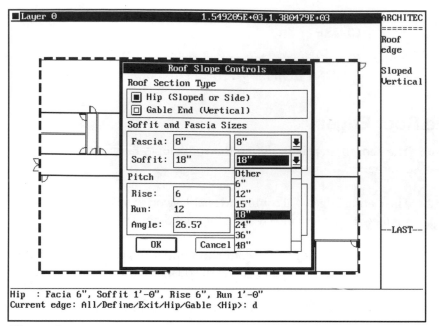

Figure 8.

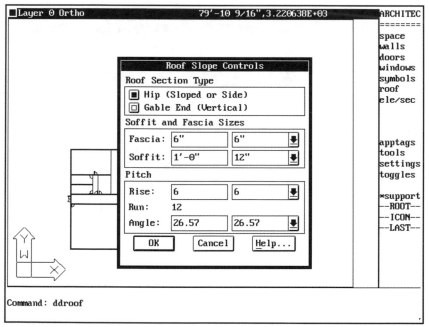

Figure 9.

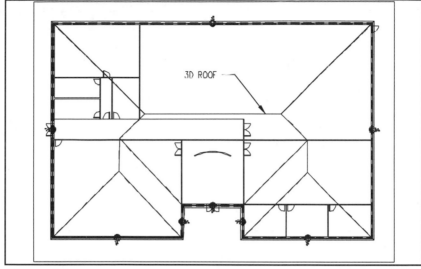

Figure 10

6. Select a Soffit width of 18" from the Soffit popup list as shown in Figure 8, or enter a value in the Soffit: edit box.

7. Verify that Roof Section Type is toggled to Hip. Enter 8 in the Rise: edit box as shown in Figure 9, or select it from the popup list.

8. The roof command assigns a roof symbol containing the roof information to each roof plane as shown in Figure 10.

Architec>Roof>Define Edge - All

> Select polyline perimeter roof edge: [**select the polyline**]

> Processing — please wait.

> Checking edges for slope symbols — 1 of 8

> Gable: Fascia 6", Soffit 6"

> Hip : Fascia 6", Soffit 1'-0", Rise 6", Run 1'-0"

> Current edge: All/Define/Exit/Hip/Gable Hip:**D**

Note: Dialog box opens to change settings for Fascia height, Soffit height and Rise. Enter the new values.

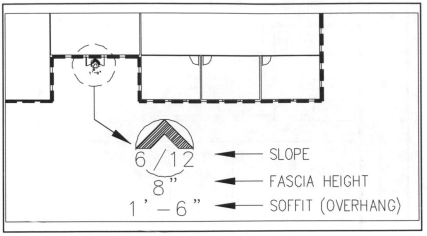

Figure 11.

> Hip : Fascia 8", Soffit 1'-6", Rise 8", Run 1'-0"

> Current edge: All/Define/Exit/Hip/Gable Hip:**[Enter]**

> Checking edges for slope symbols — 2 of 8.

Note: Hit Enter to continue checking edges for slope symbols for all roof edges. The last roof prompt is as indicated below.

> Processing completed.

If Duplicate Slope is OFF, a roof symbol appears with a rubberbanding line connected to the crosshairs, assigning the fascia height and soffit overhang as you define the roof plane at each roof edge. Otherwise, the symbol will appear automatically at all the roof planes.

9. The roof symbol values shown in Figure 11 can be altered later by selecting Update Slope Symbols in the Roof menu under the Architec pull-down menu.

Creating a 3D Roof

1. Select Draw Roof from Roof under the Architec pull-down menu.

2. The Draw Roof command automatically activates the Autosave command and saves the current drawing prior to being executed.

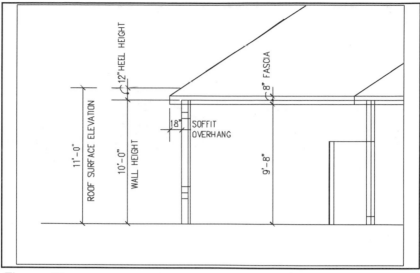

Figure 12.

3. Draw a 3D roof with the roof elevation at the perimeter line 11'. The perimeter line and other roof terms are shown in Figure 12.

Architec>Roof>Draw Roof

> DO

> Save the drawing ROOF? Yes/No/Save_as <Yes>: **Y**

> Processing completed

> Roof surface elevation = UCS height + wall height + heel height

Note: If the perimeter line is on the outside wall edge, roof surface elevation includes the height of the wall and the distance from the top of the outside wall face (top of bearing plate) to the roof plane (as shown in Figure 12).

> Enter roof elevation above UCS at perimeter line <8'-6">: **11'**

> Enter roof type 2d/3d/Both <Both>: **3D**

> Select polyline perimeter roof edge: [**select polyline**]

> Select other lines as cutting planes <none>: [**Enter**]

> Processing — please wait

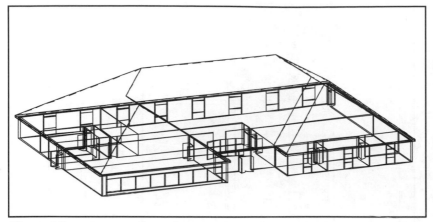

Figure13.

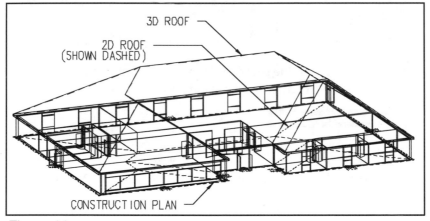

Figure 14.

> Checking edges for slope symbols — 8 of 8

> Intersecting planar regions — 8 of 8

> Processing — please wait

> Merging parallel planes...

> Drawing roof planes...

> Processing completed

4. The 3D roof is shown in plan view (Figure 10) and isometric view in Figure 13.

***TIP – Roofs

1. The roof can be converted from 3D to 2D with the Convert 3D to 2D command under the Roof submenu in the Architec pull-down menu. If the roof is a block, it must be exploded first. The 2D roof is constructed at 0 elevation as shown in Figure 14.

   Architec>Roof>Convert 3D to 2D

2. The Update Slope Symbols allows you to edit slope symbols by selecting the tag shown previously in Figure 11 and changing the roof elevation, fascia, slope and/or soffit.

3. When the toggle for 3D roof is ON, a roof is created as a block on layer RFBLOCK with dashed framing lines on layer RFFRAME below the roof block.

4. The Display Toggles submenu, shown in Figure 15, controls the RFINFO layer for the Roof Info tag, RFPERIM for roof perimeter and framing.

   Settings>Display Toggles>Roofs-Framing/Roofs-Info/Roofs-Outline

***Tip – Save/Save As

1. We have completed this session.

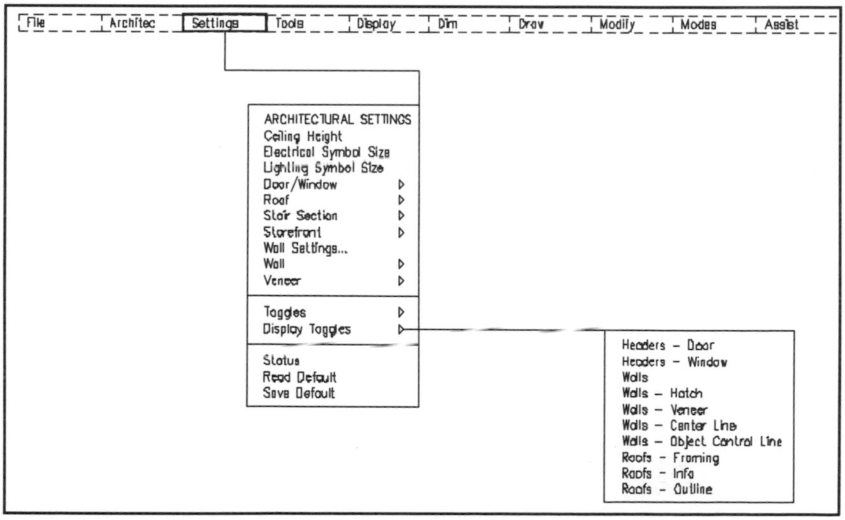

Figure 15

2. Pick Exit AutoCAD from the File pull-down menu to end Session 4, or continue to Session 5.

3. If you proceed, invoke the AutoCad Save command to save the SESSION4 drawing, then enter the Save As command.

4. Save As creates a new drawing from your existing drawing. Enter the new drawing name SESSION5 at the Save current changes: prompt.

Session 5
Draft Elevation

In this lesson, you will use the plan drawing with roof created in Session 4 to create a draft elevation, and insert window and door elevation details.

Begin a New Drawing

1. Select Save As... from the File pull-down menu to open the Save Drawing As dialog box shown in Figure 1.

2. Save the SESSION4 drawing in the C:\ASG6TUT\SESSION4 directory to the filename SESSION5 in the C:\ASG6TUT\SESSION5 directory as shown in Figure 1.

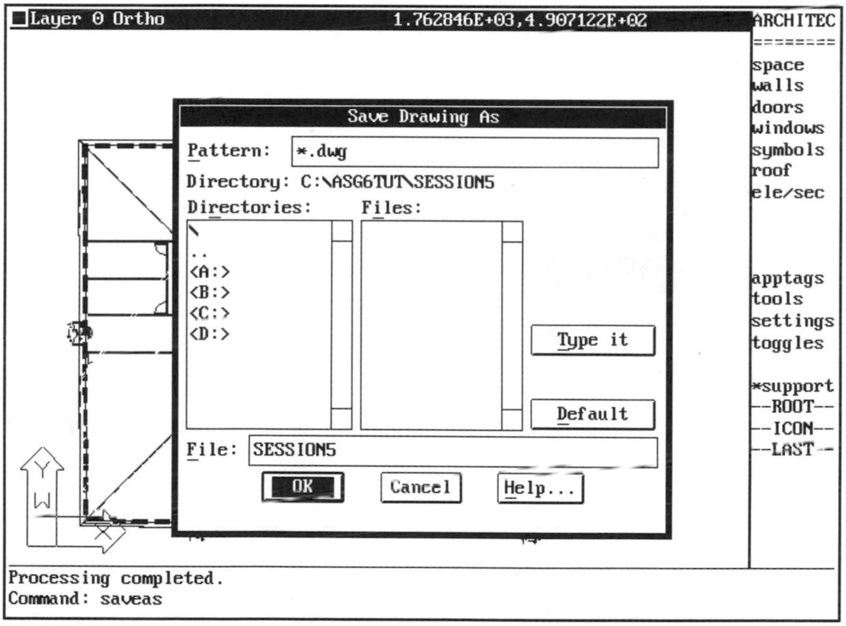

Figure 1.

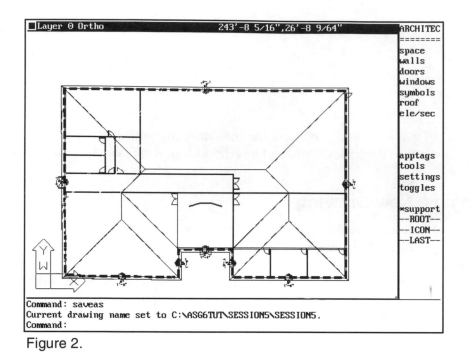

Figure 2.

Modify Layers

1. Freeze the layers created from the roof setup.

2. Select Modify Layers from the Modes pull-down menu and freeze the RFINFO, RFPERIM and RFFRAME layers.

   Modes>Modify Layers

Draft Elevation

1. Create a draft elevation of the front face of the building 6'-0" above the construction plane.

2. Select Draft Elevation under Elevation/Section from the Architec pull-down menu as shown in Figure 3.

3. Place the draft elevation on your current drawing below the floor plan. (You may have to invoke the AutoCAD Pan command to shift the display screen).

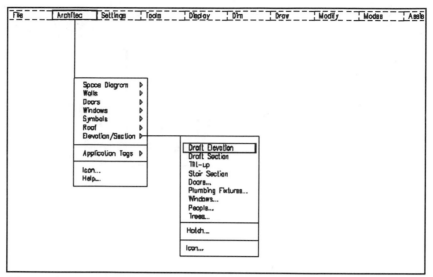

Figure 3.

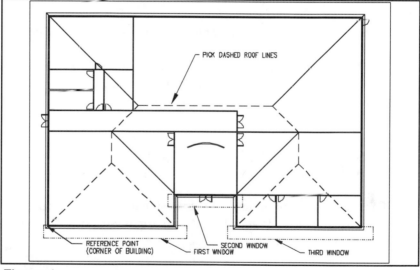

Figure 4.

4. Pick the roof lines shown dashed. Then select the three exterior front building walls using the window selection set method as shown in Figure 4.

5. As prompts appear, select reference points and camera location for the draft elevation.

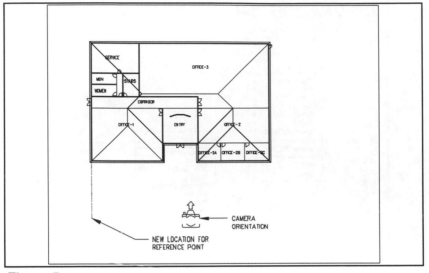

Figure 5.

6. Select the left exterior corner of the building as a reference point.

7. A rubberbanding line appears prompting for a new location (where the draft elevation will be drawn). Extend the line to an area below the floor plan as shown in Figure 5.

8. The command then displays a camera icon, requesting a point and orientation for setting the viewing angle that the elevation is viewed from as shown in Figure 5.

9. The final prompt offers an option to designate the height above the construction plane for viewing the elevation. An enlarged view describing the construction plane is shown in Figure 6.

10. After completing the draft elevation, add or extend lines to clean up the elevation.

Architec>Elevation/Section>Draft Elevation

> Store this elevation in a separate file Yes/No <Yes>: **N**

> Select objects to include in the elevation:

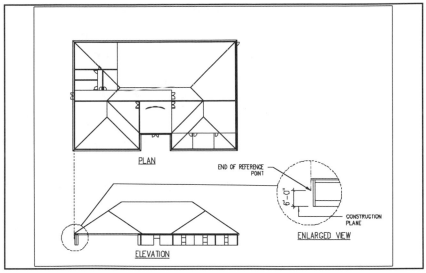

Figure 6.

> Select objects: 1 selected, 1 found [**select one of the dashed roof lines shown on Figure 4**]

Note: The roof lines must not be polylines.

> Select objects: 1 selected, 1 found [**select roof line**]

> Select objects: 1 selected, 1 found [**select roof line**]

> Select objects: 1 selected, 1 found [**select roof line**]

> Select objects: 1 selected, 1 found [**select roof line**]

> Select objects: 1 selected, 1 found [**select roof line**]

> Select objects: 1 selected, 1 found [**select roof line**]

> Select objects:**W** [**first window as shown in Figure 4**]

> First corner: Other corner: 30 found

> Select objects: **W** [**second window**]

> First corner: Other corner: 35 found

> Select objects: **W** [**third window**]

> First corner: Other corner: 40 found

> Select objects: [**Enter**]

> Pick reference point on the floor plan: **ENDP** of [**select front left intersection of building as shown in Figure 4**]

> Pick new location for reference point <56'-4",-6'-1",0">: [**select new point as shown in Figure 5**]

Note: After the rubberbanding line appears connected to the crosshairs, select a point below the plan. A camera image then appears on the crosshairs to select a viewing angle.

> Pick insertion point: [**place the camera as shown in Figure 5**]

> Pick rotation angle <0.0">: [**orient camera with puck**]

> Enter height above construction plane: **6'**

Note: The draft elevation with an enlarged view of the reference line as it relates to the construction plane is shown in Figure 6.

> Processing — please wait.

> Processing completed.

Clean Up Elevation

1. The Draft Elevation command uses lines from the plan drawing to create a preliminary elevation.

2. Draw additional lines to complete the elevation.

3. The storefront window does not appear in the elevation because it is a block. Select Windows... under Elevation/Section from the Architec pull-down menu to open the Window Details icon and draw new windows.

4. An enlarged view of the draft elevation before and after cleanup is shown in Figure 7.

Details

1. ASG provides a substantial library of details and hatch patterns for elevations and sections.

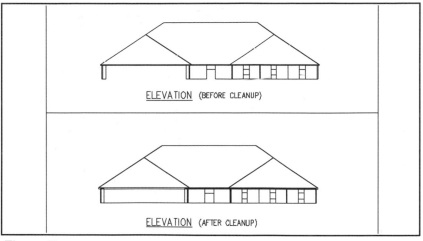

Figure 7.

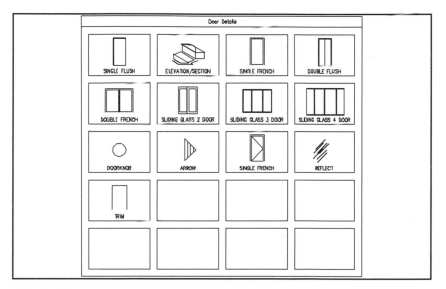

Figure 8.

2. There are five icon menus that can be selected from Elevation/Section under the Architec pull-down menu to draw elevation details.

3. Icon menus to select elevation and section details for Doors, Plumbing, Windows, People, and Trees are shown in Figures 8 through 13.

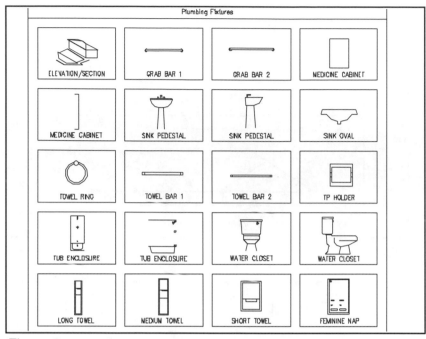

Figure 9.

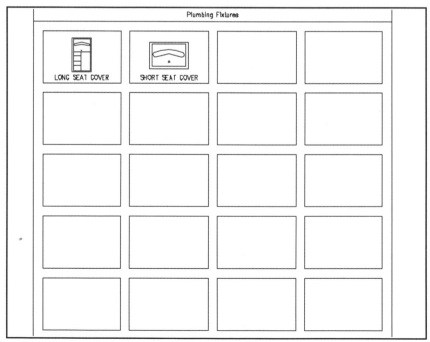

Figure 10.

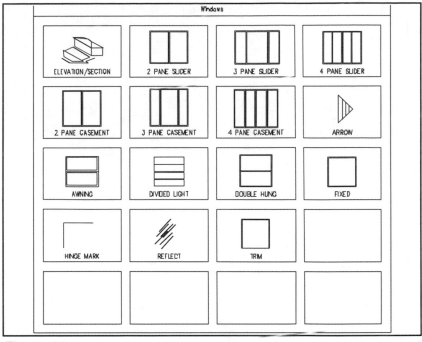

Figure 11.

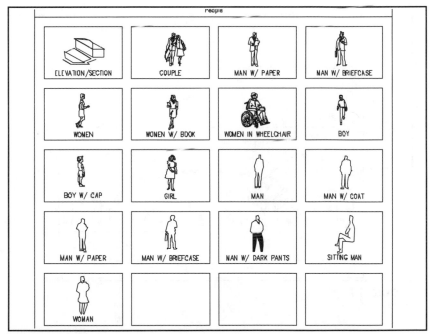

Figure 12.

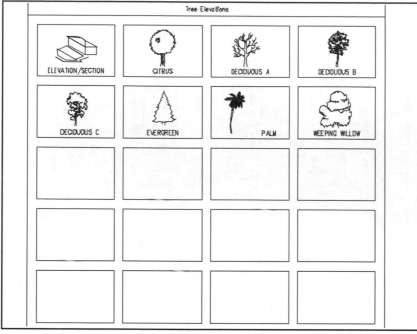

Figure 13.

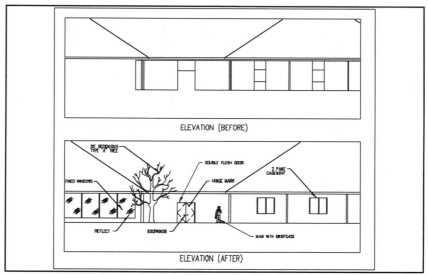

Figure 14.

Window Details – 2 Pane Casement

1. Figure 14 shows the draft elevation *before* and *after* adding Windows, a Door, People, and other details.

2. The casement windows in Figure 14 are selected from the Windows icon menu shown previously in Figure 3.

3. Select the 2 Pane Casement command shown in Figure 11 to draw the casement window shown in Figure 14.

   Architec>Elevation/Section>Window...>2 Pane Casement

   > DO

   > Pick lower left corner point of opening (ENDpoint): **INT** of [**select the bottom left corner of a window opening created by the draft elevation**]

   > Pick upper right corner of opening (ENDpoint): **INT** of [**select the top right corner of a window opening created by the draft elevation**]

   > Enter side stile width <1 1/2">: **1-1/2**

   > Enter top and bottom stile width <1 1/2">: **1-1/2**

   > Enter reveal width <1/4>: **1/4**

   > Enter width of left window or sliding glass door <half>: **HALF**

   > Processing completed.

4. Erase the horizontal and vertical draft window lines framing each opening after inserting each detail window.

Window Details – Fixed

1. Insert a series of Fixed 8'-8" x 6'-10 9/16" windows (to replicate the Storefront windows) along the left side of the elevation, accepting the defaults for side, top, and bottom stile widths.

2. Insert the first Fixed window at the lower left corner of the Storefront opening as shown in Figure 15, relocate it, and then use the AutoCAD Array command

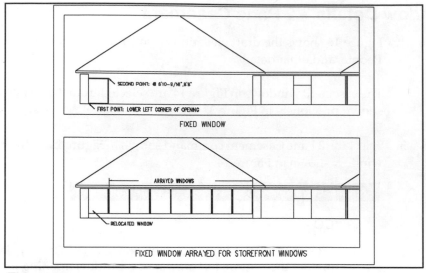

Figure 15.

(specifying 1 row, 8 columns, with distance of 6'-11 9/16") to duplicate the additional windows.

Architec>Elevation/Section>Window...>Fixed

> DO

> Pick lower left corner point of opening (ENDpoint): [**select a point as shown in Figure 15 at lower left corner of storefront opening area along the construction plane)**]

> Pick upper right corner of opening (ENDpoint): **@6'10-9/16", 8'8"** [**selecting top right corner of a window opening**]

> Enter side stile width <1 1/2">: **1-1/2**

> Enter top and bottom stile width <1 1/2">: **1-1/2**

> Enter reveal width <1/4>: **1/4**

> Processing completed.

3. Use the AutoCAD Move command from the Modify pull-down menu to relocate the window.

Modify>Move

4. Invoke the AutoCAD Array command from the Modify pull-down menu to duplicate the windows.

`Modify>Array`

> Array

> Select objects: **W [use the window selection set to pick all the fixed window lines]**

> First corner: Other corner: 8 found

> Rectangular or Polar array (R/P)
> : **R**

> Number of rows: (—) : **1**

> Number of columns: (III): **8**

> Distance between columns (III): **6'-11-9/16"**

5. Add reflect marks from the Windows icon menu for window graphics. To add storefront window details, you may also draw some vertical and horizontal construction lines to frame the storefront window openings (similar to those erased at the casement windows) as the command prompts for lower left and upper right corners of the opening.

Door Details

1. To insert a double flush door, hinge mark and doorknob, select the appropriate details from the Door Details icon menu shown in Figure 8 under the Elevation/Section menu.

2. An example of the Door command prompts is provided below.

3. Erase lines created from the draft elevation after drawing the door.

`Architec>Elevation/Section>Door...>Double Flush`

> DO

> Enter door width '-0": **6'**

> Enter door height '-0": **6'-8"**

> Enter trim width 1/2": **1-1/2"**

> Pick insertion point: **INT** of [**lower left corner of door opening**]

> Processing completed.

Trees

1. Select a 25′ Deciduous A tree from the Tree Elevation icon menu shown in Figure 13.

2. An example of the tree command prompt is provided below.

```
Architec>Elevation/Section>Trees...>Deciduous A
```

> DO

> Initial load — please wait.

> Enter tree height: 300 **[select 25' from side menu]**

> Pick insertion point: **NEA** to **[select tree location as shown in Figure 14]**

The Finished Elevation

1. A finished version of the drawing with additional elevation symbols is shown in Figure 16.

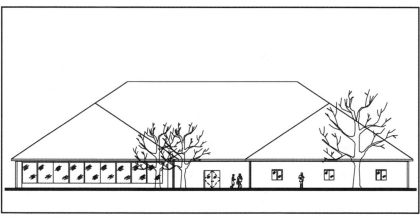

Figure 16.

2. Some symbols are blocks and cannot be edited to hide elements or structures. However, the AutoCAD Break command can be used to trim window frames and roof outlines to accommodate tree branches.

Ending Session 5

1. We have now completed Session 5.

2. Save your drawing, and type End at the AutoCAD command prompt, or pick Exit AutoCAD from the File pull-down menu to exit Session 5. To begin Session 6, you will copy the drawing from Session 4.

Session 6
Annotations and Tags

In this lesson, you will edit the plan drawing from Session 4 to add general notes, edit text, create box notes, apply leadered text, and insert a north arrow, level symbol, and tags.

Begin a New Drawing

1. Open the AutoCAD screen to begin a new drawing.

2. Pick Discard Changes when the Drawing Modification dialog box opens.

3. Select the completed drawing from Session 4 (in the C:\ASG6TUT\SESSION4 directory) as the prototype drawing for Session 6.

4. Save the drawing as SESSION6 in the C:\ASG6TUT\SESSION6 directory as shown in Figure 1.

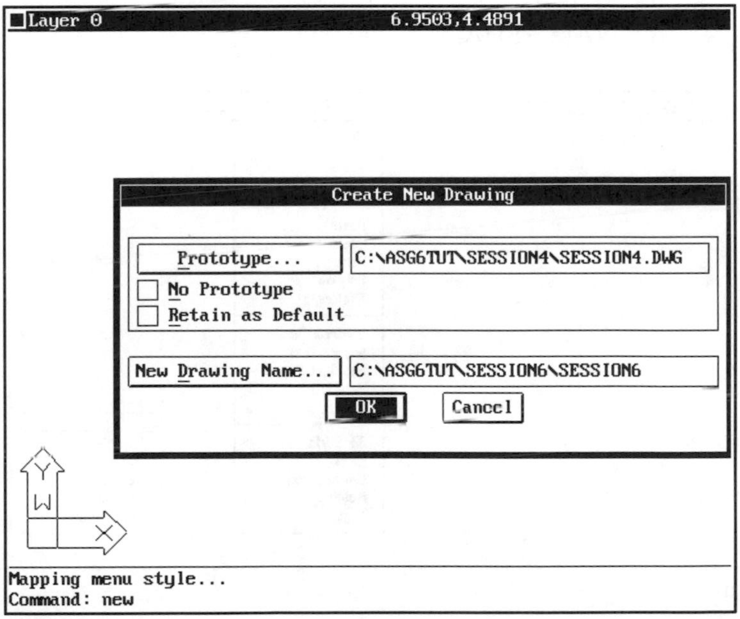

Figure 1.

5. Use the Modify Layers command from the Modes pulldown menu to turn off the following layers in the Layer Control dialog box: RFBLOCKS, RFFASCIA, RFFRAME, RFINFO, RFPERIM, RFSOFFIT, ROOFF3D.

Annotate Overview

1. The Annotate submenu under the Draw pulldown menu as shown in Figure 2 includes a text editor as well as tools for creating notes, schedules, specifications.

2. Use the Notes command to create a list of General Notes for the drawing.

3. Notes writes text into an ASCII file format (compatible with most software programs).

4. The Notes command prompts for a file name and a maximum number of characters per line. Specify a name (maximum of 8 characters) for the notes file. ASG automatically assigns a .NOT file extension and sequential numbers. (ASCII files can be revised with an ASCII text editor.) Enter GENERAL as the name of the file for this exercise, specify a 30 character line length, and type the following notes:

    ALL STUDS SHALL BE 16" O.C.
    ALL WALLS SHALL BE PLUMB.

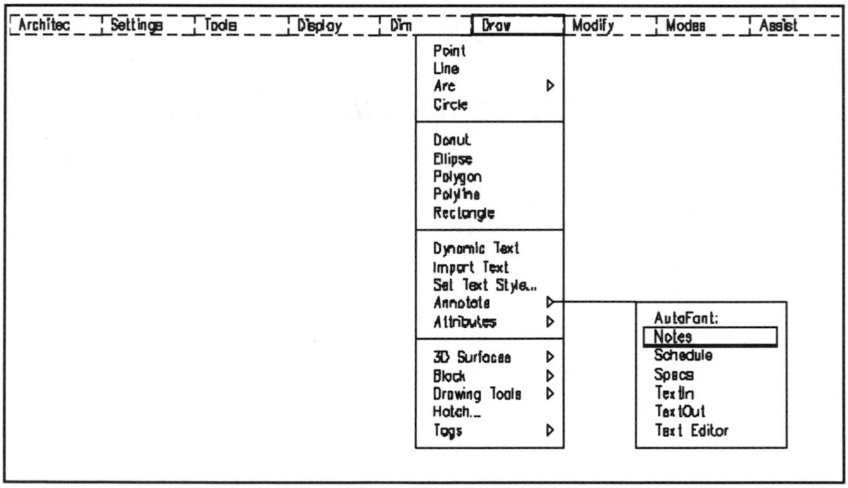

Figure 2.

DOOR MATERIAL SHALL BE 30% COREBOARD.
ALL DOORS SWING 90 DEGREES MAX.

5. A guide consisting of dots and spaces appears above the text for reference to line or character length. If the text extends beyond the guide, it will appear on a second line.

6. The text file can be imported into the drawing with the TextIn command.

Notes

1. Select Notes from the Annotate menu under the Draw pulldown menu. Type the general notes listed in item 4 in the Annotate Overview section above.

Draw>Annotate>Notes

> NOTES

> Enter (NOT) file name or . for none <.>: **GENERAL**

> Enter maximum number of characters per line <14>: **30**

> NOTE #1
  <. . . .^. . . .^. . . .^. . . .^. . . .^. . . .^>
  : **ALL STUDS SHALL BE 16" O.C.** [**Enter**]

> NOTE #2
  <. . . .^. . . .^. . . .^. . . .^. . . .^. . . .^>
  : **ALL WALLS SHALL BE PLUMB.** [**Enter**]

> NOTE #3
  <. . . .^. . . .^. . . .^. . . .^. . . .^. . . .^>
  : **DOOR MATERIAL SHALL BE 30% COREBOARD.** [**Enter**]

> NOTE #4
  <. . . .^. . . .^. . . .^. . . .^. . . .^. . . .^>
  : **ALL DOORS SWING 90 DEGREES MAX.** [**Enter**]

> NOTE #5
  <. . . .^. . . .^. . . .^. . . .^. . . .^. . . .^>
  [**Enter**]

> Processing completed.

2. The ASCII file that you have just created with the Notes command is now on your hard drive with the filename GENERAL.NOT. It can be inserted into a drawing with the TextIn command.

3. When inserted into a drawing, the title GENERAL NOTES will appear above the notes.

4. The GENERAL.NOT file can be edited with an ASCII text editor or the DOS Eit command after inserting it into the drawing. It can also be viewed with the DOS Type command:

> Command: TYPE

> File to list: GENERAL.NOT

TextIn

1. Insert the GENERAL.NOT file into the drawing.

2. @NUMBER = 2.   Notes are inserted on the current layer with the current text style.

3. Select TextIn from the Annotate submenu to insert the GENERAL.NOT file on the right side of the drawing, as shown in Figure 3. Use ASG's "auto" as the distance between lines.

Draw>Annotate>TextIn

> TEXTIN

> Enter file name or . for none <.>: **GENERAL.NOT**

Note: Include the NOT extension for the file name. Any ASCII file name can be inserted into the drawing. The Notes command only creates files with .NOT extensions.

> Enter distance between lines <auto>: [**Enter**]

> Pick start point or Align/Center/Fit/Middle/Right/Style: [**pick a point near the upper right corner of the drawing to begin the text file as shown in Figure 3**]

> Enter height <2'>: **1'**

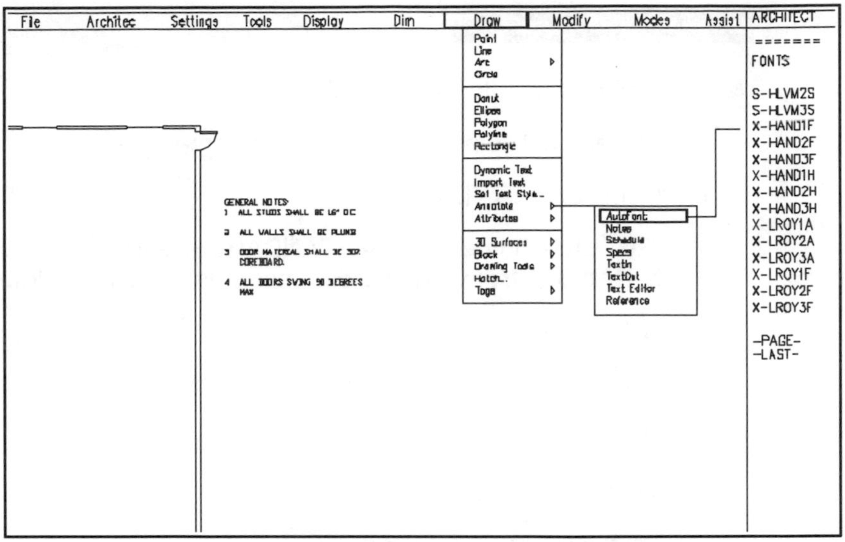

Figure 3.

Note: The height of text can be assigned by picking two points, specifying a distance, or using ASG's automatic selection.

> Enter rotation angle <0.0>: **0**

> Build text into a block Yes/No <No>: **NO**

> Processing complete.

Text Style

1. Change the text style before adding additional notes to the drawing.

2. Pick AutoFont: from the Annotate cascading submenu under the Draw pull-down menu to display various styles on the side screen menu.

3. Pick at the bottom of the side screen menu to scroll the menu up until X-HAND1F appears, as shown in Figure 3.

4. Selecting AutoFont: invokes the Style command, which prompts for text height, width factor, and obliqueing angle. It also offers options to create text that reads backwards and upside-down.

> **Draw>Annotate>AutoFont:**

> > Command: AutoFont

> > Make a font selection from the screen menu.

> > Command: STYLE

> > Text style name (or ?) <STANDARD>: X-HAND1F **[select X-HAND1F from side screen menu as shown in Figure 3]**

> > New style.

> > Font file: C:/ASG6/X-FONTS/X-HAND1F

> > Height '-0": **[Enter]**

> > Width factor : **[Enter]**

> > obliqueing angle : **[Enter]**

> > Backwards? **[Enter]**

> > Upside-down **[Enter]**

> > X-HAND1F is now the current style.

5. A list of ASG fonts can be found in the ASG documentation.

Additional Notes

1. Add the following note #5 to the GENERAL.NOT file:

   WALLS SHALL BE 5/8" GYPSUM WALLBOARD

2. To add note #5 use the same file name (the last file name created appears as the default file name) so that the next sequential number is automatically assigned.

3. The new note will be appended to the existing GENERAL.NOT file. To update the general notes in the drawing, erase them and then select the TextIn command again to reinsert the new notes. (The ERASE command is under the Modify pulldown menu.)

4. The note appears with X-HAND1F as the current text style, as shown in Figure 4.

> **Modify>Erase**

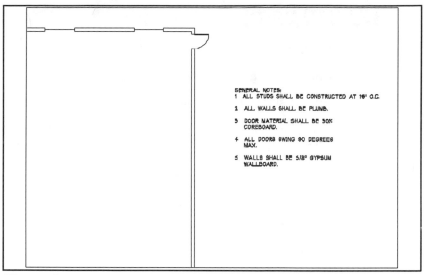

Figure 4.

Draw>Annotate>Notes

> NOTES

> Enter (NOT) file name or . for none <.>: **GENERAL.NOT**

> Type file to screen Yes/No <No>: **NO**

Note: If you enter YES to this prompt, the text screen of the notes will appear.

> Enter starting number for reference notes <5>: [**Enter**]

Note: Notice that the next sequential note number is automatically assigned.

> NOTE #5
  <. . . .^. . . .^. . . .^. . . .^. . . .^. . . .^>
  : **WALLS SHALL BE 5/8" GYPSUM WALLBOARD.** [**Enter**]

> NOTE #6
  <. . . .^. . . .^. . . .^. . . .^. . . .^. . . .^>
  : [**Enter**]

> Processing completed.

5. Select the TextIn command and reinsert the revised GENERAL note file into the drawing.

Draw>Annotate>TEXTIN

> Command: TEXTIN

> Enter file name or . for none <.>: **GENERAL.NOT**

> Enter distance between lines <auto>: [**Enter**]

> Pick start point of Align/Center/Fit/Middle/Right/Style: [**pick a point to begin the revised text file as shown in Figure 4**]

> Enter height <2'>: **1'**

> Enter rotation angle <0.0>: **0**

> Build text into a block Yes/No <No>: **N**

> Processing complete.

Text Editor

1. Zoom into the upper right portion of the drawing to edit note #1.

2. Select the Text Editor command from the Annotate menu to edit note #1 of the general notes.

3. The text

   1. ALL STUDS SHALL BE 16" O.C.

   will appear at the bottom of the screen within brackets with a vertical bar above. While holding down the Ctrl key, use the right and left arrow keys to move the text. The vertical bar indicates where the changes will be made. Figure 5 shows note #1 revised from

   1. ALL STUDS SHALL BE 16" O.C.

   to

   1. ALL STUDS SHALL BE CONSTRUCTED AT 16" O.C.

Draw>Annotate>Text Editor

Revise note #1 to read:

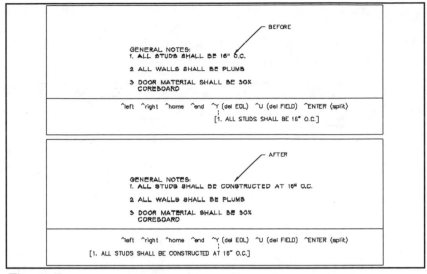

Figure 5.

1. ALL STUDS SHALL BE CONSTRUCTED AT 16″ O.C.

> TextED

> Select text to edit <none>:

> Select objects: [**select note #1**] 1 selected, 1 found

> Select objects: [**Enter**]
  ^left ^right ^home ^end ^Y(del EOL)^U(del FIELD)
  ^ENTER(split)
  |

  [ALL STUDS SHALL BE CONSTRUCTED AT 16″ O.C.] [**Enter**]

Note: The following indicates how to manipulate the line of text using the keyboard Ctrl key with the arrow, Home, or End key:

^left	Ctrl + left arrow	One character to the left
^right	Ctrl + right arrow	One character to the right
^home	Ctrl + HOME key	Beginning of line
^end	Ctrl + END key	End of line
^Y (del EOL)	Ctrl + Y key	Deletes to end of line.
^U (del FIELD)	Ctrl + U key	Deletes entire line
^Enter (split)	Ctrl + Enter key	Splits single line into two lines.

Tag Overview

1. ASG offers a full palette of typical Architectural tag types as shown in Figure 6. The tag types are customizable.

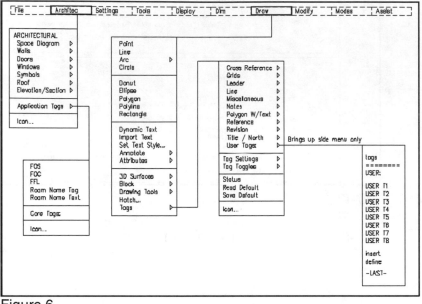

Figure 6.

2. The entire library of tags is shown in Figure 7.

3. Figures 8 through 13 show some Tag icon menus from the Draw pulldown menu for cross references, grids, line types, miscellaneous tags, notes, and polygons with text.

4. Figure 14 identifies specific Application Tags located under the Architec pulldown menu.

5. If Autolayer is on, Tags are inserted on layer SYM. Otherwise, they are placed on the current layer.

6. Tag size and color, as well as text tag height, are controlled from Tag Settings and Tag Toggles menus as shown in Figure 15, or Status under the Tags cascading menu.

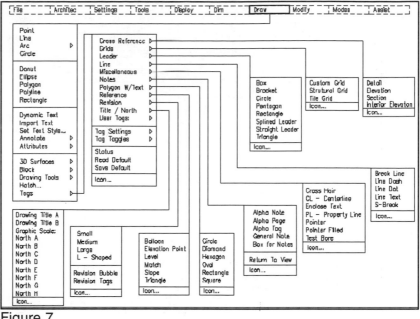

Figure 7.

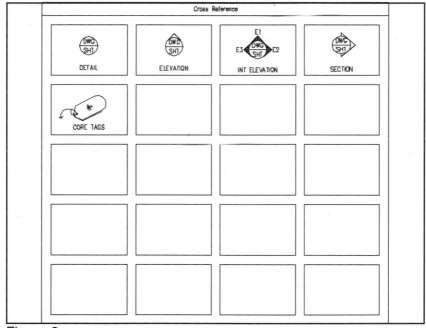

Figure 8.

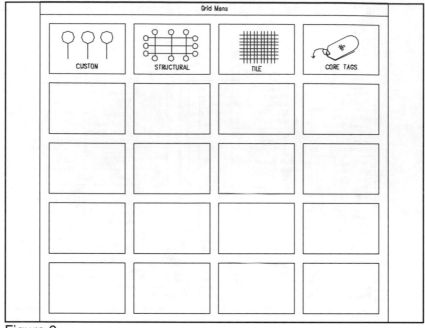

Figure 9.

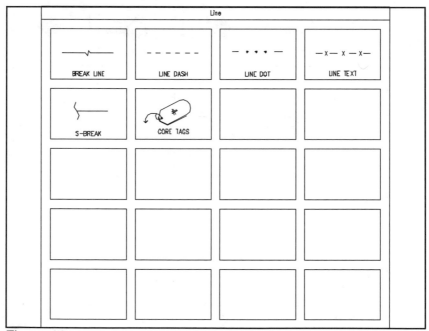

Figure 10.

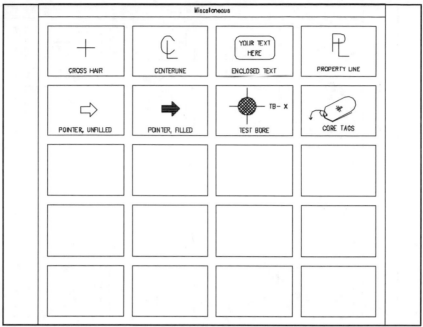

Figure 11.

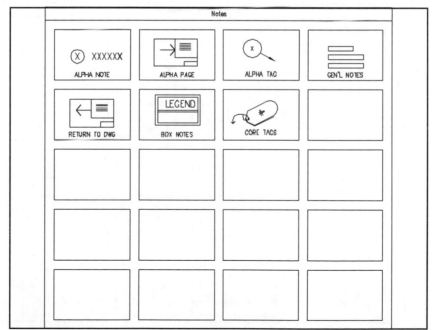

Figure 12.

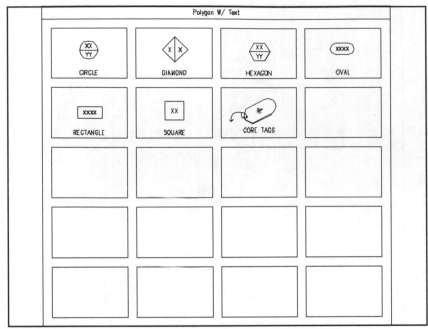

Figure 13.

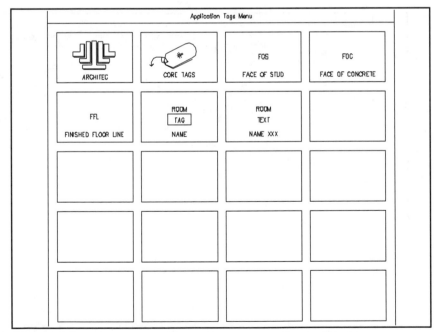

Figure 14.

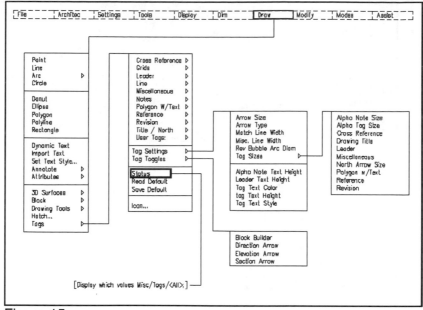

Figure 15.

Alpha Tag

1. Label the wall using a circular tag, which ASG calls Alpha Tag, containing the Letter A as shown in Figure 16.

2. Select Tags, then Notes, from the Draw pulldown menu, as shown in Figure 17, or the icon menu shown in Figure 18, to place an Alpha Tag into the drawing.

> **Draw>Tags>Notes>Alpha Tag**

>   DO

>   Pick item to tag: **NEA to [select the wall as shown in Figure 16 to locate the starting point of the leader**

>   Pick insertion point: [**select a location for the circular tag**]

Note: After the tag appears ghosted and attached to the crosshairs, insert it into the drawing.

>   Enter alpha note <A>: **A**

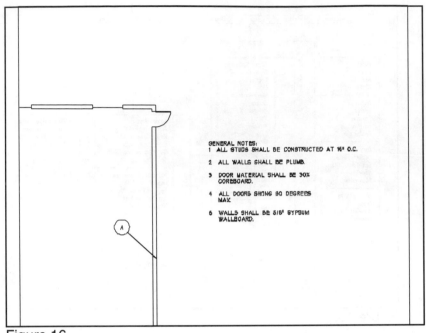

Figure 16.

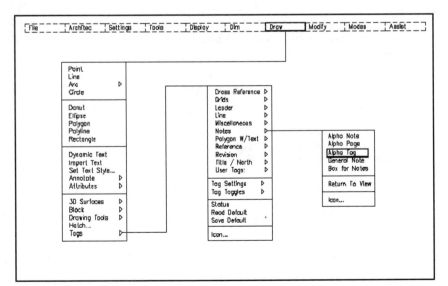

Figure 17.

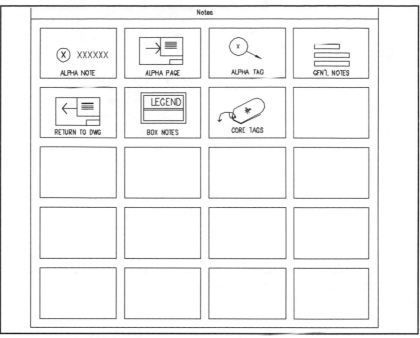

Figure 18

Note: A leader line with an arrow appears connected to the tag after insertion into the drawing.

> Processing completed.

Box Notes

1. Create a box for wall notes. Select Box for Notes from the same Notes submenu.

2. Label the box WALL NOTES using the dynamic option and picking two points as described in Figure 19.

   Draw>Tags>Notes>Box for Notes

   > DO

   > Pick lower left corner of the box or Dynamic <none>:**D**

Note: The Dynamic option allows you to pick two points on the screen, to indicate an approximate size.

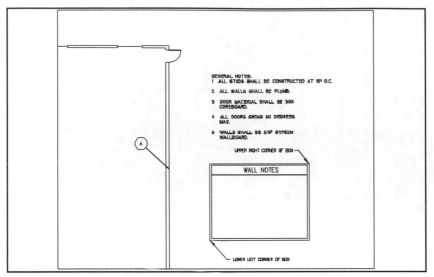

Figure 19.

> Enter title of the box <WALL>: **WALL NOTES**

Note: The text height for the title of the Box for Notes is determined by the Final plotted scale height. (Use the Detailed... pick button in the Drawing Setup dialog box to set title text height.)

> Enter lower left corner of the box: [**pick lower left corner (shown in Figure 19) as the first point**]

> Enter upper right corner of box: [**pick upper right corner as the second point**]

> Processing completed.

Alpha Note

1. Insert a note for an Alpha Tag into the note box as shown in Figure 20.

2. Select Alpha Note from the Notes submenu, or Notes icon menu shown in Figure 18, then pick a location for the tag in the WALL NOTES box. Type the following text after the circle appears:

    8" EXTERIOR WALL

3. The snap mode becomes active to insert tags in alignment.

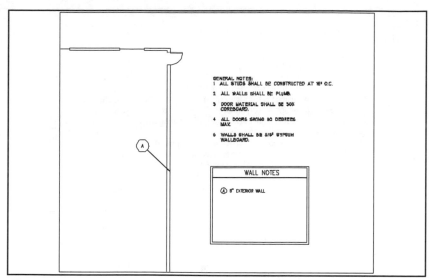

Figure 20.

Draw>Tags>Notes>Alpha Note

> DO

> Pick center of circle for alpha note: [**select location for tag as shown in Figure 20**]

> Enter letter for alpha note <A>: **A**

> Enter text <none>: **8" EXTERIOR WALL**

> Text: [**Enter**]

> Processing completed.

4. To change Alpha Note text height and tag diameter, select Tag Settings, then Tag Sizes under the Tags menu, as shown in Figure 15. The same settings are available from the Tag Status display, as shown in Figure 21 by choosing letters A and B.

Draw>Tags>Tag Settings>Tag Sizes>Alpha Note Size /Alpha Tag Size

or

Draw>Tags>StatusA,B

```
Display which values Misc/Tags/All <All>: T


TAG SETTINGS STATUS:
-----------------------------------------------------------------
(a) Alpha note plotted    size/diameter...............................  1/2"
(b) Alpha tag plotted    size/diameter............................... 1/2"
(c) Cross Reference tag plotted diameter.......................... 1/2"
(d) Drawing Title bubble plotted diameter.......................... 5/8"
(e) Leader tag plotted size............................................ 1/2"
(f) Miscellaneous tag plotted size/diameter...................... 3/16"
(g) North Arrow plotted size.......................................... 1/2"
(h) Polygon W/Test plotted size/diameter.......................... 1/2"
(i) Reference tag plotted size/diameter.......................... 1/4"
(j) Revision tag plotted size........................................ 1/4"



Enter settings/toggle letter(s) to change or RETURN for graphics screen:
```

Figure 21.

The note and tag sizes will not change on the screen, but they will be plotted at the increased size.

Adjusting Tag and Text Size

1. Customize tag text and size adjustments using the Tag Settings and Tag Toggle menus, shown previously in Figure 15.

2. These same setting options are in the Tags Status display shown in Figure 21 or the Misc Status display shown in Figure 22.

    `Draw>Tags>Tag Settings>Tag Sizes>Cross Reference/Drawing Title>Leader>Miscellaneous>North Arrow Size/ Polygon w/Text/`

or

    `Draw>Tags>Status>T`

Straight Leader with Arrow

1. Insert a straight leadered line to label the exit door.

2. Pick Tags from the Draw pulldown menu, then Leader to display the cascading menu shown in Figure 23.

```
Display which values Misc/Tags/All <All>: M


MISC TAG SETTINGS STATUS:
------------------------------------------------------------
(a) Arrow type.................................................... 3/16"
(b) Arrow size................................................... ARROW
(c) Match Line plotted width.................................... 0.05
(d) Miscellaneous line plotted with............................ 0"
(e) Revision Bubble arc diameter............................... 3/4"


(f) Alpha Note text height...................................... 1/8"
(g) Leader Text height.......................................... 1/8"
(h) Tag Text color.............................................. 4 Cyan
(i) Tag Text height............................................. 1/8"


TAGS TOGGLES STATUS:
------------------------------------------------------------
(j) Section arrow............................................... FILLED
(k) Section direction arrow.................................... FILLED
(l) Elevation arrow............................................ FILLED
(m) Block builder.............................................. OFF


Enter settings/toggle letter(s) to change or RETURN for graphics screen:
```

Figure 22.

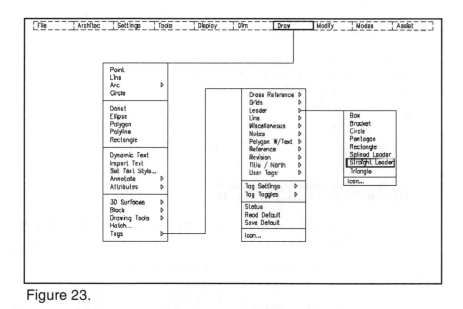

Figure 23.

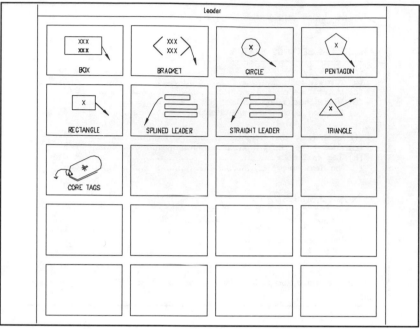

Figure 24.

3. Select Straight Leader directly from this menu, or open the Leader icon menu shown in Figure 24 and double click the icon. Pick a point near the exit door, as shown in Figure 25.

4. The command automatically toggles ortho mode on to maintain a vertical leader alignment position. Press F8 to toggle ortho off, and place the leadered text as shown in Figure 25 with the label "EXIT DOOR."

Draw>Tags>Leader>Straight Leader

>   Pick leader start point: **[select point near door as shown in Figure 25]**

>   To point or Arrow : **[Pick a second point]**

>   **Note:**   An osnap menu appears at the side screen. Ortho mode will automatically be set to on. Press F8 if you want a diagonal line.

Note: To draw a series of connected leadered lines with an arrow, choose the Arrow command from the side screen menu (at this prompt), then pick the

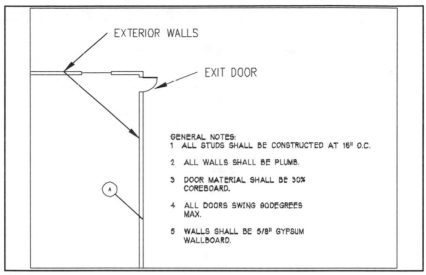

GENERAL NOTES:
1 ALL STUDS SHALL BE CONSTRUCTED AT 16" O.C.

2 ALL WALLS SHALL BE PLUMB.

3 DOOR MATERIAL SHALL BE 30% COREBOARD.

4 ALL DOORS SWING 90DEGREES MAX.

5 WALLS SHALL BE 5/8" GYPSUM WALLBOARD.

Figure 25.

next point on your screen. Continue picking "Arrow" from the side screen for each sequential leadered arrow segment, then press enter to end the command. The example shown in Figure 25 is labeled EXTERIOR WALLS.

> To point or Arrow : **[Enter]**

> Enter text: **EXIT DOOR**

> Text: **[Enter]**

***TIP – Changing Arrow Types

1. ASG provides an assortment of Dim Arrow Types as shown in Figure 26. Choosing Arrow Type from Tag Settings under the Tags menu, as shown in Figure 27, opens the Dim Arrow Types icon menu. The Dim Arrow Types icon menu is also available from the side screen menu.

2. The note labeled "EXIT DOOR" shown previously in Figure 25 with arrow type ARROW is shown in Figure 28 with the arrow type changed to ASG-AR10.

Draw>Tags>Tag Settings>Arrow Type

***TIP – Using the HSLASH Arrow for Dimensioning

1. The HSLASH dimension arrow is shown in Figure 28 as a standard architectural dimensioning tick.

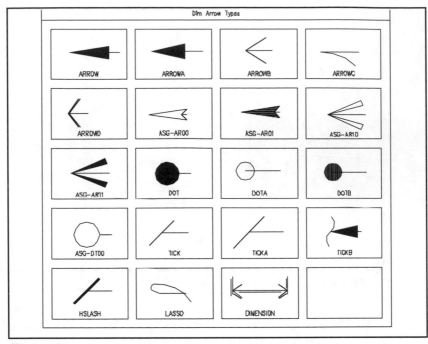

Figure 26.

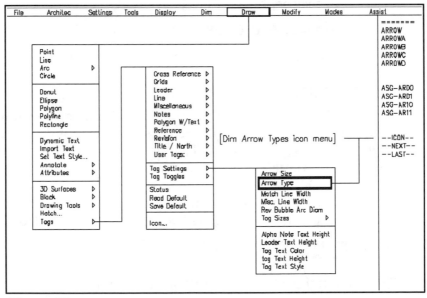

Figure 27.

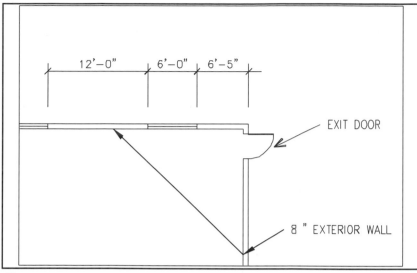

Figure 28.

2. To use the HSLASH in this manner, first select the tick from the icon menu to define the block in the drawing database, then enter HSLASH as the name of the DIMBLK variable.

    Note: The Dimtsz dimension variable must be set to 0 for tick marks to appear.

North Arrow Tag

1. Insert a north arrow at the bottom right corner of the drawing, as shown in Figure 29.

    Note: The 0 orientation for all North arrow blocks causes the North arrow and text to face to the right, even though the Title/North Icon pulldown menu shows the arrow blocks facing up. The text orientation is always the same as the arrow; if a block is inserted with North facing toward the bottom of the drawing sheet, the text "NORTH" will also be facing upside-down.

2. Select Title/North under Tags from the submenu shown in Figure 30, or the icon shown in Figure 31, then the North E icon.

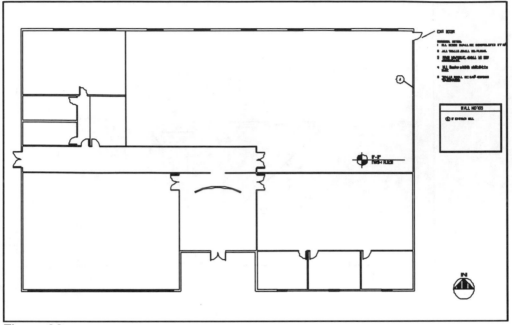

Figure 29.

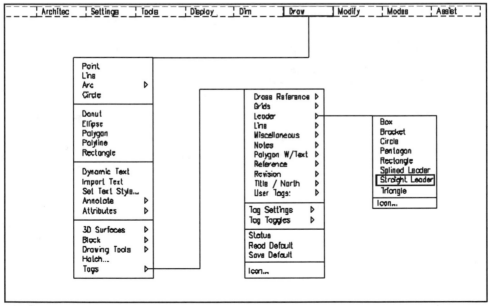

Figure 30.

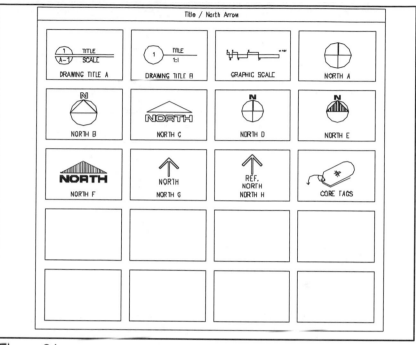

Figure 31.

3. Respond to the prompts by picking the insertion point and rotation angle.

    `Draw>Tags>Title/North>North E`

    > DO

    > Pick insertion point: [**pick point at bottom right corner of drawing as shown in Figure 29**]

    > Enter rotation angle <0.0>: [**use ortho on to orient arrow to top of drawing**]

    > Processing completed.

Level

1. Insert the Level tag from the Reference submenu shown in Figure 32, or the Reference icon menu shown in Figure 33, into the drawing at a plotted scale of 1/2".

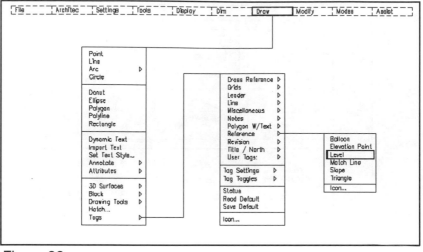

Figure 32.

2. Change the plotted scale size of reference tags by selecting letter I in the Tag Status display (see Figure 21) under Tags in the Draw pulldown menu.

> Enter reference tag plotted size/diameter <1/4">: **1/2**

Note: You may want to repeat this exercise to retrieve the default value 1/4" scale.

3. Select Level from the Tags submenu, under Reference, to place the symbol, as shown in Figure 29, into the drawing.

Note: The Reference Icon menu illustrated in Figure 33 is more detailed then the actual ASG Reference Icon. Additional text is shown above and below leader lines to more accurately identify the command.

4. As the level tag prompts for a starting point of a leader line, a ghosted image of the symbol appears on the screen with a rubberbanding line.

5. Drag the image to the left of the screen to create a line where text can be inserted above and below, as shown in Figure 29.

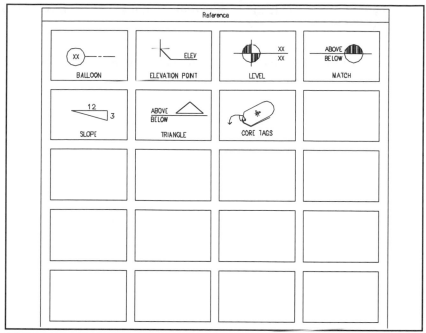

Figure 33.

6. Identify the finish floor level as 0'-0" above the leader line, and the level being referenced as FINISH FLOOR below the leader line.

Draw>Tags>Reference>Level

> DO

> Pick leader start point: [**pick start point of leader line as shown in Figure 29; a ghosted image of the level tag appears**]

> Pick insertion point: [**drag ghosted image of level tag to the left, locating the position of tag**]

> Enter text above leader line <->: **0'-0"**

> Enter text below leader line <->: **FINISH FLOOR**

End Session 6

1. We have now completed session 6.

2. Pick Exit AutoCAD from the File pulldown menu or type the AutoCAD END command, saving Session 6.

3. In the next session we will use 2D and 3D symbols to draw stairs, furniture, and plumbing fixtures.

Session 7
Symbols

In this session we will follow procedures for creating 2D and 3D symbols. The text and illustrations will familiarize you with ASG's Symbol Libraries. The exercises will demonstrate how to draw different types of stairs, insert plumbing fixtures and furniture, and convert symbols from 2D to 3D.

Main Symbol Groups

Selecting Symbols

1. The main symbol groups in the Architec pull-down menu include Appliances, Electrical, Furniture, Lighting/Ceiling, Plumbing, Site, Stairs, and Structural, as shown in Figure 1.

2. Symbols can be selected from the pull-down menu, screen menu, icon menu, and the tablet template. You can preview symbols by selecting the Library Slide

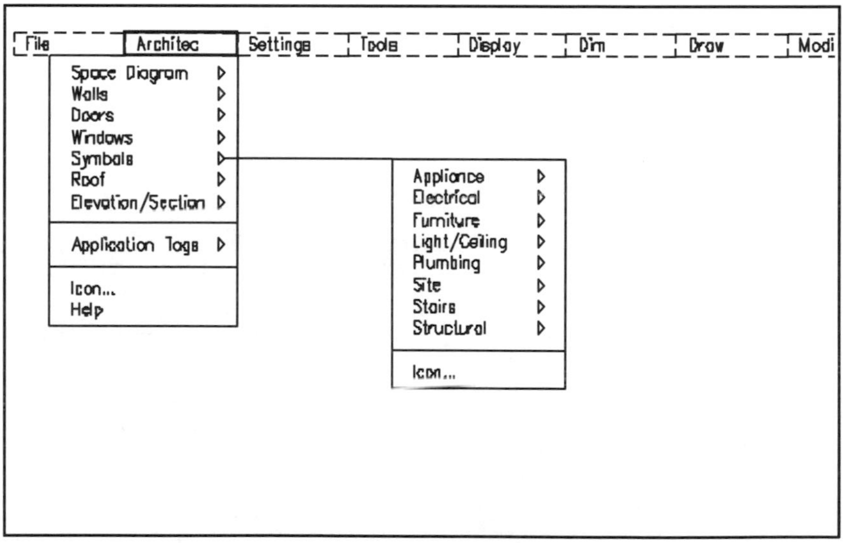

File	Architec	Settings	Tools	Display	Dim	Draw	Modi

Space Diagram ▷
Walls ▷
Doors ▷
Windows ▷
Symbols ▷ ─── Appliance ▷
Roof ▷ Electrical ▷
Elevation/Section ▷ Furniture ▷
Light/Ceiling ▷
Application Togs ▷ Plumbing ▷
Site ▷
Icon... Stairs ▷
Help Structural ▷

Icon...

Figure 1.

command in each symbol group under the Architec pull-down menu, as shown in Figure 2. A sample of the Electrical Library Slide is shown in Figure 3.

3. All icon symbols outlined in blue activate a submenu of additional symbols, as illustrated in the Symbols icon box in Figure 7.

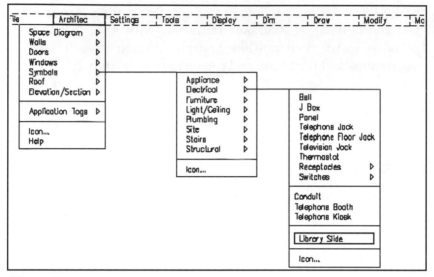

Figure 2.

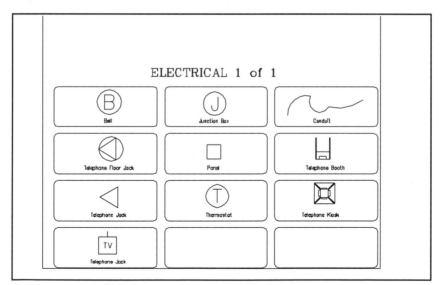

Figure 3.

Symbol Settings and Toggles

1. The Settings menu controls Ceiling Height, Electrical symbol size, and Lighting symbol size, as shown on the Architectural Settings menu in Figure 4.

2. The Toggles submenu on the Settings menu controls 2D-3D symbols, 2-Point Insertion, Attribute Dialogue boxes, and Attribute Prompting, as shown on the submenu in Figure 4.

3. Some symbols have associated blocks with Schedule attributes which can be turned on and off. The prompt appears at the command line or, if Attribute Dialogue Box is on, a dialogue box appears.

4. Settings and toggles can also be changed from the Status display options under the Settings pull-down menu. The values displayed include Basic, Door, Roof, Stair, Storefront, Wall, Window and Veneer.

5. Most symbols are available in 2D and 3D. They can be converted by selecting the Convert 3D to 2D or Convert 2D to 3D command from the Tools pull-down menu shown in Figure 5. The tools pull-down menu also provides commands for controlling attributes, manipulating doors or windows, and creating schedules.

```
┌─────────────────────────────────────────────────────────────────────────────┐
│ File      Architec   Settings   Tools      Display    Dim      Drow    Modify   Modes │
│                     ARCHITECTURAL SETTINGS                                     │
│                     Ceiling Height                                            │
│                     Electrical Symbol Size                                    │
│                     Lighting Symbol Size                                      │
│                     Door/Window        ▷    ┌──────────────────────┐          │
│                     Roof               ▷    │  2D - 3D Symbols      │          │
│                     Stair Section      ▷    │  2-Pt Insert          │          │
│                     Storefront         ▷    │  Attribute Dialogue Box│         │
│                     Wall Settings...        │  Attribute Prompt     │          │
│                     Wall               ▷    │  Icon                 │          │
│                     Veneer             ▷    └──────────────────────┘          │
│                                                                               │
│                     Toggles            ▷                                       │
│                     Display Toggles    ▷    ┌──────────────────────┐          │
│                     Status                  │  Headers - Door       │          │
│                     Read Default            │  Headers - Window     │          │
│                     Save Default            │  Walls                │          │
│                                             │  Walls - Hatch        │          │
│                                             │  Walls - Veneer       │          │
│                                             │  Walls - Center Line  │          │
│                                             │  Walls - Object Control Line│     │
│                                             │  Roofs - Framing      │          │
│                                             │  Roofs - Info         │          │
│                                             │  Roofs - Outline      │          │
│                                             └──────────────────────┘          │
└─────────────────────────────────────────────────────────────────────────────┘
```

Figure 4.

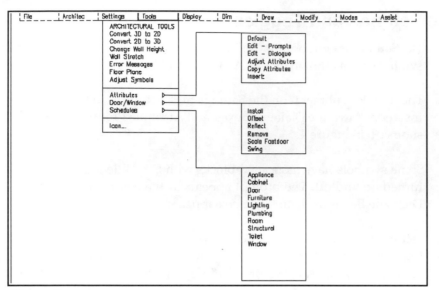

Figure 5.

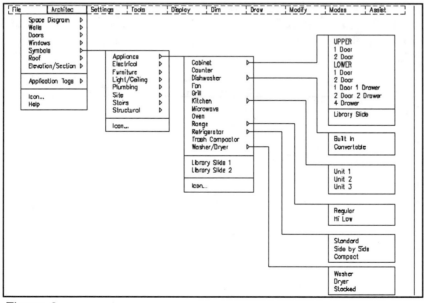

Figure 6.

Symbol Subgroups

ASG has eight main symbol menu groups, each of which includes symbol submenu groups. Symbols can be selected directly from the abbreviated description in the submenu, or from the Icon menu as shown in the following figures.

<u>Appliances</u>

Appliance pull-down menu	Figure 6
Appliance Symbol Menu	Figure 7

<u>Electrical</u>

Electrical pull-down menu	Figure 8
Electric Symbol Menu	Figure 9
Electric Symbol Menu	Figure 10

<u>Furniture</u>

Furniture pull-down menu	Figure 11
Furniture Symbol Menu	Figure 12
Furniture Symbol Menu	Figure 13
Chairs Symbol Menu	Figure 14
Desks Symbols icons	Figure 15

<u>Light/Ceiling</u>

Light/Ceiling pull-down menu	Figure 16
Light/Ceiling Symbol Menu	Figure 17

<u>Plumbing</u>

Plumbing pull-down menu	Figure 18
Plumbing Symbol Menu	Figure 19
Plumbing Symbol Menu	Figure 20
Plumbing Symbol Menu	Figure 21

<u>Site</u>

Site pull-down menu	Figure 22
Site Symbol Menu	Figure 23
Site Symbol Menu	Figure 24
Site Symbol Menu	Figure 25

<u>Stairs</u>

Stairs pull-down menu	Figure 26
Stair Symbol Menu	Figure 27

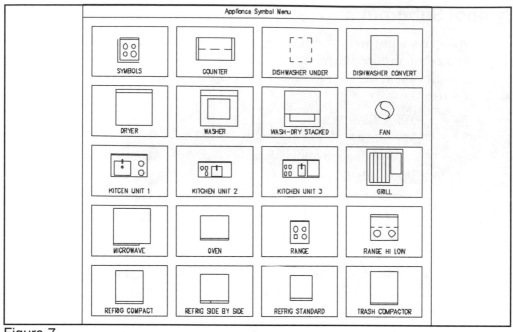

Figure 7.

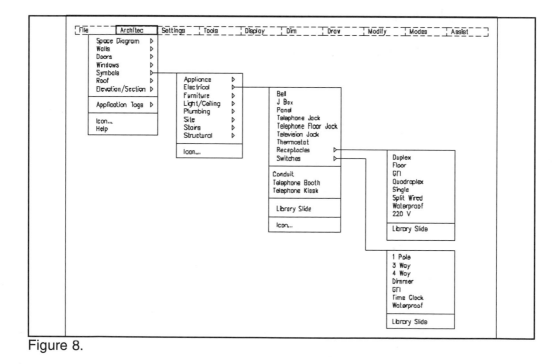

Figure 8.

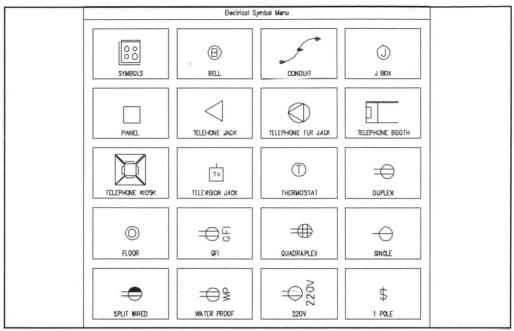

Figure 9.

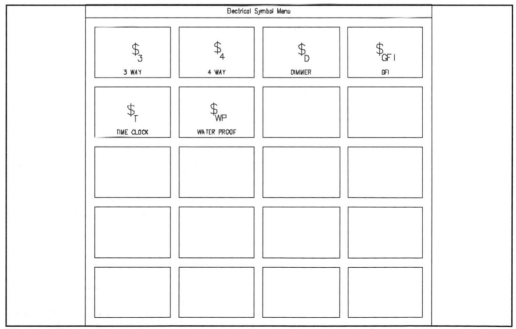

Figure 10.

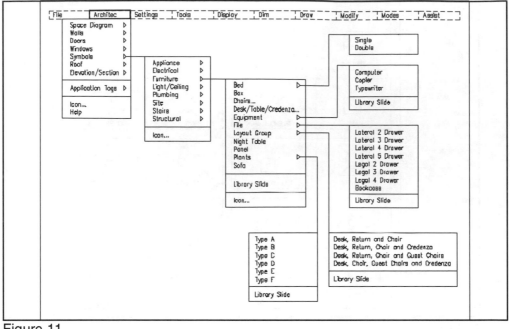

Figure 11.

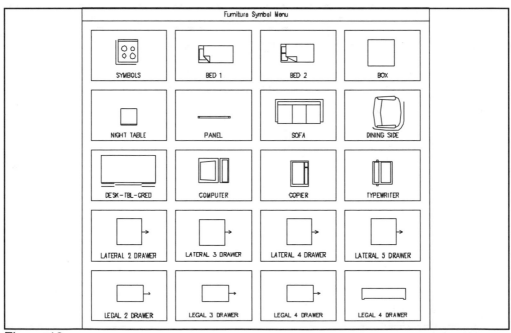

Figure 12.

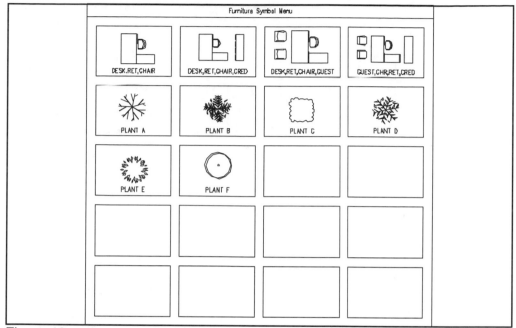

Figure 13.

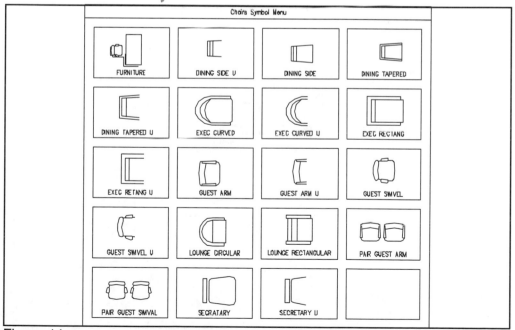

Figure 14.

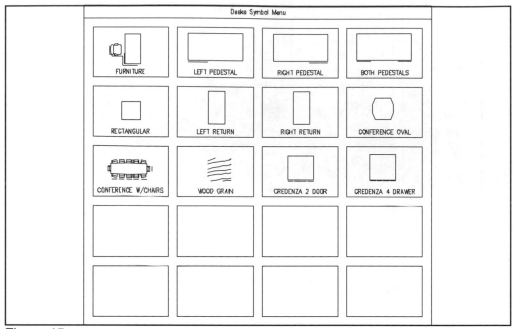

Figure 15.

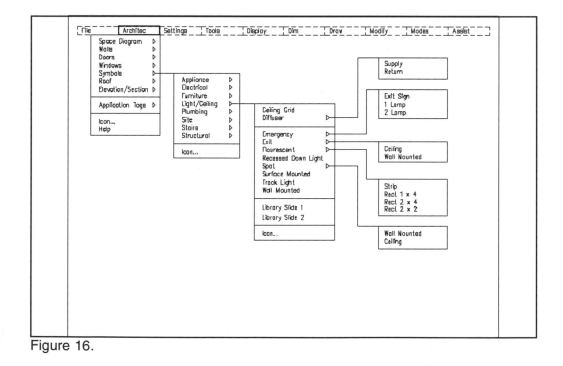

Figure 16.

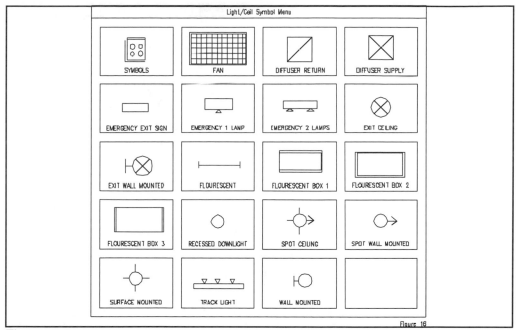

Figure 17.

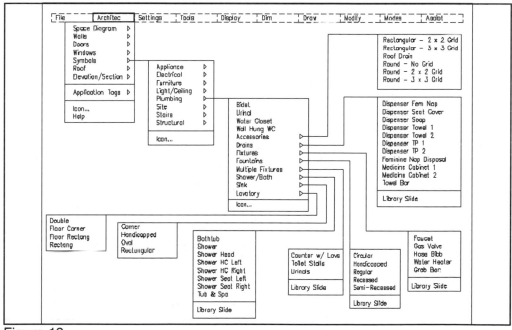

Figure 18.

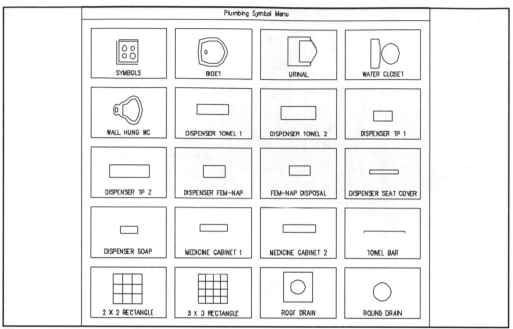

Figure 19.

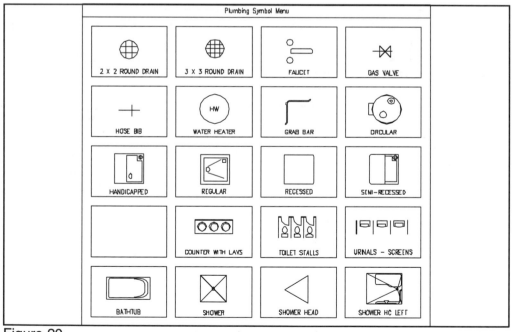

Figure 20.

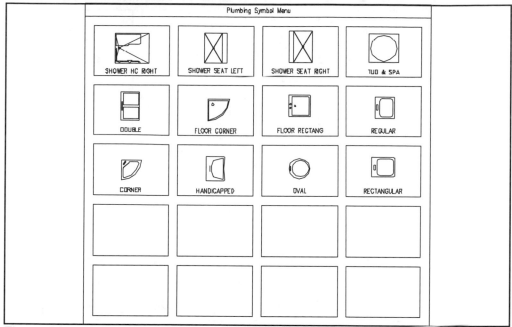

Figure 21.

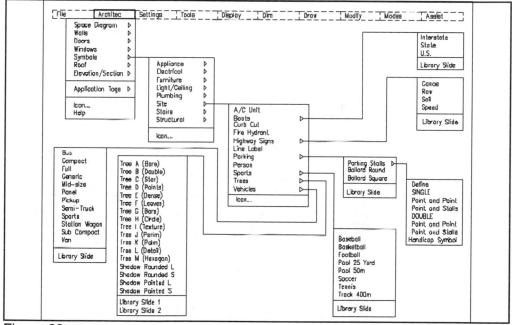

Figure 22.

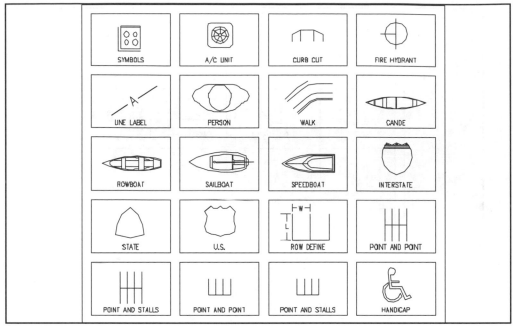

Figure 23.

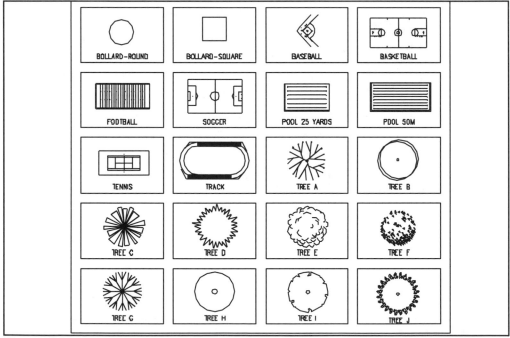

Figure 24.

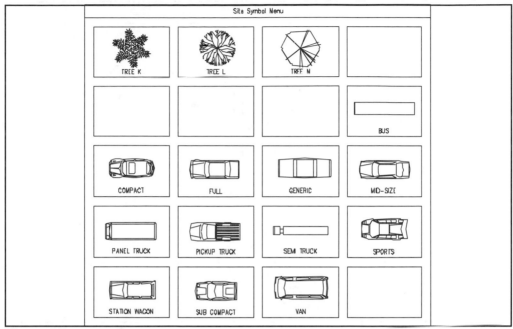

Figure 25.

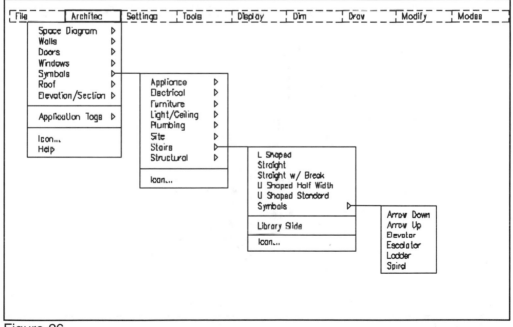

Figure 26.

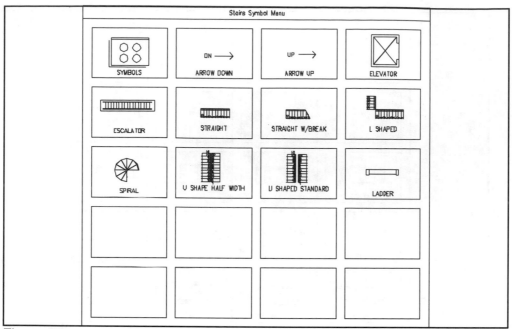

Figure 27.

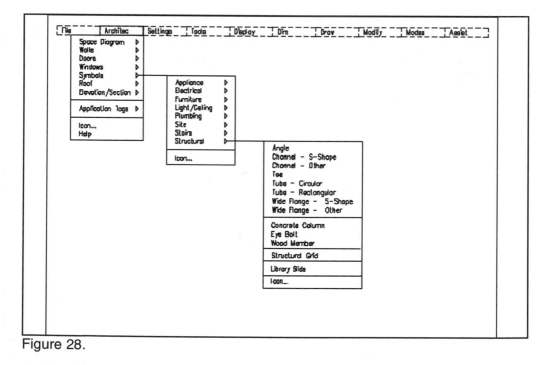

Figure 28.

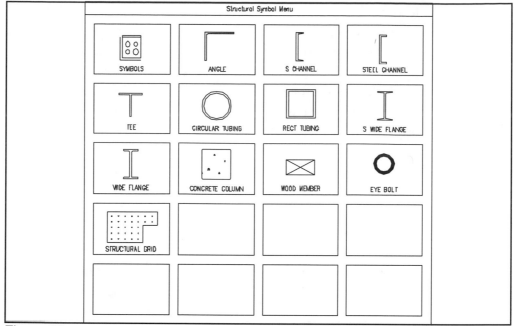

Figure 29.

Settings and Toggles Display Values

1. ASG symbol values can be changed by selecting the abbreviated description from the Settings and Toggles cascading submenus or by using one of the eight Status display options.

2. Settings and Toggles submenus, as well as the Status display command options, are located under the Settings pull-down menu, as shown in Figure 30.

Roof

- Roof submenu — Figure 34
- Roof Status display — Figure 35

Stair

- Stair Section submenu — Figure 36
- Stair Status display — Figure 37

Storefront

- Storefront submenu — Figure 38
- Storefront Status display — Figure 39

Wall

- Wall submenu — Figure 40
- Wall Status display — Figure 41

Veneer

- Veneer submenu — Figure 42
- Veneer Status display — Figure 43

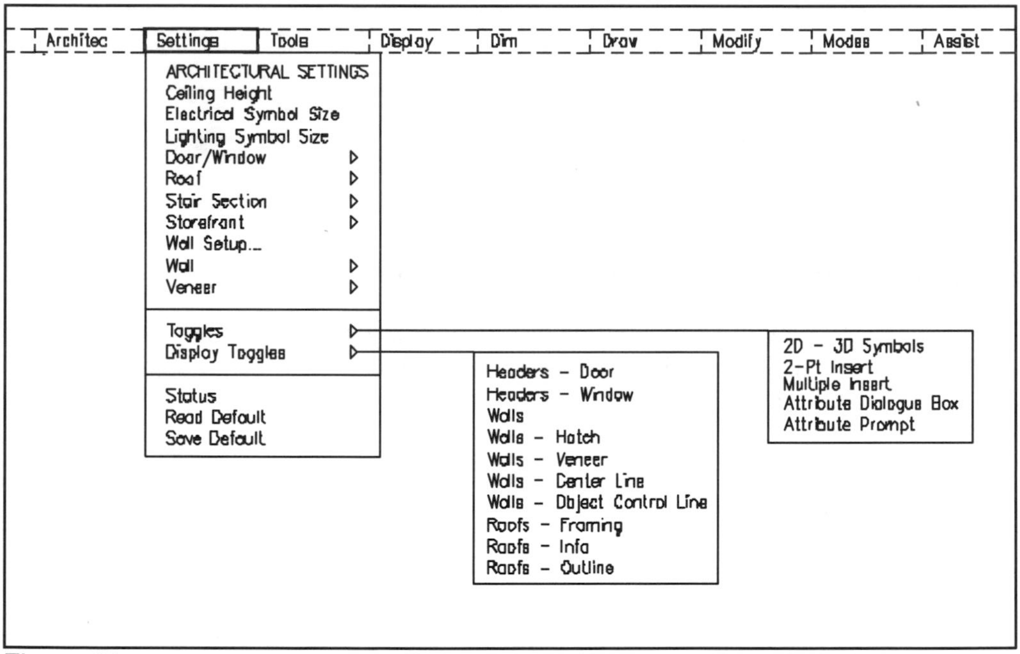

Figure 30.

Display which values Basic/Door/Roof/STAir/STOrefront/WAll/Window/Veneer/All <All>: B

ARCHITECTURAL STATUS:
```
--------------------------------------------------------------
SETTINGS
(a) Ceil Ht     Ceiling height.................................... 96.0
(b) ElSymSiz    Electrical symbols size.......................... 0.1875
(c) LiSymSiz    Lighting symbols size............................ 0.1875
TOGGLES:
(d) 2D - 3D     2D - 3D Symbols................................. 2D
(e) 2-Pt Ins    2-Pt Insert..................................... OFF
(f) AttDioBx    Attribute dialogue box.......................... OFF
(g) AttPrmpt    Attribute prompt................................ OFF
(h) Icon        Automatically display icon menu................. off
DISPLAY TOGGLES:
(i) Door        Door headers.................................... None
(j) Window      Window headers.................................. None
(k) Walls       Walls........................................... None
(l) Hatching    Wall hatching................................... None
(m)Veneers      Wall veneers.................................... None
(n) Info        Roof information................................ None
(o) Outline     Roof outline.................................... None
```

Enter settings/toggle letter(s) to change or RETURN for graphics screen:

Figure 31.

Display which values Basic/Door/Roof/STAir/STOrefront/WAll/Window/Veneer/All <All>: B

ARCHITECTURAL STATUS:
```
--------------------------------------------------------------
SETTINGS
(a) Ceil Ht     Ceiling height.................................... 96.0
(b) ElSymSiz    Electrical symbols size.......................... 0.1875
(c) LiSymSiz    Lighting symbols size............................ 0.1875
TOGGLES:
(d) 2D - 3D     2D - 3D Symbols................................. 2D
(e) 2-Pt Ins    2-Pt Insert..................................... OFF
(f) AttDioBx    Attribute dialogue box.......................... OFF
(g) AttPrmpt    Attribute prompt................................ OFF
(h) Icon        Automatically display icon menu................. off
DISPLAY TOGGLES:
(i) Door        Door headers.................................... None
(j) Window      Window headers.................................. None
(k) Walls       Walls........................................... None
(l) Hatching    Wall hatching................................... None
(m)Veneers      Wall veneers.................................... None
(n) Info        Roof information................................ None
(o) Outline     Roof outline.................................... None
```

Enter settings/toggle letter(s) to change or RETURN for graphics screen:

Figure 32.

Display which values Basic/Door/Roof/STAir/STOrefront/WAll/Window/Veneer/All <All>: D

ARCHITECTURAL STATUS:

DOOR / WINDOW SETTINGS
(a) DoorSwng   Door Swing... 90 DEG
(b) InsPoint   Insert point.. CENTER
(c) IntOsnap   Initial osnap... NEArest
(d) RotAngle   Rotation angle... PROMPT
(e) Sil Ht D   Sill height door.. 0"
(f) Sil Ht W   Sill height window... 3'

DOOR / WINDOW TOGGLES:
(g) Fastdoor   Fastdoor... OFF
(h) HatClean   Hatching cleanup.. OFF
(i) MatchD/W   Match door/window layer.................................... OFF
(j) SilHdr D   Sill /Hdr Door... None
(k) SilHdr W   Sill /Hdr Window.. SILL

Enter settings/toggle letter(s) to change or RETURN for graphics screen:

Figure 33.

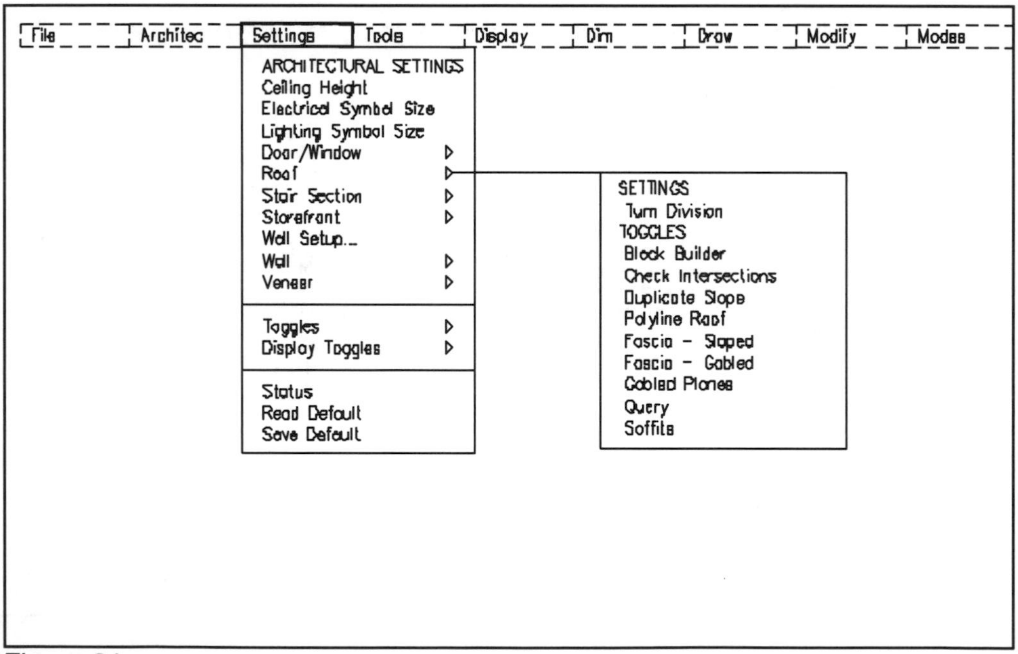

| File | Architec | Settings | Tools | Display | Dim | Draw | Modify | Modes |

ARCHITECTURAL SETTINGS
Ceiling Height
Electrical Symbol Size
Lighting Symbol Size
Door/Window   ▷
Roof   ▷
Stair Section   ▷
Storefront   ▷
Wall Setup...
Wall   ▷
Veneer   ▷

Toggles   ▷
Display Toggles   ▷

Status
Read Default
Save Default

SETTINGS
  Turn Division
TOGGLES
  Block Builder
  Check Intersections
  Duplicate Slope
  Polyline Roof
  Fascia - Sloped
  Fascia - Gabled
  Gabled Planes
  Query
  Soffits

Figure 34.

```
Display which values Basic/Door/Roof/STAir/STorefront/WAll/Window/Veneer/All <All>: R


ARCHITECTURAL STATUS:
------------------------------------------------------------
ROOF SETTINGS
(a) TurnDiv    Number of degrees per turn division.........  22.5
               (Specifies how arc'ed roofs are segmented).

ROOF TOGGLES:
(b) BlockBld   Build completed roofs into a block..............  ON
(c) CheckInt   Check for intersections of common roofs...  ON
(d) DupSlope   Duplicate slope values...........................  ON
(e) PolyRoof   Polyline outline each roof plane..............  OFF
(f) FasciaSl   Draw edge fascia on sloped roof edges......  ON
(g) FasciaGa   Draw edge fascia on gabled roof edges......  ON
(h) Gable      Draw gabled planes...............................  ON
(i) Soffits    Draw soffits on roof edges......................  ON




Enter settings/toggle letter(s) to change or RETURN for graphics screen:
```

Figure 35.

| Architec | Settings | Tools | Display | Dim | Draw | Modify | Modes | Assist |

```
          ARCHITECTURAL SETTINGS
          Ceiling Height
          Electrical Symbol Size
          Lighting Symbol Size
          Door/Window          ▷
          Roof                 ▷
          Stair Section        ▷
          Storefront           ▷          HANDRAIL
          Wall Setup...                     Diameter/Width
          Wall                 ▷            Height
          Veneer               ▷          STAIRS AND STEPS
                                            Maximum Riser Height
          Toggles              ▷            Nosing Size
          Display Toggles      ▷            Nosing Type
                                            Riser Thickness
          Status                            Stair Construction
          Read Default                      Stair Location
          Save Default                      Tread Location
                                            Width of Stair
                                          STRINGER
                                            Effective Depth
                                            Plumb Cut Distance
                                            Work Line Depth
```

Figure 36.

```
Display which values Basic/Door/Roof/STAir/STOrefront/WAll/Window/Veneer/All <All>: STA


ARCHITECTURAL STATUS:
------------------------------------------------------------------------
STAIR SECTION SETTINGS
(a) StrConst    Stair construction type............................ Type 1
                Type 1: Wood, Open riser, Full stringer.
(b) StrLocat    Stair location.................................... Interior
(c) MaxRiser    Maximum allowable riser height.................. 7"
(d) EffDepth    Effective depth of stringer..................... 3 1/2"
(e) WorkLine    Work line depth................................. 1"

(f) Width       Width of stair including stringer............... 3'-6"
(g) TredThik    Thickness of tread.............................. 1 1/8"
(h) RiseThik    Thickness of riser.............................. N/A
(i) RiseType    Riser type...................................... N/A
(j) NoseType    Nosing type..................................... Square
(k) NoseSize    Nosing overhang length.......................... 1"
                Nosing thickness................................ N/A

(l) HRailHt     Handrail height at nosing....................... 2'-10"
(m) HRailDia    Handrail diameter or width...................... 1 1/2"
(n) PlumbCut    Distance from riser to stringer end............. 3"

Enter settings/toggle letter(s) to change or RETURN for graphics screen:
```

Figure 37.

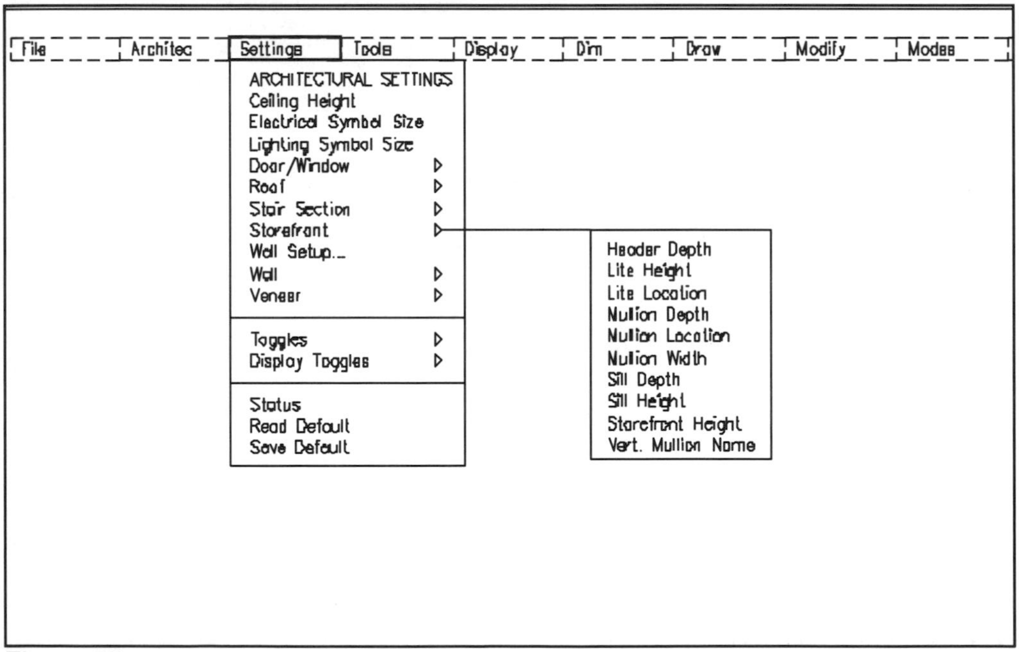

Figure 38.

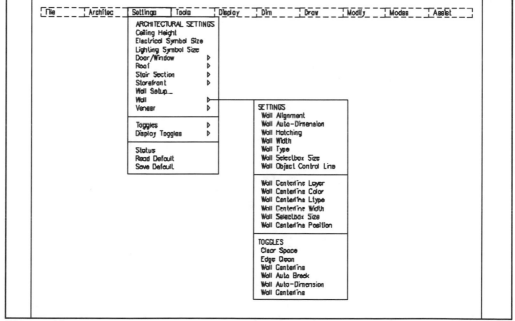

Display which values Basic/Door/Roof/STAir/STOrefront/Wall/Window/Veneer/All <All>: STO

ARCHITECTURAL STATUS:

STOREFRONT SETTINGS
(a) Hdr Dpth   Header depth.. 5 1/2"
(b) Lite Ht   Lite height... 6'
(c) Lite Loc   Lite location (Interior, Middle, Exterior)........ Middle
(d) Mul Dpth   Mullion depth... 5"
(e) Mul Loc   Mullion location (Same as lite location)...... Middle
(f) Mul Wt   Mullion width... 2"
(g) Sil Dpth   Sill depth.. 5 1/2"
(h) Sil Ht   Sill height... 6"
(i) StrfntHt   Storefront height... 8'
(j) VrtMulNm   Vertical mullion name (Default or User)...... Default

Enter settings/toggle letter(s) to change or RETURN for graphics screen:

Figure 39.

Figure 40.

```
Display which values Basic/Door/Roof/STAir/STOrefront/WAll/Window/Veneer/All <All>: WA


ARCHITECTURAL STATUS:
------------------------------------------------------------
WALL SETTINGS
(a) Wall Alg     Wall alignment.................................... Center
(b) Auto-Dim    Auto-Dimension distance.......................... OFF
(c) Wall Hat     Wall hatching pattern............................ None
(d) Wall Ht      Wall height...................................... 10'
(e) Wall Th      Wall width (thickness of wall)................... 6"
(f) WallCCol    Wall centerline's color.......................... 5
(g) WallCLtp    Wall centerline's linetype....................... HIDDEN
(h) WallCWid    Wall centerline width............................ 2"
(i) WallSbox    Wall selection box size.......................... 6
(j) WallCLyr    Wall centerline layer............................ ARWALLCEN
(k) WallCLPs    Wall center line position........................ Wall


WALL TOGGLES:
(l) ClrSpace    Clear space...................................... OFF
(m) EdgClean    Edge clean....................................... OFF
(n) WallCLin    Wall centerline.................................. ON
(o) WallABrk    Wall- Automatically break at start or end.      OFF
(p) WallOCL     Wall Object Control Line......................... OFF


Enter settings/toggle letter(s) to change or RETURN for graphics screen:
```

Figure 41.

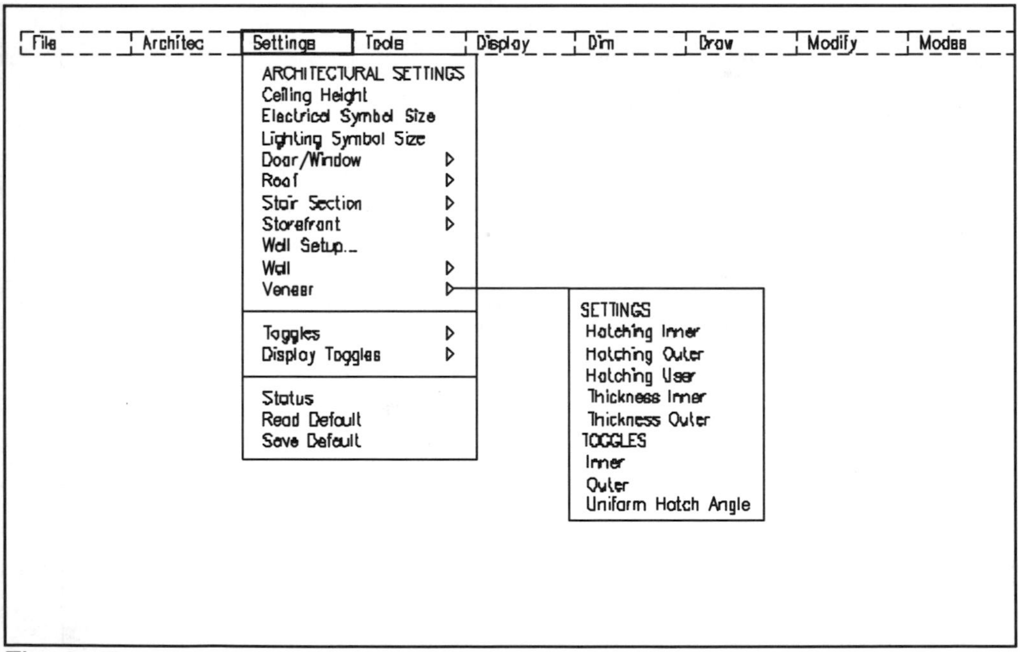

Figure 42.

```
Display which values Basic/Door/Roof/STAir/STOrefront/WAll/Window/Veneer/All <All>: V


ARCHITECTURAL STATUS:
-----------------------------------------------------------------
VENEER SETTINGS
(a) HatInner   Inner veneer hatching pattern....................... None
(b) HatOuter   Outer veneer hatching pattern....................... None
(c) HatUser    User veneer hatching pattern........................ None
(d) WidInner   Inner veneer width (thickness of veneer)...... 1"
(e) WidOuter   Outer veneer width (thickness of veneer)..... 2"

VENEER TOGGLES:
(f) Inner      Inner veneer............................................... OFF
(g) Outer      Outer veneer............................................... OFF
(h) HatAngle   Uniform hatch angle..................................... ON


Enter settings/toggle letter(s) to change or RETURN for graphics screen:
```

Figure 43.

Tools

To edit and manipulate entities ASG provides the following Tools: 2D and 3D Symbol Conversion, Change Wall Height, Wall Stretch, Error Messages, Floor Plane, Adjust Symbols, Attributes, Doors/Windows, and Schedules.

Tools	
Tools pull-down menu	Figure 44
Architectural Tools Menu	Figure 45
Architectural Tools Menu	Figure 46

Architec	Settings	Tools	Display	Dim	Draw	Modify	Modes	Assist

Convert 3D to 2D
Convert 2D to 3D
Change Wall Height
Wall Stretch
Error Messages
Floor Plane
Adjust Symbols

Attributes ▷
Door / Window ▷
Schedules ▷

Icon...

Appliance
Cabinet
Door
Furniture
Lighting
Plumbing
Room
Structural
Toilet
Window

Install
Offset
Reflect
Remove
Scale Fastdoor
Swing

Default
Edit – Prompts
Edit – Dialogue
Adjust Attributes
Copy Attributes
Insert:

Figure 44.

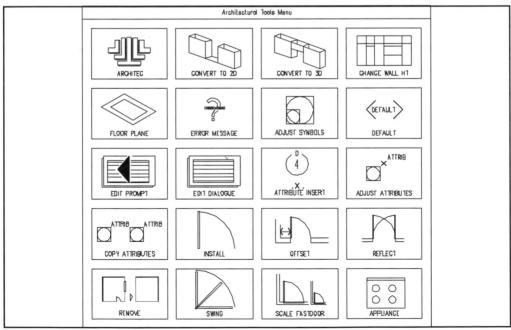

Figure 45.

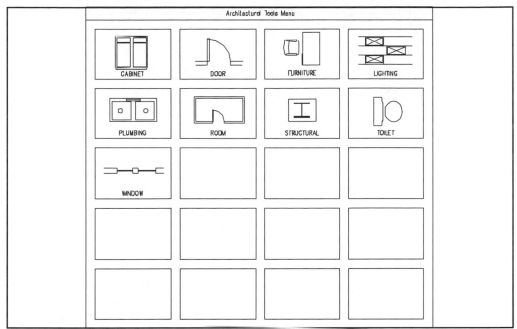

Figure 46.

Overview of Stair Exercise

1. Create a series of new drawings using the completed drawing from Session 4 as a prototype drawing.

2. Begin a new drawing called 2DSTAIR to draw a 2D straight stair.

3. Begin a new drawing called USTAIR to draw a 2D U shaped stair.

4. Save the SESSION 4 drawing as SESSION 7 to draw a 3D stair, insert furniture in the entry area, and add plumbing fixtures, including toilet, sinks, and toilet partitions.

Stair Terms

1. Stair terms and handrail types are shown in Figures 47 and 48.

2. Stairs are not created as blocks and can't be converted from 2D to 3D in the drawing. As you are prompted for a 2D or 3D stair type, select 3D only if required for your presentation.

3.   The following list compares the available 2D and 3D prompts.

Stairs:

Stair width	2D	3D
Landing width	2D	3D
Tread depth	2D	3D
Floor-to-floor height	2D	3D
Carriage thickness		3D
Size of nosing		3D
Shape of nosing		3D
Wall thickness	2D	3D
Center wall	2D	3D
Handrails	2D	3D
Handrail clearance	2D	3D
Handrail diameter	2D	3D
Handrail height		3D
Balusters		3D
Number of steps in bottom run	2D	3D
Number of steps in top run	2D	3D
Number of steps in mid-landing	2D	3D

2D Stair Drawing

1.   Select New from the File pull-down menu to open the Create New Drawing dialog box.

2.   Choose the Prototype... pick box to display the Prototype Drawing File subdialog box.

3.   Double click on the SESSION4 drawing from the ASG6TUT\SESSION4 directory, as shown in Figure 49, to accept it as a prototype.

4.   When the Create New Drawing dialog box reappears, select the Retain as Default box and then enter the path and drawing name in the New Drawing Name... edit box.

5.   Type C:\ASG6\SESSION4\2DSTAIR, as shown in Figure 50, then pick OK.

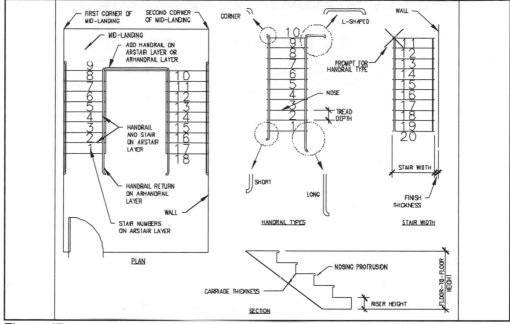

Figure 47.

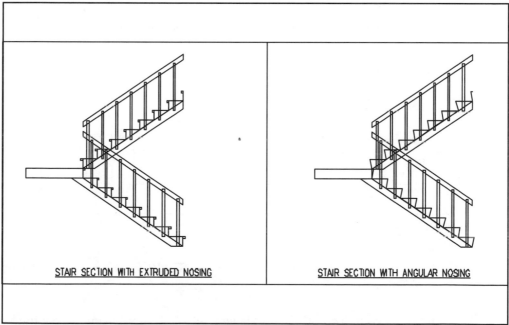

Figure 48.

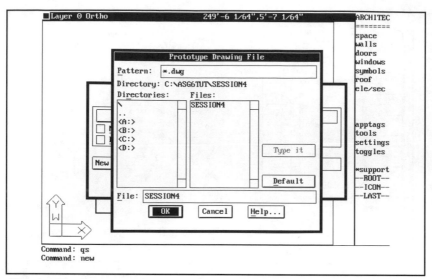

Figure 49.

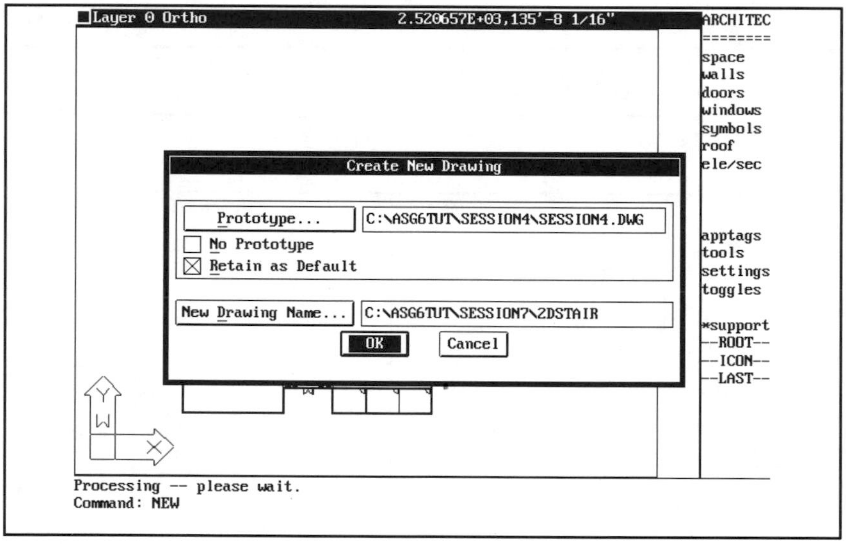

Figure 50.

6. If the roof layers are still turned off, the 2DSTAIR drawing should appear, as it is in Figure 51.

7. If you need to turn off the roof layers, select Modify Layers... from the Modes pull-down menu to display the Layer Control dialog box.

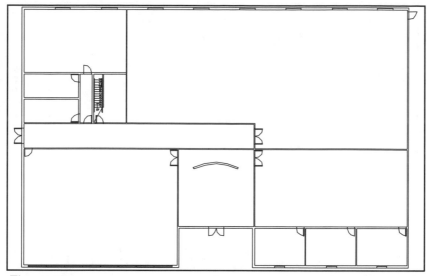

Figure 51.

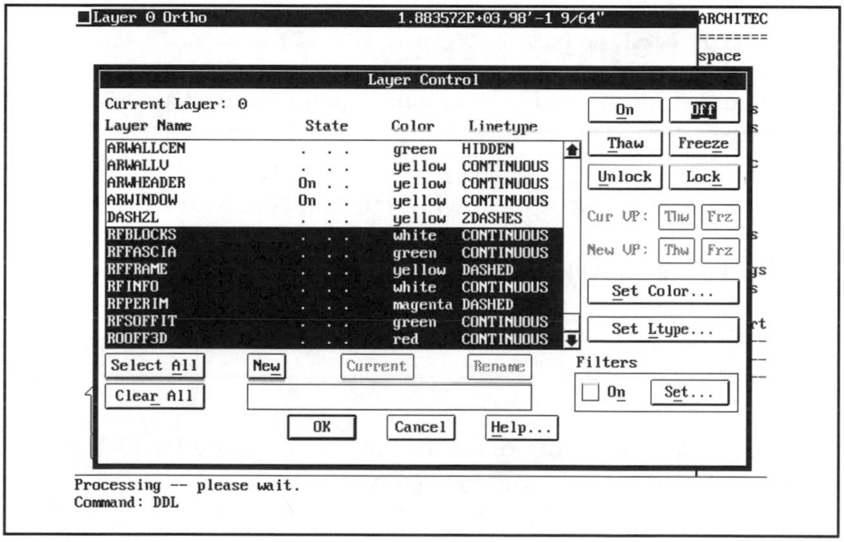

Figure 52.

8. Turn off all the roof layers, as shown in Figure 52, then pick OK. The drawing should now appear as it is in Figure 53.

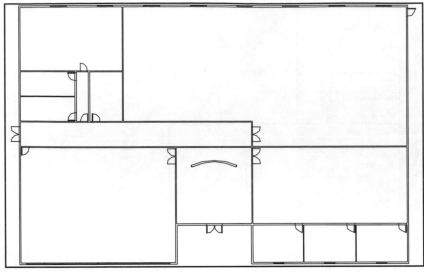

Figure 53.

Set Plotted Text Height

1. Stair symbols are treated as notations and are inserted at a size relative to the drawing scale.

2. All 2D Stairs drawings appear with stair numbers within the tread depth.

3. The final plotted text height controls the size of stair numbers.

4. Select Setup under the File pull-down menu to display the cascading menu, then pick Setup....

5. When the Drawing Setup dialog box appears, choose the Detail... pick box to open the Detailed Scales subdialog box.

6. Enter the value 1/16 in the Height: edit box as shown in Figure 54, then pick OK to close each dialog box.

***TIP – Save as Default

1. Save the new settings as the default.

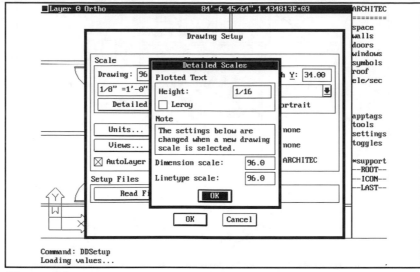

Figure 54.

2. Select Save Default from the Settings pull down menu and respond to the default prompt.

3. Replace the Architec.cfg with the same name.

4. If you end the drawing session before completing any of the stair exercises, all of the previous settings will be recalled.

Settings>Save Default

> Enter ARCHITECTURAL (CFG) file to write, or Dir/Help/eXit ARCHITEC: **ARCHITEC**

> Replace file C:\ASG6\ARCHITEC\ARCHITEC.CFG Yes/No :**Y**

> Processing completed

Straight Stairs

1. Draw a 2D Straight stair in the STAIRS space.

2. To create the stair in place, drawing a diagonal reference line will help establish the exact start point of the stairs. This line will extend from the bottom left corner of the STAIR space to the coordinate 3'6,6'. Start the stair at this

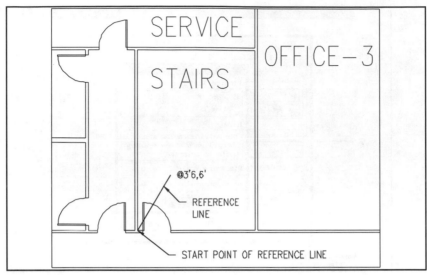

Figure 55.

coordinate, as shown in Figure 55. The LINE command is under the Draw pull-down menu.

Draw>Line

> Command: LINE

> From point: **INT** of [**bottom left corner of STAIRS space as shown in Figure 55**]

> To point: **@3'6,6'**

> To point: [**Enter**]

3. To draw a stair, select Symbols from the Architec pull-down menu, then Stairs, then Straight, as shown in Figure 56, or the Stair Symbol Menu, as shown in Figure 57.

4. This command will draw 2D straight stairs with the start point at the bottom right of the stairs. Specify the following information: 3'6 width of tread, 10.75" depth of tread, 10' floor to floor height, and 0 thickness for the surface of walls. Indicate that you want handrails and accept the default settings. Specify 13 steps.

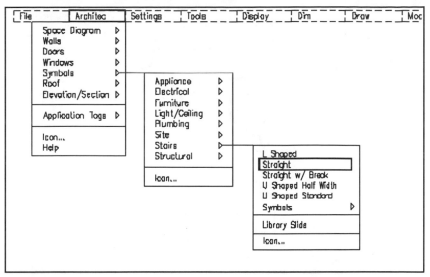

Figure 56.

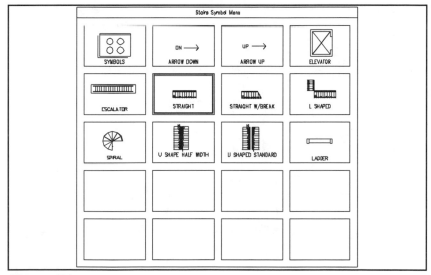

Figure 57.

5. Although the stair specifications do not satisfy code requirements, the exercise is intended simply to illustrate the process. Experiment with drawing a 2D stair based on your local code requirements.

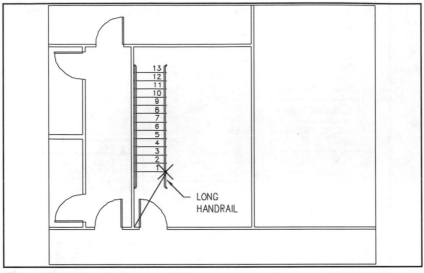

Figure 58.

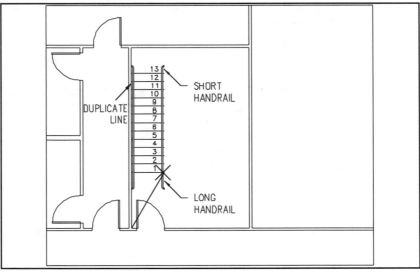

Figure 59.

6. An X appears at each corner of the stair, as shown on Figure 58, for inserting a handrail type. Select from the side screen menu the long handrail type for the bottom and short handrails at the top of the stairs. There are five handrail return types: short, long, L-shaped, corner, and user (not shown in Figure 47). The user option must be a block that you created before executing the stair routine.

7. The completed 2D stair is shown in Figure 59.

| Architec>Symbols>Stairs>Straight |

| Architec>Symbols>Stairs>Icon>Straight |

> DO

> Enter Stair type 2D/3D/Both <2D>: **2D**

> Pick bottom right point: [**ENDP**] of [**select endpoint of reference line**]

> Indicate direction of the top of the stairs: [**pick a point toward top of your drawing**]

> Enter width (from side to side) of the tread <3'-8">: **3'6**

> Enter depth (from front to rear) of the tread <11">: **10.75**

> Enter floor-to-floor height <12'-0">: **10'**

> Enter thickness of the finish on the stair well walls <5/8">: **0**

Note: The 5/8" default thickness assumes you want to add a line on each side of the stairs representing 5/8" gypsum wallboard after drawing the stair.

> Do you want handrails Yes/No <Yes>: **Y**

> Enter clearance between the wall and the handrail <1 1/2">: **1-1/2**

> Enter diameter of the handrail <1 1/2">: **1-1/2**

> Enter number of steps <20>: **20**

Note: Pressing enter at this command line will give you the riser height. The assignment indicates 13 steps, so change this information as indicated below.

> Based upon 20 stairs and 10'-0" floor-to-floor height, the riser height will be 6".

> Would you like to try again Yes/No <No>: **Y**

> Change Number of stairs or Floor-to-floor height <Number>: [**enter**] [**or select number of stairs from side menu**]

> Enter number of steps: **13**

> Based upon 13 stairs and 10'-0" floor-to-floor height, the riser height will be 9.23076925.

Note: If the riser height does not satisfy the requirements, you can try again.

Would you like to try again Yes/No <No>: **N**

> The handrail return will be placed at the X mark...

> Enter handrail type Long/Short/L-Shaped/Corner/User/ Again: **L [as shown in Figure 58, bottom right handrail]**

> The handrail return will be placed at the X mark...

Note: Typically, long handrails are at the bottom of the stairs and short handrails are at the top.

> Enter handrail type Long/Short/L-Shaped/Corner/User/ Again: **L [bottom left handrail]**

> The handrail return will be placed at the X mark...

> Enter handrail type Long/Short/L-Shaped/Corner/User/ Again: **S [as shown in Figure 59 for the top right handrail]**

> The handrail return will be placed at the X mark...

> Enter handrail type Long/Short/L-Shaped/Corner/User/ Again: **S**

> The handrail return will be placed at the X mark...

> Processing completed.

Note: A line is drawn on layer ARSTAIR over the ARWALL layer wall line at the left side of the stair only, extending from the bottom tread to the top tread. You may want to erase this duplicate line.

Complete the Stairs

1. Complete the stairs by drawing a 4" thick wall on the right side of the stairs and erasing the reference line.

2. Select Wall Settings... from the Settings pull-down menu to display the Wall Settings dialog box, or status, WA, from the settings pull-down menu to display wall settings and toggles.

```
■Layer 0 Ortho                86'-5 3/4",  1.459198E+03      ARCHITEC
                                                             ========
                                                             space
            ┌──────────────────── Wall Settings ────────────────────┐
            │                            Wall Alignment           s │
            │  Width:     [4"  ] [4"  ]▼  ┌─────────────────────┐  s │
            │  Height:    [10'-0"][10'-0"]▼ │■ Outer Wall        │    │
            │  Select Box:[6"  ] [6"  ]▼  │☐ Outer Veneer      │  c │
            │  Settings                   │☑ Center             │    │
            │    ┌─Types...─┐ ┌─Hatch...─┐ │☐ Inner Veneer     │    │
            │    ┌─Caps...──┐ ┌─Layer...─┐ │☑ Inner Wall        │  s │
            │  Toggles                    │☑ Other             │  gs │
            │   ☒ Auto Break              │ [2.0000]           │  s │
            │   ☐ Auto DIM    [10'-0"]    │ [        ]         │    │
            │   ☐ Centerline  [Settings...] └─────────────────┘  rt │
            │   ☐ OCL         [Settings...] Veneer Settings        │
            │                              ☐ Outer veneer Thickness[2"] │
            │                              ☐ Inner veneer Thickness[1"] │
            │              [  OK  ] [Cancel] [Help...]             │
            └──────────────────────────────────────────────────────┘
Command: ddwall
```

Figure 60.

```
■Layer 0 Ortho                86'-5 3/4",  1.459198E+03      ARCHITEC
                                                             ========
                                                             space
            ┌──────────────────── Wall Settings ────────────────────┐
            │                            Wall Alignment           s │
            │  Width:     [4"  ] [4"  ]▼  ┌─────────────────────┐  s │
            │  Height:    [10'-0"][10'-0"]▼ │■ Outer Wall        │    │
            │  Select Box:[6"  ] [6"  ]▼  │☐ Outer Veneer      │  c │
            │  Settings                   │☑ Center             │    │
            │    ┌─Types...─┐ ┌─Hatch...─┐ │☐ Inner Veneer     │    │
            │    ┌─Caps...──┐ ┌─Layer...─┐ │☑ Inner Wall        │  s │
            │  Toggles                    │☑ Other             │  gs │
            │   ☒ Auto Break              │ [2.0000]           │  s │
            │   ☐ Auto DIM    [10'-0"]    │ [        ]         │    │
            │   ☐ Centerline  [Settings...] └─────────────────┘  rt │
            │   ☐ OCL         [Settings...] Veneer Settings        │
            │                              ☐ Outer veneer Thickness[2"] │
            │                              ☐ Inner veneer Thickness[1"] │
            │              [  OK  ] [Cancel] [Help...]             │
            └──────────────────────────────────────────────────────┘
Command: ddwall
```

Figure 61.

3. Enter 4″ in the Width: edit box, then activate the Outer Wall ratio button in the Wall Alignment section, as shown in Figure 60, or enter the values in the wall status box as shown in Figure 61.

4. Outer Wall draws the left side of the wall as the outer side.

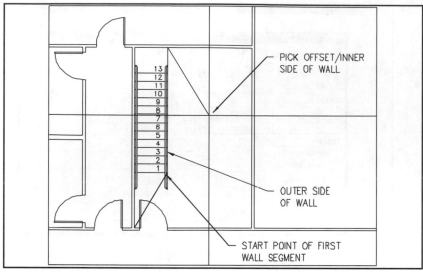

Figure 62.

5.   Toggle Auto Break on to clean up wall intersections as they are drawn.

6.   Select the Cap Settings... pick box, or select End Caps from the walls on the Architec pull-down menu, to cap the end of the wall.

7.   Pick OK to close each dialog box and the Continuous Wall command will automatically execute the prompt to Pick start point for the first wall segment Autopt.

8.   Add a wall on right side of the stairs as shown in Figures 62 and 63.

SettingsWall Settings...{Wall Settings dialog box}

> DO

> Pick start point for the first wall segment <Autopt>: **ENDP** of [**endpoint of first riser, as shown in Figure 62**]

> Next point of wall or ALign/AUtopt/CAps/CLose/Fillet/ Relative/Wall/Undo: **PER** to [**wall at top of stairs**]

> Pick offset/inner side of wall:[**pick right side of wall, as shown in Figure 63**]

Note: A temporary green line will appear.

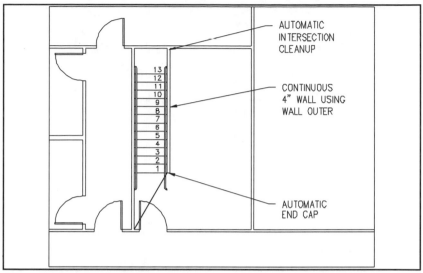

AUTOMATIC
INTERSECTION
CLEANUP

CONTINUOUS
4" WALL USING
WALL OUTER

AUTOMATIC
END CAP

Figure 63.

> Pick next point of wall or ALign/AUtopt/CAps/CLose/Fillet/ Relative/Wall: [**Enter**]

Note: Type REDRAW to refresh the screen if the left wall line does not appear.

> Processing completed.

9. Complete the stair, as shown in Figure 64, by adding the UP arrow symbol below the first stair tread. Select the UP arrow from the Stair cascading or icon menu shown previously in Figures 56 and 57. Erase the reference line.

Architec>Symbols>Stairs>**Arrow UP**

or

Architec>Symbols>Stairs>Icon>**Arrow UP**

> DO

> Pick insertion point:[**select point below the bottom tread, as shown in Figure 64**]

> Enter rotation angle <0.0>: [**drag arrow upward with cursor**]

> Processing completed.

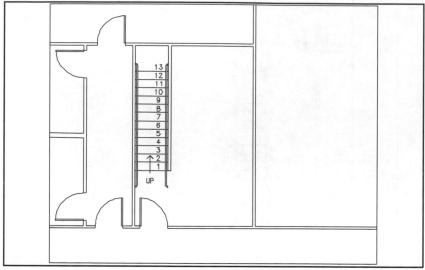

Figure 64.

***TIP – Read Default

1. If you exit the drawing session now, restore the saved architectural settings.

2. Select Read Default from the Settings pull-down menu and accept the default.

3. The values were saved under the path and filename C:\ASG6\ARCHITEC\ ARCHITEC.CFG from the previous Tip. (See Tip - Save Default.)

4. Entering the D option of the command allows you to choose from a list of saved values displayed on the side screen menu.

Settings>Read Default

> Enter ARCHITECTURAL (CFG) file to write, or Dir/Help/eXit ARCHITEC: **ARCHITEC**

> Processing completed.

2D U-Shaped Standard Stair

1. Select New from the File pull-down menu to begin a new drawing called 3DSTAIR.

2.   Enter the path and drawing name in the Create New Drawing dialog box. The drawing from Session 4 should still be set as the prototype drawing with an X in the box adjacent to Retain as Default box, as shown in Figure 65.

3.   First, verify that the Final Plotted Text Height is still 1/16". Then, zoom into the same STAIRS space.

4.   From the Architec pull-down menu, select Symbols, then Stairs, then U Shaped Standard.

5.   When prompted for stair type, select 2D.

6.   Draw a 2D stair, as shown in Figure 66. The start point of the mid-landing is at the left top corner of the STAIR space. Proceed across to the opposite corner of the space, then select a point toward the door when prompted for the direction of the bottom of the stairs.

7.   Specify the following information: 3'-8" landing and tread width, 11" tread depth, 10' floor to floor height and 0 thickness for the surface of the walls.

Architec>Symbols>Stairs>U Shaped Standard

Architec>Symbols>Stairs>Icon>U Shaped Standard

>   DO

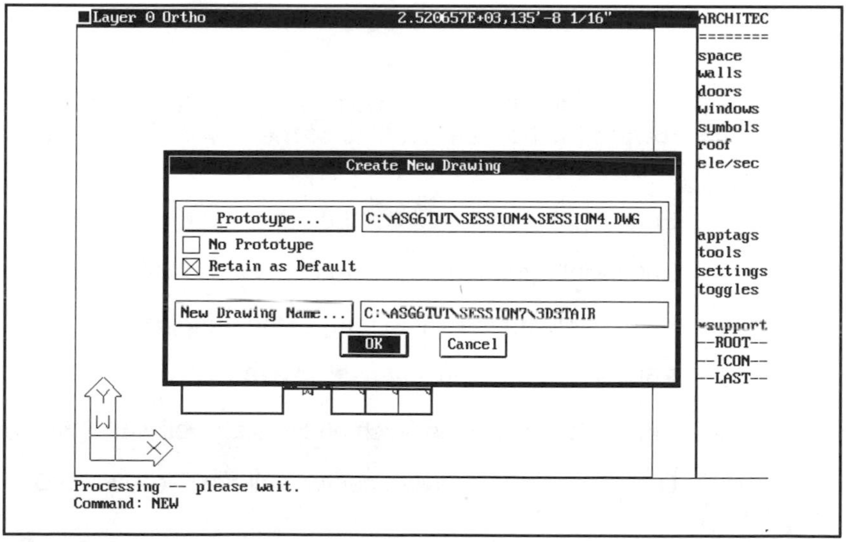

Figure 65.

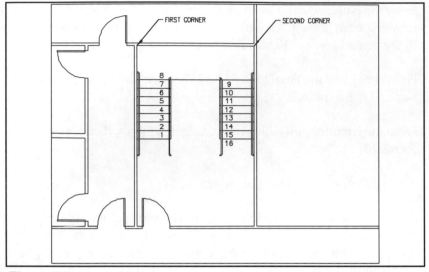

Figure 66.

> Enter Stair type 2D/3D/Both <2D>: **2D**

> Pick first corner of the mid-landing: **INT** of [**top left corner of STAIR space**]

> Pick second corner of the mid-landing: **INT** of [**top right corner of STAIR space, as in Figure 66**]

Note: A heavy polyline will appear with a rubberband connected to your crosshairs.

> Indicate direction of the bottom of the stairs: [**pick a point toward the bottom left side of the STAIRS space to begin tread #1 near the door**]

> Enter landing width <3'-8">:**3'8**

> Enter width (from side to side) of the tread <3'-8">:**3'8**

> Enter depth (from front to rear) of the tread <11">:**11**

> Enter floor-to-floor height <12'-0">:**10'**

> Enter thickness of the finish on the stair well walls <5/8">:**0**

> Does the stairwell have a center wall Yes/No <No>:**NO**

Note: If you respond Yes, you will be prompted: Enter thickness of finish on center walls <5/8">:

> Do you want handrails Yes/No <Yes>: **Y**

> Enter clearance between the wall and the handrail<1 1/2">: **1-1/2**

> Enter diameter of the handrail <1 1/2">: **1-1/2**

> Enter number of steps in the bottom run <10>: **8**

> Enter number of steps in the top run <10>: **8**

> Enter number of steps in the mid-landing <0>:**0**

> Based upon 16 stairs and 10'-0" floor-to-floor height, the riser height will be 7-1/2".

> Would you like to try again Yes/No: **N**

> The handrail return will be placed at the X mark...

> Enter handrail type Long/Short/L-Shaped/Corner/User/ Again:**L [select Long from side menu]**

> The handrail return will be placed at the X mark...

> Enter handrail type Long/Short/L-Shaped/Corner/User/ Again:**L [select Long from side menu]**

> The handrail return will be placed at the X mark...

> Enter handrail type Long/Short/L-Shaped/Corner/User/ Again:**C [select Corner from side menu]**

> The handrail return will be placed at the X mark...

> Enter handrail type Long/Short/L-Shaped/Corner/User/ Again:**S [select Short from side menu]**

> The handrail return will be placed at the X mark...

> Enter handrail type Long/Short/L-Shaped/Corner/User/ Again:**C [select Corner from side menu]**

> The handrail return will be placed at the X mark...

> Enter handrail type Long/Short/L-Shaped/Corner/User/ Again:**S [select Short from side menu]**

> The handrail return will be placed at the X mark...

> Enter handrail type Long/Short/L-Shaped/Corner/User/ Again:L [**select Long from side menu**]

> The handrail return will be placed at the X mark...

> Enter handrail type Long/Short/L-Shaped/Corner/User/ Again:L [**select Long from side menu**]

> Processing completed.

Note: The 2D U Shaped Stair handrails and returns are shown in Figure 67.

8. Complete the stair by adding lines on layer ARHANDRAIL or ARSTAIR to connect the corner handrails between the stairs at the mid-landing, and the UP arrow at the bottom of tread #1, as shown in Figure 67.

3D U-Shaped Standard Stair

1. Select New from the File pull-down menu to begin a new drawing called SESSION7.

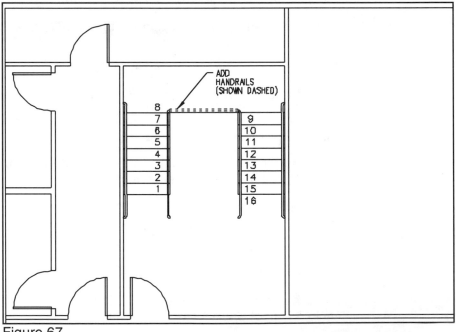

Figure 67.

2. Enter the path and drawing name in the Create New Drawing dialog box shown in Figure 68. The drawing from Session 4 should still be set as the prototype drawing with an X in the box adjacent to Retain as Default.

3. From the Architec pull-down menu, select Symbols, then Stairs, then U Shaped Standard.

4. The prompts for drawing a 3D stair are similar to a 2D stair. Tread numbers do not appear on the 3D stairs.

5. Select the same beginning points for the mid-landing at the top left and right corners of the Stair space, as shown in Figure 69. Then pick a point toward the door when prompted for the direction of the bottom of the stairs.

6. Specify the following information: 3'-8" landing and tread width, 11" tread depth, 10' floor to floor height and 0 thickness for the surface for the surface of the walls.

7. The carriage thickness (stringer width at rear of step) is 5", with a 1 1/2" extruded nosing.

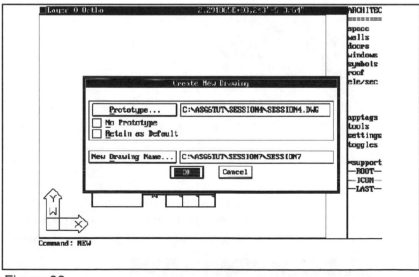

Figure 68.

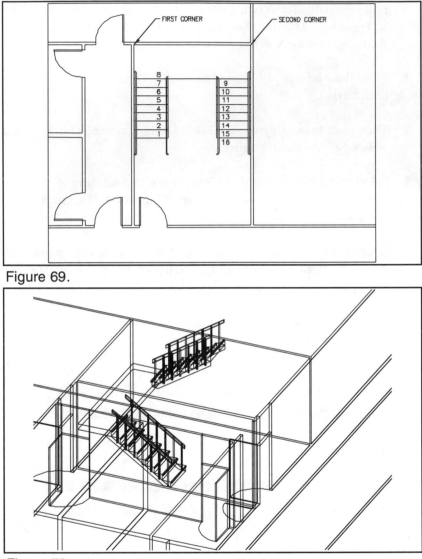

Figure 69.

Figure 70.

8. Accept the default handrail height (although it does not meet code requirements) with balusters. Enter 8 steps for both top and bottom runs, with no step at the mid-landing. A partial isometric view is shown in Figure 70.

Architec>Symbols>Stairs>U Shaped Standard

Architec>Symbols>Stairs>Icon>U Shaped Standard

> DO

> Enter Stair type 2D/3D/Both <2D>: **3D**

> Pick first corner of the mid-landing: **INT** of [**point 1, as shown in Figure 69**]

> Pick second corner of the mid-landing: **INT** of [**point 2**]

> Indicate direction of the bottom of the stairs: [**pick a point toward the stair door opening**]

> Enter landing width <3'-8">:**3'8**

> Enter width (from side to side) of the tread <3'-8">:**3'8**

> Enter depth (from front to rear) of the tread <11">:**11**

> Enter floor-to-floor height <12'-0">:**10'**

> Enter thickness of the carriage <5">:**5**

> Enter distance that the nosing protrudes <1 1/2">:**1-1/2**

> Nosing type Extruded/Angular <Extruded>:**E**

> Enter thickness of the finish on the stair well walls <5/8">:**0**

> Does the stairwell have a center wall Yes/No <No>:**N**

Note: If you respond Yes, you will be prompted: Enter thickness of finish on center walls <5/8">:

> Do you want handrails Yes/No <Yes>: **Y**

> Enter clearance between the wall and the handrail <1 1/2">: **1-1/2**

> Enter diameter of the handrail <1 1/2">: **1-1/2**

> Enter height of the handrail <2'-8">: **2'8**

> Do you want balusters Yes/No <Yes>: **Y**

> Enter number of steps in the bottom run <10>: **8**

> Enter number of steps in the top run <10>: **8**

> Enter number of steps in the mid-landing <0>:**0**

> Based upon 16 stairs and 10'-0" floor-to-floor height, the riser height will be 7-1/2".

> Would you like to try again Yes/No: **N**

> Processing completed.

9. Repeat the 3D stair command based on your local code requirements for handrail height.

Overview of Plumbing Fixtures Exercise

1. In this exercise, you will add plumbing fixtures to the men's and women's restrooms.

2. First, insert all the plumbing fixtures in the women's toilet room.

3. After completing the women's room, mirror those fixtures that are duplicated both places to the men's room. Add urinals to complete the men's room.

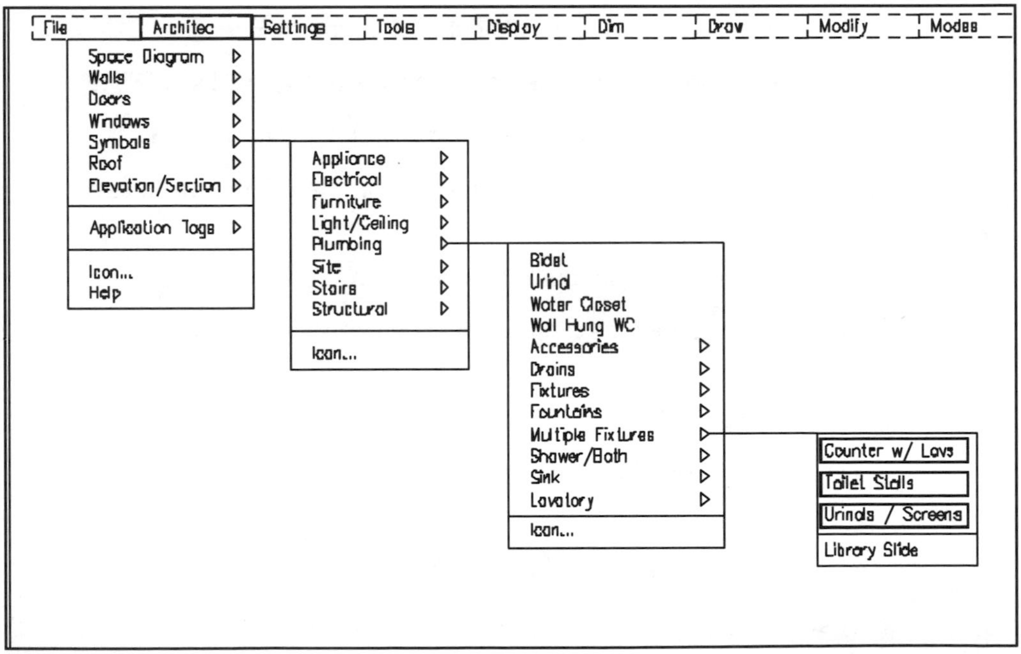

Figure 71.

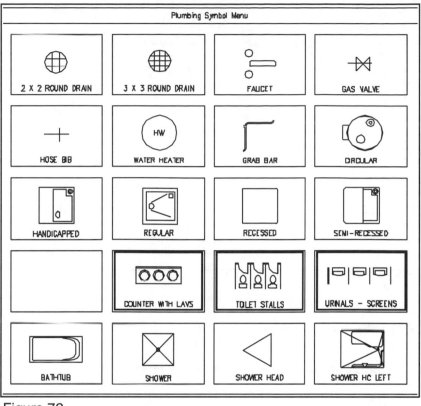

Figure 72.

4. Select Symbols from the Architec pull-down menu, and then Plumbing, as shown in Figure 71, or the Plumbing Symbol icons shown in Figure 72.

5. The submenu displays all the plumbing symbols, including the Multiple Fixtures symbols used for this exercise.

Women's Toilet Room

1. Insert one handicap toilet, two regular toilet stalls, and a counter with two sinks in the women's room.

2. Toilet paper holder, mirrors, handicap handrails, and similar accessory symbols are available for insertion into the plan from the Accessories submenu.

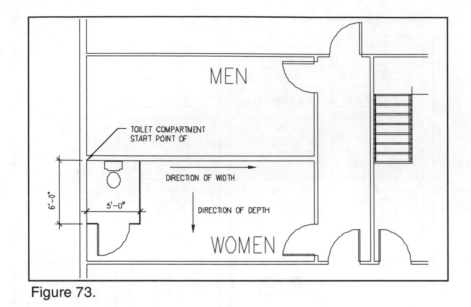

Figure 73.

Handicapped Toilet Stall

1. Insert a handicap toilet specifying a compartment width of 5′ and a compartment depth of 6′, with 0 wall finish.

2. Select Toilet Stalls from the Multiple Fixtures menu.

3. The Toilet Stalls command prompts for the stall size, toilet type, partition location, and door swing.

4. Begin drawing the stall at the top left corner of the room and proceed to the right, as shown in Figure 73.

   Architec>Symbols>Plumbing>Multiple Fixtures>Toilet Stalls

   > DO

   > Pick start point of toilet compartment: **INT** of [**top left corner of women's room**]

   > Indicate direction of width: [**select point to the right**]

   > Indicate direction of depth: [**select point toward the bottom of screen as shown in Figure 73**]

> CURRENT VALUES: Compartment: Width: 36, Depth: 60, Door: 24

> Partition: Thickness: 1, Floor: 12, Height: 60, Finish: 5/8

> Enter value to change CW/CD/D/PT/PF/PH/W: **CW**

> Enter compartment width <3'-0">: **5'**

Note: Each value must be changed individually. After selecting the compartment width, the current values will appear again confirming the previous selection and ready for additional changes. This selection changes the compartment width from 36" to 60". (Your default values may be different from those indicated in this exercise.)

> CURRENT VALUES: Compartment: Width: 60, Depth: 60, Door: 24

> Partition: Thickness: 1, Floor: 12, Height:60, Finish:5/8

> Enter value to change CW/CD/D/PT/PF/PH/W: **CD**

> Enter compartment depth <5'-0">: **6'**

Note: CD changes compartment depth from 5' to 6'.

> CURRENT VALUES: Compartment: Width: 60, Depth: 72, Door: 24

> Partition: Thickness: 1, Floor: 12, Height: 60, Finish: 5/8

> Enter value to change CW/CD/D/PT/PF/PH/W:**D**

> Enter door width <2'-0">: **3'**

Note: D changes door width from 2' to 3'

> CURRENT VALUES: Compartment: Width: 60, Depth: 72, Door: 36

> Partition: Thickness: 1, Floor: 12, Height: 60, Finish: 5/8

> Enter value to change CW/CD/D/PT/PF/PH/W:**W**

> Enter wall finish thickness <5/8">: **0**

Note: W changes wall finish thickness to 0. If 5/8" is selected, the toilet partition stall is drawn 5/8" from the wall line.

> CURRENT VALUES: Compartment: Width: 60, Depth: 72, Door: 36

> Partition: Thickness: 1, Floor: 12, Height: 60, Finish: 5/8

> Enter value to change CW/CD/D/PT/PF/PH/W: [**Enter**]

> Enter number of compartments <1>: **1**

> Enter type of toilet <Floor>: **Floor**

> Enter toilet width: 20 [**select 20 x 30 from side menu**]

> Enter toilet depth:30 [**dimension furnished automatically from initial selection**]

> Enter toilet height: 16 [**dimension furnished automatically from initial selection**]

Note: The values furnished may not satisfy code requirements. Check with your local code for correct values.

> Does the first compartment have a beginning partition Yes/No <Yes>: **N**

> Does the last compartment have an end partition Yes/No <Yes>: **Y**

> Processing -- please wait.

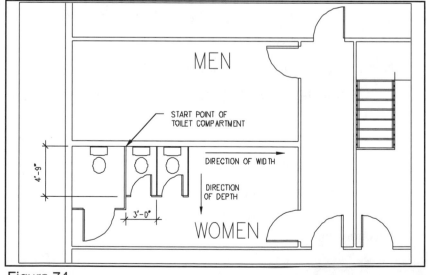

Figure 74.

> Would you like to change the door swing Yes/No <No>: **Y**

> Would you like to change the door swing Yes/No <No>: [**Enter**]

> Processing completed

Additional Toilet Stalls

1. Highlight the Architec pull-down menu to open the previous Toilet Stalls menu, then double click Architec to repeat the command for additional toilet stalls.

2. Insert 2 additional toilet stalls, each 3' wide and 4'-9" deep with 2' wide doors as shown in Figure 74.

Architec>Symbols>Plumbing>Multiple Fixtures>Toilet Stalls

> DO

> Pick start point of toilet compartment: INT of [**top left corner of women's toilet stall as shown in Figure 74**]

> Indicate direction of width: [**select point to the right**]

> Indicate direction of depth: [**select point toward the bottom of screen**]

> CURRENT VALUES: Compartment: Width: 60, Depth: 72, Door: 36

> Partition: Thickness: 1, Floor: 12, Height: 60, Finish: 0

> Enter value to change CW/CD/D/PT/PF/PH/W: **CW**

> Enter compartment width <5'-0">: **3'**

> CURRENT VALUES: Compartment: Width: 36, Depth: 72, Door: 36

> Partition: Thickness: 1, Floor: 12, Height: 60, Finish: 0

> Enter value to change CW/CD/D/PT/PF/PH/W: **CD**

> Enter compartment depth <6'-0">: **4'9'**

> CURRENT VALUES: Compartment: Width: 36, Depth: 57, Door: 36

> Partition: Thickness: 1, Floor: 12, Height: 60, Finish: 0

> Enter value to change CW/CD/D/PT/PF/PH/W: **D**

> Enter door width <3'-0">: **2'**

> CURRENT VALUES: Compartment: Width: 36, Depth: 57, Door: 24

> Partition: Thickness: 1, Floor: 12, Height: 60, Finish: 0

> Enter number of compartments <1>: **2**

> Enter type of toilet <Floor>: **FLOOR**

> Enter toilet width <1'-8">: **1'8**

> Enter toilet depth <2'-6">: **2'6**

> Enter toilet height <1'-4">: **1'4**

> Does the first compartment have a beginning partition Yes/No <Yes>: **N**

> Does the last compartment have an end partition Yes/No <Yes>: **Y**

> Processing – please wait.

> Would you like to change the door swing Yes/No <No>:**N** @PROMPT = Processing completed.

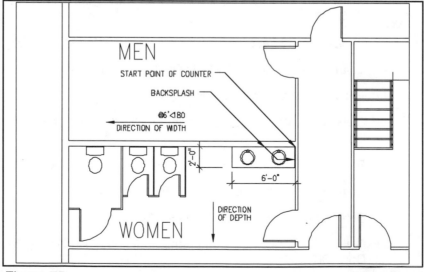

Figure 75.

Lavatories

1. The lavatories command prompts for the countertop and backsplash sizes, backsplash location, and type and number of lavatories.

2. Add a 6' wide by 24" deep countertop with 2 lavatories 16" wide x 17" deep, as shown in Figure 75, by selecting Counter with Lavs from the Multiple Fixtures pull-down or icon menu.

    Architec>Symbols>Plumbing>Multiple Fixtures>Counter w/ lavs

    > Enter counter type 2D/3D/Both <2D>: **2D**

    > Pick start point of the counter: **INT** of [**select top right corner of women's room, as shown in Figure 75**]

    > Pick endpoint of the counter: **@6'<180**

    > Indicate direction of depth: [**select a point toward bottom of screen**]

    > CURRENT VALUES: Counter: Depth: 24, Finish: 0

    > Splash: Start: 3/4, Back: 3/4, End: 3/4.

    > Enter value to change CD/FT/SS/SB/SE: **SE**

    > Enter splash guard thickness at the end point <3/4">: **0**

    Note: SE changes the backsplash thickness from 3/4" to 0 on the the left side of the counter where no wall exists.

    > CURRENT VALUES: Counter: Depth: 24, Finish:0

    > Splash: Start: 3/4, Back: 3/4, End: 0.

    > Enter value to change CD/FT/SS/SB/SE: [**enter**]

    > Verify the specified counter length <6'-0">: **6'**

    > Enter number of lavatories: **2**

    > Enter lavatory type Handicap/Oval/Rectang/User <Oval>: [**enter**]

    > Enter lavatory width: **16** [**select 16 x 17 from side menu**]

    > Enter lavatory depth: **17** [**dimension furnished automatically from initial selection**]

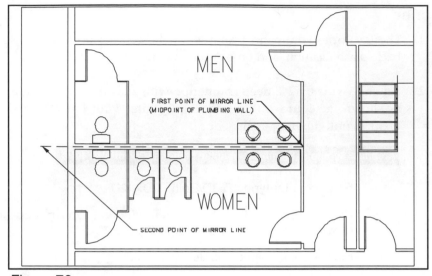

Figure 76.

> Enter lavatory height: **6 [dimension furnished automatically from initial selection]**

> Enter height above the floor <3'-0">: **32 [dimension furnished automatically from initial selection]**

> Processing – please wait.

> Processing completed.

Men's Toilet Room

1. Most plumbing fixtures are installed along a common plumbing wall.

2. Instead of drawing fixtures for each room, copy the fixtures by mirroring them along a common line, and then add fixtures if necessary.

3. Mirror the handicap stall and the countertop along the common plumbing wall, as shown in Figure 76. Pick each element of the figures you wish to mirror.

Modify>Mirror

Urinals

1. Add 2 urinals in the Men's room, as shown in Figure 77.

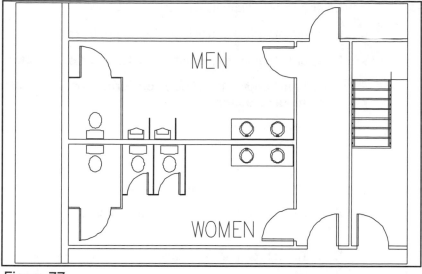

Figure 77.

2.   Select Urinals/Screens from the Multiple Fixtures menu and respond to the prompts for location, number, size and screen positions.

ArchitecSymbolsPlumbingMultiple FixturesUrinals/Screens

> DO

> Pick start point of the urinal compartments: **INT** of [**bottom outside corner of handicap stall along wall line**]

> Indicate direction of width: [**select a point toward right side of screen**]

> Indicate direction of depth [**select a point toward top of screen**]

> CURRENT VALUES: Stall: Width: 30, Finish: 0.

> Screen: Width: 24, Thickness: 3/4, Floor: 12, Height: 42.

> Enter value to change W/F/SW/ST/SF/SH: [**Enter**]

Note: If your default finish value is not 0, you can't select a value of 0 for (F) Wall Finish. The message "Value must be positive and nonzero" appears even though zero is an option on the side screen menu. If you want a value of 0 try to use any small fractional positive number.

> Enter number of urinals <1>: **2**

> Enter urinal type Default/User <Default>: **[Enter]**

> Enter urinal width: 18 [**select 18" x 12" from side menu**]

> Enter urinal depth: 12 [**dimension furnished automatically from initial selection**]

> Enter urinal height: 24 [**dimension furnished automatically from initial selection**]

> Enter height above the floor: 24   [**dimension furnished automatically from initial selection**]

> Does the first compartment have a beginning screen Yes/No <Yes>: **N**

> Does the last compartment have an end screen Yes/No <Yes>: **Y**

> Processing -- Please wait.

> Processing completed.

Overview of Furniture Exercise

1. Choose all the furniture by selecting Symbols, then Furniture, under the Architec pull-down menu, as shown in Figure 78.

2. The submenu displays all the furniture symbols including the Sofas, Chairs, and Tables symbols used for this exercise.

3. Symbol names similar to Chairs and Desk/Table/Credenza are displayed with three dots indicating that they open icon menus.

4. The symbol names Bed, Equipment and so on, appear with arrows, signifying that they display a cascading submenu.

5. Peruse Basic Status from the Settings pull-down menu to confirm 2D Symbols is ON (letter D), as shown in Figure 31. (Later we will convert the furniture to 3D symbols.)

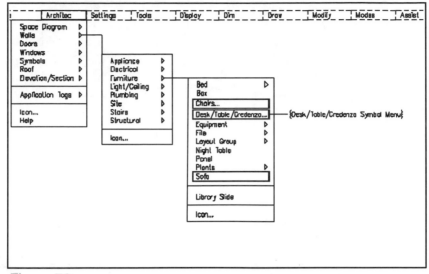

Figure 78.

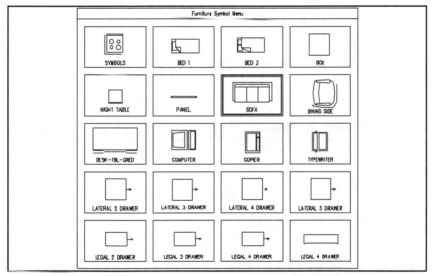

Figure 79.

Sofa

1. Select Furniture from the Architec pull-down menu to display the cascading submenu, as shown in Figure 78, or the Furniture Symbol Menu icon in Figure 79.

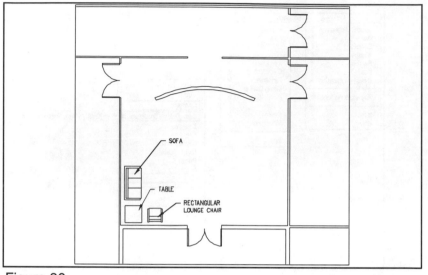

Figure 80.

2. Choose Chairs... to open the Chair Symbol dialog box, then double click the Lounge Rectangular icon.

3. Specify a sofa 72″ wide x 36″ deep by selecting it from the side screen.

4. Insert the sofa into the Entry area, as shown in Figure 80.

Architec>Symbols>Furniture>Chairs...>{Chair Symbol Menu>Sofa

> DO

> Enter sofa width: 72 [**select 72 x 36 from side menu**]

> Enter sofa depth: 36 [**dimension furnished automatically from initial selection**]

> Enter sofa height:16 [**dimension furnished automatically from initial selection**]

> Pick insertion point: [**locate as shown in Figure 80**]

> Enter rotation angle <0.0>: [**orient as shown in Figure 80**]

> Processing completed.

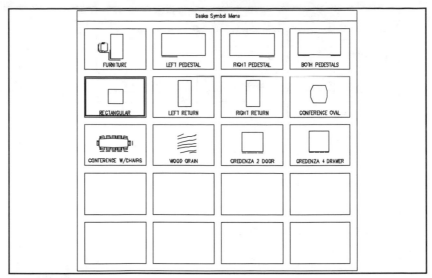

Figure 81.

Table

1. Insert a rectangular table from the Desks/Tables/Credenza submenu.

2. The Desk/Table/Credenza Menu icon opens to display the various symbols, as shown in Figure 81.

3. Double click the Rectangular Table icon, specifying a size of 36" x 36" from the command prompt, or picking the default from the screen menu.

4. Insert the symbol into the Entry area as shown in Figure 80.

Architec>Symbols>Furniture>Desk/Tables/Credenza>{Desk Symbol Menu}Rectangular

> DO

> Enter table width: 36 [select 36 x 36 from side menu]

> Enter table depth: 36 [**dimension furnished automatically from initial selection**]

> Enter table height:29 [**dimension furnished automatically from initial selection**]

> Pick insertion point: [**locate as shown in Figure 80**]

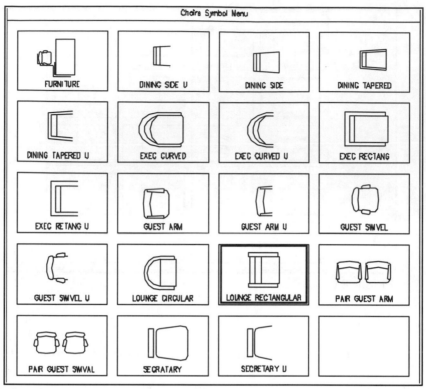

Figure 82.

> Enter rotation angle <0.0>: [**orient as shown in Figure 80**]

> Processing completed.

Chair

1. Insert a rectangular lounge chair into the Entry area as in Figure 80.

2. Specify a size of 32″ x 30″ from the Chairs submenu, or Chair Symbol Menu icon shown in Figure 82.

Architec>Symbols>Furniture>Chairs...>{Chairs Symbol Menu}Lounge Rectangular

> DO

> Enter chair width: 32 [**select 32 x 30 from side menu**]

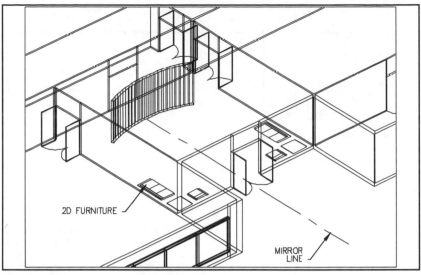

Figure 83.

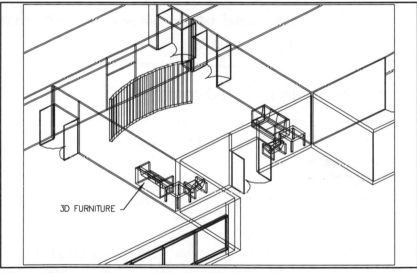

Figure 84.

> Enter chair depth: 30 [**dimension furnished automatically from initial selection**]

> Enter chair height: 16 [**dimension furnished automatically from initial selection**]

> Pick insertion point: [**locate as shown in Figure 80**]

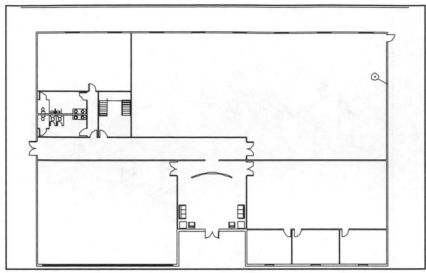

Figure 85.

> Enter rotation angle <0.0>: [**orient as shown in Figure 80**]

> Processing completed.

Converting Symbols from 2D to 3D

1. Mirror the sofa, table and chair to the opposite side of the Entry area, using the midpoint of the custom wall as the first point of the mirror line.

    Modify>Mirror

2. An isometric view of the 2D furniture and mirror centerline is shown in Figure 83.

3. Convert the 2D furniture to 3D by selecting Convert 2D to 3D from the Tools pull-down menu, shown previously in Figure 44.

4. An isometric view of the 3D furniture drawing is shown in Figure 84.

    Tools>Convert 2D to 3D

    > Pick symbol types that you want to convert.

    > Enter Done when finished.

Note: Select Furniture from the side screen menu, then pick Done. (If you wanted to convert other symbols, like the plumbing fixtures, select Plumbing from the side menu also. Pick Done after selecting the various symbol types.)

> Command: DONE

> Select objects to convert to 3D matching pattern * <all>:

> Select objects: 1 selected 1 found [**enter**]

Note: Pressing enter for the default value <all> will change all furniture in your drawing from 2D to 3D.

> Processing -- please wait.

> Processing -- please wait.

> Processing completed.

5.   The 2D furniture symbols (blocks) are replaced with 3D symbols. Similarly, the 2D symbols can be restored at any time by selecting Convert 3D to 2D from the same menu.

6.   The completed plan showing the 3D stair, furniture, and plumbing symbols is shown in Figure 85.

Save

1.   We have completed Session 7. Pick the exit AutoCAD command from the Files menu, and save your drawing when prompted.

Session 8
Schedules and Two-Way Databases

This session will guide you through inserting Door Tag symbols into the drawing for all the doors, and editing and updating the Door Tags using a two-way database. Then you will create a Door schedule in the drawing.

Begin a New Drawing

1. Begin a new drawing called SESSION8 using the completed SESSION7 drawing from Session 7 to insert Door Tag attribute blocks.

2. Select New from the File pulldown menu to begin a new drawing.

3. Pick Discard Changes when the Drawing Modification dialog box opens.

4. Select the completed drawing from Session 7 in the C:\ASG6TUT\SESSION7 directory as shown in Figure 1 to use as the prototype drawing for Session 8.

5. Enter the drawing path and name C:\ASGTUT\SESSION8\SESSION8, as shown in Figure 1.

Tags

1. Tags are available for Appliances, Cabinets, Doors, Furniture, Lighting and Plumbing Fixtures, Rooms, Structural, Toilets and Windows.

2. These tags are attribute blocks storing information that can be extracted from the drawing database, or manipulated using a two-way database.

3. Tag prompts are inserted using a dialog box, or at the command prompt line.

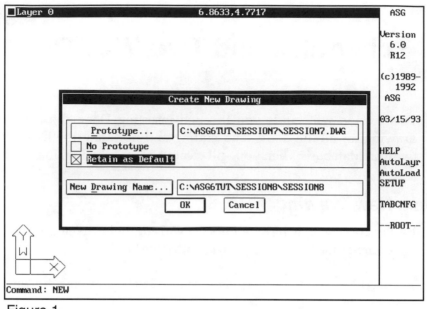

Figure 1.

Settings and Toggles

1. Enable the Attribute dialog box from Status in the Settings pulldown menu.

2. Select the Basic status display to verify the current settings for Attribute dialog box and Attribute prompt as shown in Figure 2.

3. Set Attribute dialog box ON (letter F) and attribute prompt to NUMBERS ONLY (letter G), responding with NO at the command prompt: "Do you want to be prompted for all Yes/No" as shown in Figure 3.

4. The Attribute dialog box ON setting will allow you to insert a Door tag by opening a dialog box.

5. Changing the Attribute dialog box value affects the status of the Attribute prompt.

    Note: You may have to repeat this process several times to set these values. (If the values are already set, you may want to experiment and reset them.)

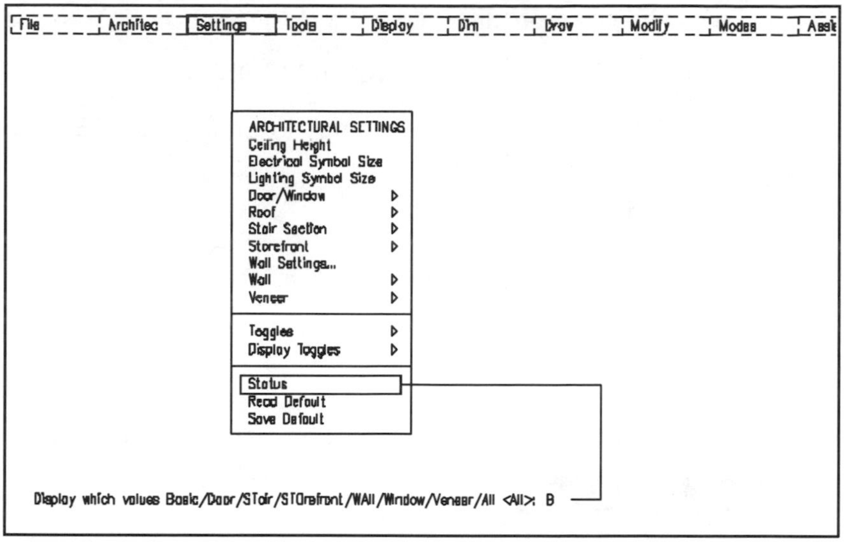

Figure 2.

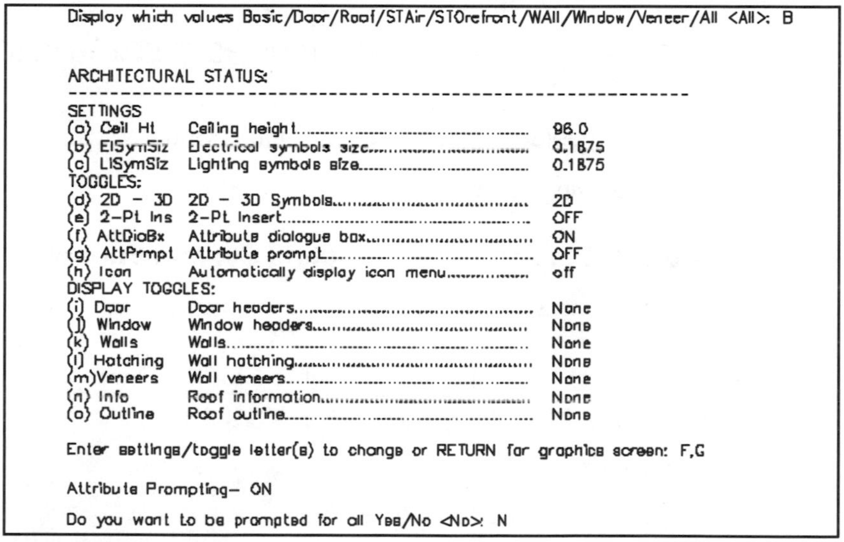

Figure 3.

`Settings>Status>B>F,G`

> Enter settings/toggle letter(s) to change or RETURN for graphics screen: **F,G**

> Attribute dialog box - ON

> Attribute prompting - OFF

Note: Repeat letter G to toggle NUMBERS ONLY.

> Enter settings/toggle letter(s) to change or RETURN for graphics screen: **G**

> Attribute prompting - ON

***TIP – Settings: Save Default/Read Default

1. Save the status of the current settings and toggles.

2. If you end the drawing session before completing this exercise, you can select Read Default from the Set/Tog pulldown menu to retrieve your saved values.

> **Settings>Save Default**

> Enter ARCHITECTURAL (CFG) file to write, or Dir/Help/eXit <Diagram>: **SCHED**

> Replace file C:\ASG6\ARCHITEC\ARCHITECTURAL (CFG) Yes/No : **Y**

> Writing default values... Default values written

> Processing completed.

***TIP – AutoCAD's Attribute Prompting System Variable

1. The Attreq system variable controls attribute prompting.

2. Check to see that the Attreq value is set to 1 for the Door number, width, and height prompts when inserting the Door tag.

> Command: ATTREQ

> New value for ATTREQ : **1**

3. Check to see that the values for the Attdia and Attmode attribute system variables are also set to 1.

Modify Layers

1. Before proceeding with this exercise, prepare the drawing so it appears as in Figure 4.

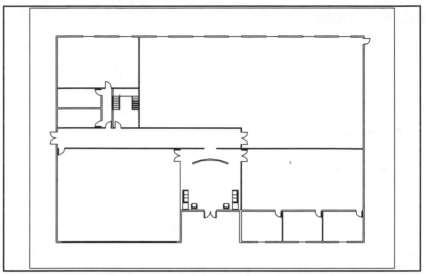

Figure 4.

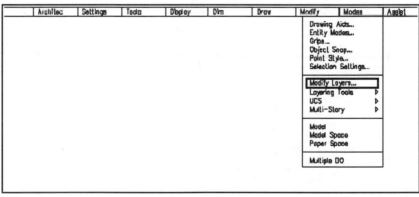

Figure 5.

2. Select Modify Layers from the Modes pulldown menu shown in Figure 5 to open the Modify Layers dialog box and turn off the following layers: ARHEADER, ARWHEADER, ARWALL1LINE, ARWALLCEN, RFBLOCKS, RFFASCIA, RFFRAME, RFINFO, RFPERIM, RFSOFFIT, ROOFF3D.

Modes>Modify Layers...>{Modify Layers}

Default Attribute Values

1. Set up an Attribute prompt with default values for the Door tag.

2. Select Default from Attributes under the Tools menu as shown in Figure 6 to display the Edit Attributes dialog box.

3. Picking DOOR from the side menu causes this Edit Attributes dialog box to appear with a period (.) for each value.

> **Tools>Attributes>Default**

> \>   Enter attribute target name or . for none <Appliance>: **DOOR**
> [**select DOOR from the side menu**]

4. Enter the following values for the Door tag defaults. The full list of door prompts can displayed by picking the Next button at the bottom of the dialog box. (Retain the period to indicate no value):

No	.
Width	6'-0"
Height	6'-8"

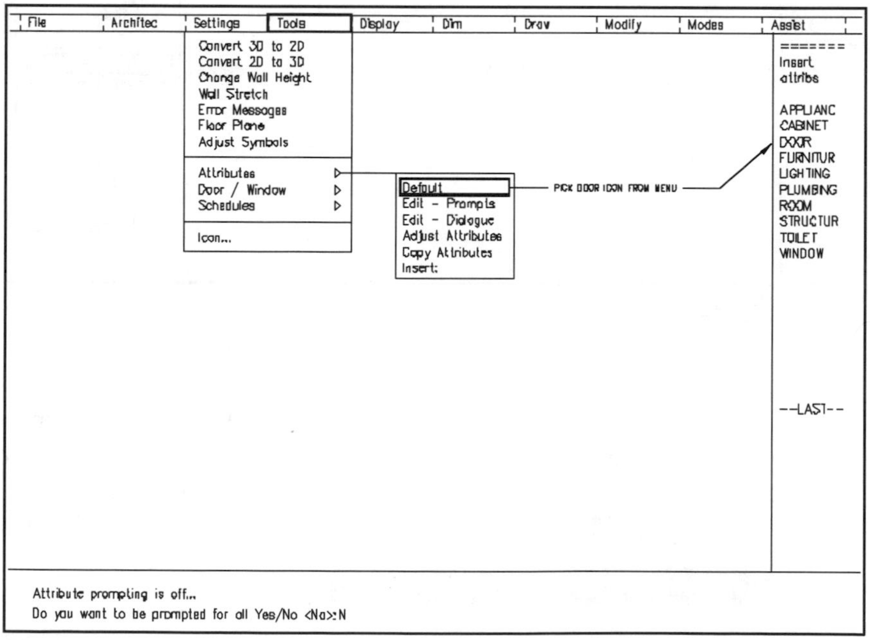

Figure 6.

Room name	.
Door type	.
Hardware group	.
Fire rating	.
Construction	ALUM.
Door glass type	TEMP.
Finish	.
Thick	.
Frame construction	.
Frame finish	.
Head detail number	.
Jamb detail number	.
Sill detail number	.
Remarks	.
Cost	.

5. Pick the OK button to exit the dialog box.

> Checking attribute default values...

> Changing attribute default values...

> Enter attribute target name or . for none <Furniture>: .

Note: Since we will only be working with the Door tag in this exercise, a period will exit the command.

> No changes made to attribute default values...

> Processing completed.

Inserting a Door Tag

1. To place the first tag, select Attributes, then Insert from the Tools pulldown menu.

2. The side screen displays a list of tag types. Respond to the prompt: Make a selection from the screen menu by picking DOOR.

3. The cursor initially appears dragging the Door tag.

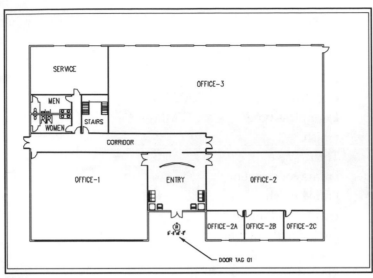

Figure 7.

4. Insert the tag in the drawing by picking a point below the Entry Door as shown in Figure 7.

5. The Edit Attributes dialog box then opens as the Enter Attributes dialog box, with the default attribute values for Width, Height, Construction and Door glass type as shown in Figure 8.

6. Add the Door number and Room name as shown below and in Figure 9.

Tools>Attributes>Insert>Door

>   DO

>   Pick insertion point: [**place Door tag as shown in Figure 7 and enter the following values in dialog box**]

        Door number   01
        Room name   ENTRY

>   Processing Completed.

7. The new values will be added to the default tag as it blinks on the screen.

```
Layer 0                          1.881426E+03,59'-1 1/64"         architec
                                                                  ========
                   ┌──────────── Edit Attributes ──────────────┐  Attrib
                   │                                            │  targets
                   │  Block name: AUD1DAS                       │
                   │                                            │  APPLIANC
                   │  Door number        [.              ]      │  CABINET
                   │                                            │  DOOR
                   │  Width              [6'-0"           ]      │  FURNITUR
                   │                                            │  LIGHTING
                   │  Height             [6'-8"           ]      │  PLUMBING
                   │                                            │  ROOM
                   │  Room name          [.              ]      │  STRUCTUR
                   │                                            │  TOILET
                   │  Door type          [.              ]      │  WINDOW
                   │                                            │
                   │  Hardware group     [.              ]      │
                   │                                            │
                   │  Fire rating        [.              ]      │
                   │                                            │
                   │  Construction       [ALUM.          ]      │
                   │                                            │
                   │  Door glass type    [TEMP.          ]      │  --LAST--
                   │                                            │
                   │  Finish             [.              ]      │
                   │                                            │
                   │   [  OK  ] [Cancel] [Previous] [Next] [Help...]
                   └────────────────────────────────────────────┘
 Enter attribute target name or  .  for none <Appliance>: Door
```

Figure 8.

```
Layer 0                          1.687645E+03,55'-5 43/64"         architec
                                                                  ========
                   ┌──────────── Enter Attributes ─────────────┐  CENter
                   │                                            │  ENDpoint
                   │  Block name: AUD1DAS                       │  INSert
                   │                                            │  INTersec
                   │  Door number        [01             ]      │  MIDpoint
                   │                                            │  NEArest
                   │  Width              [6'-0"           ]      │  NODe
                   │                                            │  PERpend
                   │  Height             [6'-8"           ]      │  QUAdrant
                   │                                            │  TANgent
                   │  Room name          [ENTRY          ]      │
                   │                                            │  .x
                   │  Door type          [.              ]      │  .y
                   │                                            │  .z
                   │  Hardware group     [.              ]      │  .xy
                   │                                            │  .xz
                   │  Fire rating        [.              ]      │  .yz
                   │                                            │
                   │  Construction       [ALUM.          ]      │  --LAST--
                   │                                            │
                   │  Door glass type    [TEMP.          ]      │
                   │                                            │
                   │  Finish             [.              ]      │
                   │                                            │
                   │   [  OK  ] [Cancel] [Previous] [Next] [Help...]
                   └────────────────────────────────────────────┘
 Command:
 Command: DO
 Pick insertion point:
```

Figure 9.

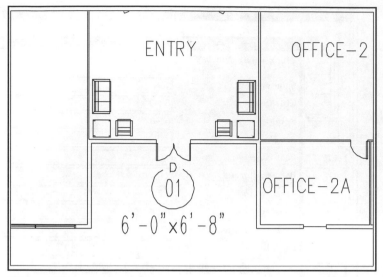

Figure 10.

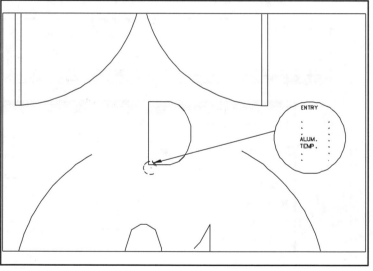

Figure 11.

Door Tag Symbol

1. An enlarged view of the Door tag symbol is shown in Figure 10. Additional attributes are displayed at the base of the letter D in the form of what looks like a dot.

2.   A magnified view of the dot is shown in Figure 11.

****TIP – Door Tag Size

1.   The Door tag size is determined by the Plotted text height.

2.   To change the size, open the Drawing Setup dialog box from the Files pull down menu under Setup.

3.   Select the Detailed... pick button to open the subdialog box and enter a new value in the Height: edit box.

Files>Setup>Setup...>{Drawing Setup}{Detailed...}

Copy Door Tag

1.   After Door tag 01 is inserted, copy this Door tag near doors 6, 7, 8 and 13 as shown in Figure 12.

2.   Select Copy from the Modify pulldown menu shown in Figure 13.

Modify>Copy

>   Command: COPY

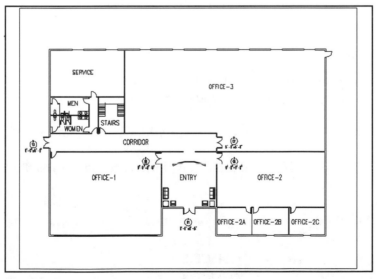

Figure 12.

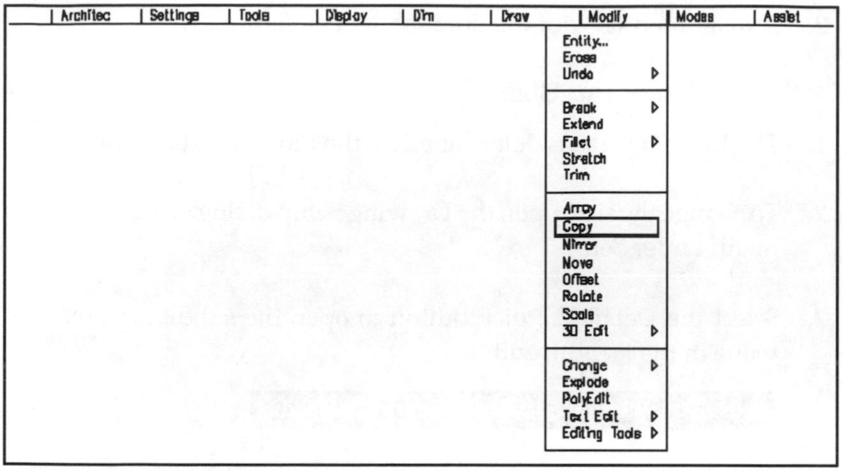

Architec	Settings	Tools	Display	Dim	Draw	Modify	Modes	Assist

Entity...
Erase
Undo   ▷

Break   ▷
Extend
Filet   ▷
Stretch
Trim

Array
Copy
Mirror
Move
Offset
Rotate
Scale
3D Edit   ▷

Change   ▷
Explode
PolyEdit
Text Edit   ▷
Editing Tools   ▷

Figure 13.

> Select objects: 1 found **[select Door tag 01]**

> Select objects: **[Enter]**

> Select objects: ase point or displacement/Multiple: **M**

> Base point: **[select point near middle of Door tag 01]**

> Second point of displacement: **[select points near doors 06, 07, 08 and 13 as shown in Figure 12]**

Edit Door Tags

1. Edit the attributes for Door tags 06, 07, 08 and 13 as listed below. (The placement of these tags in Office-1, 2, 3 and Corridor are shown in Figure 12.)

2. Select Edit-Dialogue from the Tools pulldown menu under Attributes.

3. Each tag must be edited separately. Picking the tag opens the Edit Attribute dialog box.

4. Revise the door number and room name as shown in Figure 12 and listed below:

     Door 06   OFFICE-2
     Door 07   OFFICE-3

Door 08   OFFICE-1

Door 13   CORRIDOR

Tools>Attributes>Edit - Dialogue

5.   After editing the first tag, pick OK to exit the dialog box and repeat the Attribute Editing command by pressing the space bar or entering DO at the command line.

> Command: DO

> Select attribute block: **[select another Door tag]**

> Processing completed.

Note: Default values are not saved with the tag when inserting the tag with prompt and dialog box OFF. When prompted for the door number, width and height, only these values are assigned to the tag. Any additional values must be added to the tag by editing the tag after its insertion. (For example, the Construction and Door Glass type in our default tag must be added to tags that are inserted with dialog box and prompt OFF.)

Change Tag Default Values

1.   Select new default values for the remaining tags by picking Default from the Tools pulldown menu under Attributes.

2.   Pick Door from the side menu. When the dialog box appears, make the following changes:

Tools>Attributes>Default>Door

> Enter attribute target name or . for none <Appliance>: **DOOR [select Door from the side menu and type in the new default values listed below]**

Width   3'-0"

Height   6'-8"

Construction   WOOD

> Checking attribute default values...

> Changing attribute default values...

> Enter attribute target name or . for none <Furniture>: .

> No changes made to attribute default values...

> Processing completed.

Additional Door Tags

1. Add the remaining tags directly from the Enter Attributes dialog box.

2. Pick Insert under Attributes from the Tools pulldown menu, then Door from the side menu for the first Door that contains the new attribute default values.

3. Each time the dialog box appears, replace the period for the Door number and Room name with the appropriate information listed below and as shown in Figure 14.

    Tools>Attributes>Insert>Door

    > DO

    > Pick insertion point: [**pick location of each Door tag**]

    > Processing completed

Door 02	ENTRY
Door 03	OFFICE-2A
Door 04	OFFICE-2B
Door 05	OFFICE-2C
Door 09	SERVICE
Door 10	MEN
Door 11	WOMEN
Door 12	OFFICE-1
Door 14	OFFICE-3
Door 15	STAIRS
Door 16	CORRIDOR

4. Repeat the Insert command by pressing the space bar or entering DO at the command line.

    > Command: DO

    > Pick insertion point:[**place tags in drawing as shown in Figure 14**]

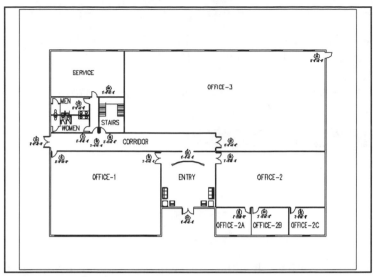

Figure 14.

> Processing completed.

Two-Way Database Overview

The Two-way option of the Schedule command updates attributes in the drawing by using a database-type screen format. Use the Two-way option to edit or extract the attributes of the tag symbols.

1. After inserting all the Door tags, use the Two-way option to make changes to the Door tags with ASG's data manager.

2. The Schedule command will exit the drawing to display a database screen where information can be reviewed or edited.

3. The F4 key provides editing features such as sorting on key fields, replacing text globally, and searching for specific information.

4. External files can also be created for importing schedules into database programs such as dBASE and R:BASE.

5. The F10 key returns you to the drawing where your Door tags are automatically updated.

Two-Way

1. Pick Door under Schedules in the Tools pulldown menu to activate this command as shown in Figure 15.

2. Choose the Two-way option from the side screen to open the Data Manager for reviewing and editing the door schedule.

   Tools>Schedules>Door>Two-way

   > Schedule/Two-way <Schedule>: **TWO-WAY** [**select from side menu**]

   > Select parts for extraction <all>:

   > Select objects: [**Enter**]

   Note: The default value <all> will search the drawing for all Door tags and import them into the internal ASG database.

   > Extracting attributes...

   > 16 records in extract file

3. The data manager will open to a screen confirming the ASG path. If the path to ASG is not correct, re-type a new path; then press Enter and the screen will open to a database as shown in Figure 16.

   > Enter full ASG path   \ASG6\   [**Enter**]

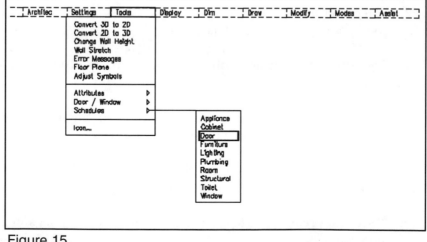

Figure 15.

C:\ASG6\ARCHITEC\S\ERASE.TXT								
Dono	Dowidth	Doheight	Doroom	Dotyp	Dohdw	Dorote	Docons	Dogloss
01	6'-0"	6'-8"	ENTRY	.	.	.	ALUM.	TEMP.
02	6'-0"	6'-8"	ENTRY	.	.	.	WOOD	.
03	3'-0"	6'-8"	OFFICE-2A	.	.	.	WOOD	.
04	3'-0"	6'-8"	OFFICE-2B	.	.	.	WOOD	.
05	3'-0"	6'-8"	OFFICE-2C	.	.	.	WOOD	.
06	6'-0"	6'-8"	OFFICE-2	.	.	.	ALUM.	TEMP.
07	6'-0"	6'-8"	OFFICE-3	.	.	.	ALUM.	TEMP.
08	6'-0"	6'-8"	ENTRY	.	.	.	ALUM.	TEMP.
09	3'-0"	6'-8"	SERVICE	.	.	.	WOOD	.
10	3'-0"	6'-8"	MEN	.	.	.	WOOD	.
11	3'-0"	6'-8"	WOMEN	.	.	.	WOOD	.
12	3'-0"	6'-8"	CORRIDOR	.	.	.	WOOD	.
13	6'-0"	6'-8"	CORRIDOR	.	.	.	ALUM.	TEMP.
14	3'-0"	6'-8"	STAIRS	.	.	.	WOOD	.

‡ 1/16   ↔ 1/19   352K free   Dono

| Next Field: →| or ^→ | Top: ^PgUp | F2: Format | F9: Edit Screen | F10: Save & Exit |
| Prev Field: | or ^← | Top: ^PgDn | F4: Utility | Functions | ESC: Abort |

Figure 16.

Note: If the first column does not list the Door numbers in sequence, you need to sort them. Place the highlighted bar on any Door number in the Dono column. (Use the up and down arrow keys to maneuver vertically, the Tab key to move horizontally toward the right and Shift-Tab keys to move horizontally toward the left).

Press the F4 key to activate the Utility Functions option on the menu bar at the top of screen. Using the right arrow key, move the highlighted bar to Utility, activating this pulldown menu as shown in Figure 17. Press Enter at the Sort by current field/column command.

Data Manager: Utility> Sort by current field/column

4. Using the down arrow key, go to Door 15 (under the Dono column), then use the Tab key to move right to the word WOOD (under the Docons column). Overwrite the value in the Docons field for No. 15 from WOOD to ALUM.

5. Use the up arrow key until you reach Door 02 then Tab over to the Docons column. Replace WOOD with a . (period) as shown in Figure 18.

6. Continue pressing the Tab key (to see the rest of the screen) until the Dormrks (Door remarks) column appears as shown in Figure 19. Replace the . (period) with CO for Cased Opening.

7. Exit the data manager by pressing the F10 key and the drawing will return to the screen, automatically updating the attributes for the Door tags.

```
┌─────────────────────────────────────────────────────────────────────────────┐
│ ┌───────────────────────────────────────────────────────────────────────────┐ │
│ │ File    Edit      Search/replace  │ Utility │  Fields                       │ │
│ ├───────────────────────────────────────────────────────────────────────────┤ │
│ │ Dono    Dowidth   Doheight   Dor┌─────────────────────────────┐ ns  Doglass │ │
│ │                                  │ Sort by current field/column │             │ │
│ │ 01      6'-0"     6'-8"     ENT  ├──────────────────────────── M.   TEMP.     │ │
│ │ 02      6'-0"     6'-8"     ENT  │ Fill field/column with value │ D    .       │ │
│ │ 03      3'-0"     6'-8"     OFF  │ Fill with incremented #      │ D    .       │ │
│ │ 04      3'-0"     6'-8"     OFF  │ XMEM utilized                │ D    .       │ │
│ │ 05      3'-0"     6'-8"     OFF  │ Color screen                 │ D    .       │ │
│ │ 06      6'-0"     6'-8"     OFF  │ Monochrome screen            │ M.   TEMP.   │ │
│ │ 07      6'-0"     6'-8"     OFFICE-3   .      .       .      ALUM.  TEMP.     │ │
│ │ 08      6'-0"     6'-8"     ENTRY      .      .       .      ALUM.  TEMP.     │ │
│ │ 09      3'-0"     6'-8"     SERVICE    .      .       .      WOOD    .         │ │
│ │ 10      3'-0"     6'-8"     MEN        .      .       .      WOOD    .         │ │
│ │ 11      3'-0"     6'-8"     WOMEN      .      .       .      WOOD    .         │ │
│ │ 12      3'-0"     6'-8"     CORRIDOR   .      .       .      WOOD    .         │ │
│ │ 13      6'-0"     6'-8"     CORRIDOR   .      .       .      ALUM.  TEMP.     │ │
│ │ 14      3'-0"     6'-8"     STAIRS     .      .       .      WOOD    .         │ │
│ ├───────────────────────────────────────────────────────────────────────────┤ │
│ │ ↕  1/16   ↔ 1/19    352K free                      Dono                      │ │
│ └───────────────────────────────────────────────────────────────────────────┘ │
│                                                                                 │
│ ┌───────────────────────────────────────────────────────────────────────────┐ │
│ │ Next Field:  →| or ^→     Top: ^PgUp    F2: Format  F9: Edit Screen  F10: Save & Exit │ │
│ │ Prev Field:   | or ^←     Top: ^PgDn    F4: Utility  Functions      ESC: Abort        │ │
│ └───────────────────────────────────────────────────────────────────────────┘ │
└─────────────────────────────────────────────────────────────────────────────┘
```

Figure 17.

```
┌─────────────────────────────────────────────────────────────────────────────┐
│ ┌───────────────────────────────────────────────────────────────────────────┐ │
│ │                    C:\ASG6\ARCHITEC\S\ERASE.TXT                             │ │
│ ├───────────────────────────────────────────────────────────────────────────┤ │
│ │ Dono   Dowidth  Doheight  Doroom     Dotyp  Dohdw  Dorate  Docons  Doglass │ │
│ │ 01     6'-0"    6'-8"    ENTRY       .      .      .       ALUM.   TEMP.    │ │
│ │ 02     6'-0"    6'-8"    ENTRY       .      .      .       ▯       .        │ │
│ │ 03     3'-0"    6'-8"    OFFICE-2A   .      .      .       WOOD    .        │ │
│ │ 04     3'-0"    6'-8"    OFFICE-2B   .      .      .       WOOD    .        │ │
│ │ 05     3'-0"    6'-8"    OFFICE-2C   .      .      .       WOOD    .        │ │
│ │ 06     6'-0"    6'-8"    OFFICE-2    .      .      .       ALUM.   TEMP.    │ │
│ │ 07     6'-0"    6'-8"    OFFICE-3    .      .      .       ALUM.   TEMP.    │ │
│ │ 08     6'-0"    6'-8"    ENTRY       .      .      .       ALUM.   TEMP.    │ │
│ │ 09     3'-0"    6'-8"    SERVICE     .      .      .       WOOD    .        │ │
│ │ 10     3'-0"    6'-8"    MEN         .      .      .       WOOD    .        │ │
│ │ 11     3'-0"    6'-8"    WOMEN       .      .      .       WOOD    .        │ │
│ │ 12     3'-0"    6'-8"    CORRIDOR    .      .      .       WOOD    .        │ │
│ │ 13     6'-0"    6'-8"    CORRIDOR    .      .      .       ALUM.   TEMP.    │ │
│ │ 14     3'-0"    6'-8"    STAIRS      .      .      .       WOOD    .        │ │
│ ├───────────────────────────────────────────────────────────────────────────┤ │
│ │ ↕  2/16   ↔ 8/19    352K free                      Docons                   │ │
│ └───────────────────────────────────────────────────────────────────────────┘ │
│                                                                                 │
│ ┌───────────────────────────────────────────────────────────────────────────┐ │
│ │ EDIT      Enter: Accept changes    CTRL-F: Next word      CTRL-T: Delete word │ │
│ │ FIELD:     Esc: Undo changes       CTRL-A: Previous word  CTRL-U: Delete line │ │
│ └───────────────────────────────────────────────────────────────────────────┘ │
└─────────────────────────────────────────────────────────────────────────────┘
```

Figure 18.

8. To view or edit the changes, select Edit-Dialog from the Tools pulldown menu under Attributes, or pick Edit under Attributes from the Draw pulldown menu, then pick a Door tag.

Tools>Attributes>Edit - Dialogue>{Edit Attribute}

or

Draw>Attributes>Edit...{Edit Attribute}

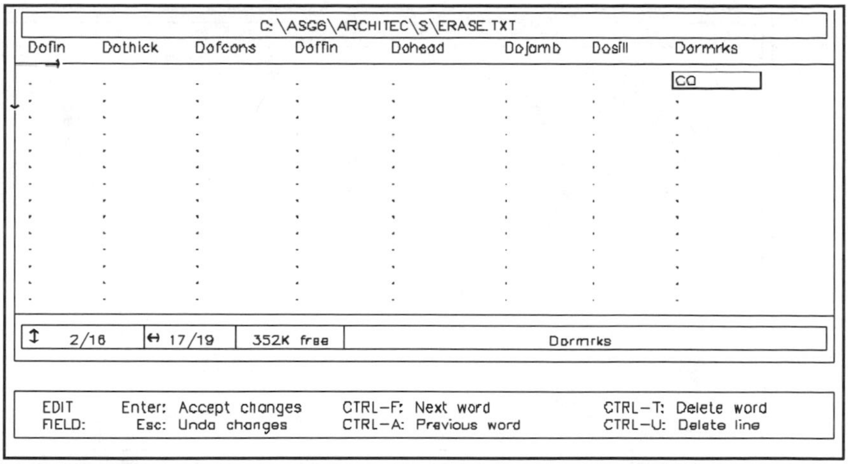

Figure 19.

or

> Command: **Ddatte**

> Select block: **[select attribute block, Edit Attribute dialog box opens, edit values]**

Schedule Overview

1. The purpose of the Schedule option is to build a schedule within the current drawing, or in a separate drawing, of all the values from the tag symbol attributes.

2. Individual schedules for Furniture, Doors, Windows, and so forth, can be created for each tag type.

3. The File pulldown menu options shown in Figure 20 import the attributes into an external database. All the schedule formats are similar, with text and graphic lines inserted on user-defined layers.

4. The attribute values from the tags are imported as text when inserted into the drawing.

File	Edit	Search/replace	Utility	Fields					
					Dotyp	Dohdw	Dorote	Docons	Doglass
Save without quitting					.	.	.	ALUM.	TEMP.
Save as ASCII file						.	.		
Create DBF on Selected Columns					.	.	.	WOOD	.
Create DBF ARRANGING Columns					.	.	.	WOOD	.
Append DBF to this file					.	.	.	WOOD	.
Append ASCII to this file					.	.	.	WOOD	.
ASCII file editor					.	.	.	ALUM.	TEMP.
Copy a file					.	.	.	ALUM.	TEMP.
Save current format					.	.	.	ALUM.	TEMP.
					.	.	.	WOOD	.
10	3'-0"	6'-8"	MEN		.	.	.	WOOD	.
11	3'-0"	6'-8"	WOMEN		.	.	.	WOOD	.
12	3'-0"	6'-8"	CORRIDOR		.	.	.	WOOD	.
13	6'-0"	6'-8"	CORRIDOR		.	.	.	ALUM.	TEMP.
14	3'-0"	6'-8"	STAIRS		.	.	.	WOOD	.

↕ 1/16	↔ 5/19	352K free	Dono

Next Field: →| or ^→	Top: ^PgUp	F2: Format F9: Edit Screen	F10: Save & Exit
Prev Field:	or ^←	Top: ^PgDn	F4: Utility Functions	ESC: Abort

Figure 20.

5. Whenever tag attribute values are edited, the recommended procedure is to erase the old schedule and reinsert a new schedule. (However, AutoCAD's Ddedit command can also be used to edit text in a schedule).

6. The column heading names in the Two-way Data Manager screen are different from the headings in the Schedule. The Schedule headings will appear at the top of each schedule inserted into the drawing.

Schedules

1. Create a Door schedule in your drawing by selecting Schedules, then Door, from the Tools menu. Then select Schedule from the side screen menu.

2. The data manager screen appears in the form of a schedule instead of a database, as shown in Figure 21.

    Note: The same editing options are still available by pressing the F4 key. Although the revisions will appear in the schedule, changes made in this schedule screen will not automatically update attribute tags.

    If the schedule is not sorted, move the highlighted bar to the No column, then press the F4 function key to display the Utility pulldown menu. Highlight Sort by current field/column, then press Enter. Exit the Schedule Data Manager by pressing the F10 function key.

```
┌──────────────────────────────────────────────────────────────────────────┐
│                      C:\ASG6\ARCHITEC\S\ERASE.TXT                          │
│ No    Width    Height    Room Name    Typ   Hdw   FireR   Cons   Glas   Fin│
│ 01    6'-0"    6'-8"    ENTRY       .     .     .     ALUM.   TEMP.    .   │
│ 02    6'-0"    6'-8"    ENTRY       .     .     .     .       .        .   │
│ 03    3'-0"    6'-8"    OFFICE-2A   .     .     .     WOOD    .        .   │
│ 04    3'-0"    6'-8"    OFFICE-2B   .     .     .     WOOD    .        .   │
│ 05    3'-0"    6'-8"    OFFICE-2C   .     .     .     WOOD    .        .   │
│ 06    6'-0"    6'-8"    OFFICE-2    .     .     .     ALUM.   TEMP.    .   │
│ 07    6'-0"    6'-8"    OFFICE-3    .     .     .     ALUM.   TEMP.    .   │
│ 08    6'-0"    6'-8"    ENTRY       .     .     .     ALUM.   TEMP.    .   │
│ 09    3'-0"    6'-8"    SERVICE     .     .     .     WOOD    .        .   │
│ 10    3'-0"    6'-8"    MEN         .     .     .     WOOD    .        .   │
│ 11    3'-0"    6'-8"    WOMEN       .     .     .     WOOD    .        .   │
│ 12    3'-0"    6'-8"    CORRIDOR    .     .     .     WOOD    .        .   │
│ 13    6'-0"    6'-8"    CORRIDOR    .     .     .     ALUM.   TEMP.    .   │
│ 14    3'-0"    6'-8"    STAIRS      .     .     .     WOOD    .        .   │
│                                                                            │
│ ↕  1/16    ↔ 5/19    352K free    │          Door number                   │
│                                                                            │
│                                                                            │
│  Next Field:  → | or ^→     Top: ^PgUp    F2: Format F9: Edit Screen  F10: Save & Exit │
│  Prev Field:    | or ^←     Top: ^PgDn    F4: Utility  Functions      ESC: Abort       │
└──────────────────────────────────────────────────────────────────────────┘
```

Figure 21.

3.   Respond Yes to the "Import schedule into drawing" prompt.

4.   Place the Door schedule in the drawing below the floor plan using a wide 3" polyline for the border.

5.   The entire plan with the schedule is shown in Figure 22.

Tools>Schedules>Door

>   Schedule/Two-way <Schedule>: **SCHEDULE** [**select from side menu**]

>   Quantify records Yes/No <No>: **NO**

>   Select parts for extraction <all>:

>   Select objects: [**Enter**]

>   Extracting attributes...16 records in extract file.

>   Directory for output is C:\ASG6\ARCHITEC\S...

>   Enter ASCII (SCH) file to write, or Dir/Help/eXit <DOTEMP>: [**Enter**]

Note: Press [**Enter**] when the data manager screen appears confirming the ASG path.

> Replace file C:\ASG6\ARCHITEC\S\DOTEMP.SCH Yes/No <No>: **Y**

Note: A similar prompt usually appears each time you enter the Data Manager program to replace or revise a schedule .

> Schedule file C:\ASG6\ARCHITEC\S\DOTEMP.SCH created...

> Import schedule into drawing Yes/No <Yes>: **Y**

> Pick upper left corner of schedule: [**select a point in lower portion of drawing as shown in Figure 22**]

> Enter border line width or Plotted <0">: **3**

> Do you want nodes Yes/No <No>: **N**

Note: A Yes response will insert a node point at the start of each record or line.

> Enter basic layer for text <ARNOTE>: [**Enter**]

> Enter basic layer for line <ARNOTE>: **GUIDELINES**

Note: ASG allows you to create a new layer at this command prompt. GUIDELINES is typed as a new layer.

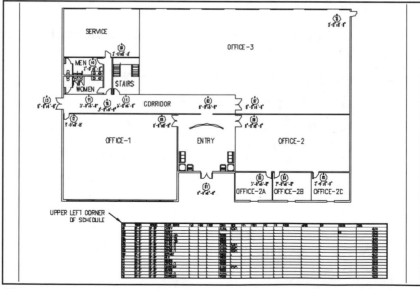

Figure 22.

> Build schedule into blocks Yes/No <Yes>: **NO**

> Processing completed.

6. Open the Modify Layer dialog box if you wish to change the color of the newly created Guidelines layer.

Exit AutoCAD

1. We have now completed Session 8.

2. Select Exit AutoCAD from the File pulldown menu to end Session 8.

In this session, you will use the Multi-story command to turn the one-story office building into a three-story building.

Begin a New Drawing

1. Select Open from the File pulldown menu to display the Open Drawing dialog box.

2. Open the completed SESSION7 drawing from Session 7 as shown in Figure 1.

3. Select Saveas from the File pulldown menu to Display the Save Drawing As dialog box.

4. Save the drawing as SESSION9 in the \ASG6TUT\SESSION9 subdirectory as shown in Figure 2.

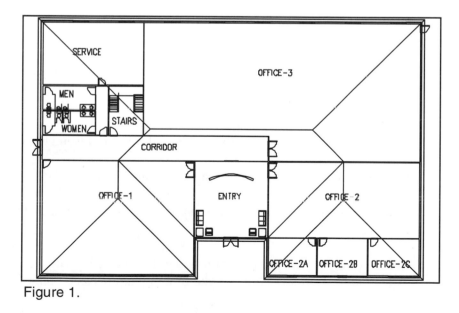

Figure 1.

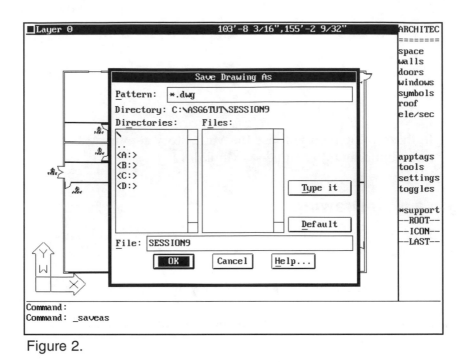

Figure 2.

5. The command line will display the prompt: Current drawing name set to C:\ASG6TUT\SESSION9\SESSION9.

Overview of Multi-Story

1. Erase some roof and door layers in the drawing created in Session 8.

2. Purge the erased and unused layers.

3. Set up two vertical viewports to work in both Plan and Isometric view.

4. Build, set and save level and elevation defaults.

5. Copy the existing single node layer names to a two node multi-story layering name convention.

6. Create a three-story building with a new two node layering convention for Walls, Doors, Windows, Furniture, Plumbing fixtures, and Stairs.

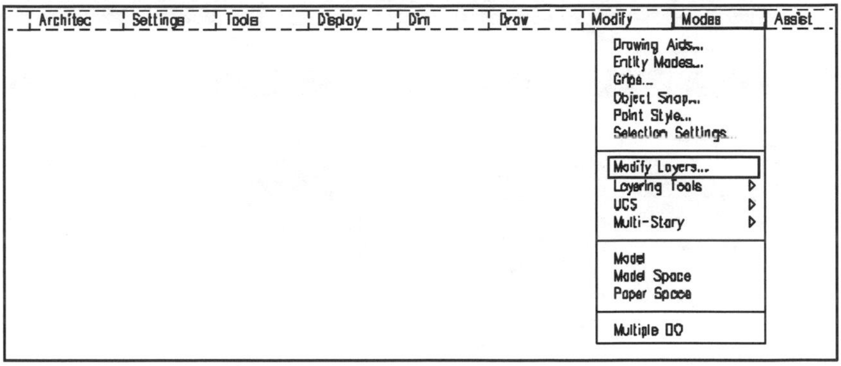

Figure 3.

7. Copy all entities from the first level to the second level maintaining unique layer names for each level.

8. Remove doors from second story walls, then copy the second level to the third level.

9. Move the roof from the first level to the third level.

Modify Layers

1. Select Modify Layers from the Modes pull-down menu as shown in Figure 3 to open the Layer Control dialog box.

2. Choose the Select All pick box to highlight all the layers, then select the Off pick box to turn all the highlighted layers off similar to Figure 4.

3. With all layers off, clear the dialog box by selecting Clear All to unhighlight all the layers similar to Figure 5.

4. Peruse the layering list, and select layers 0, ARDOORSPEC, ARWALL1LINE, REINFO AND RFPERIM, then pick ON as shown in Figure 6 to make these layers visible in the drawing. (Thaw layer ARWALL1LINE if it is still frozen.)

5. Pick OK to exit the dialog box.

6. The drawing should appear similar to Figure 7.

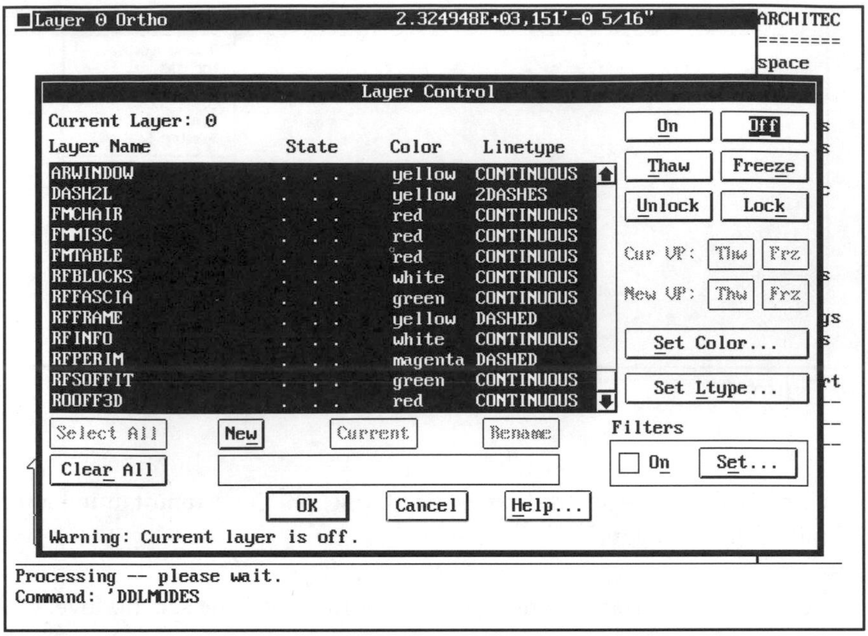

Figure 4.

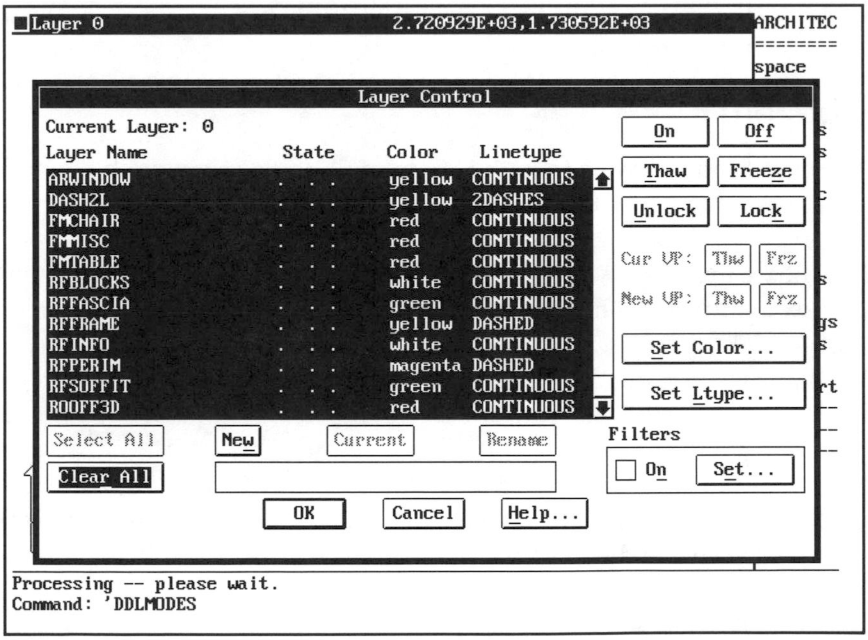

Figure 5.

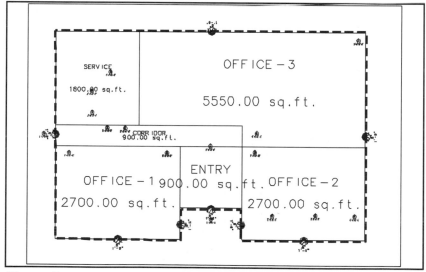

Figure 6.

Figure 7.

Erase and Purge Layers

1. Select Erase from the Modify pull-down menu and remove all the visible layers from the drawing.

    Modify>Erase

    > Erase

    > Select object: **C**

    > First corner: **[pick point at lower left corner of drawing]**
    > Other corner: **[pick point at upper right corner of drawing]**

    > Select object: **[Enter]**

2. Open the Layer Control dialog box to turn all remaining layers on.

    Modes>Modify Layers...>{Layer Control}

3. Choose the Select All pick box to highlight all the layers, then pick On.

4. Pick OK to exit the dialog box.

5. The drawing should appear as shown in Figure 8.

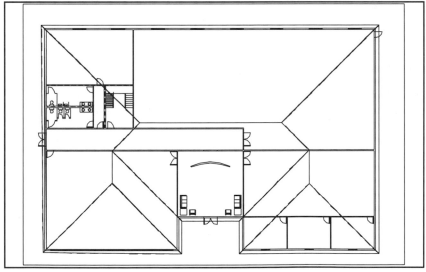

Figure 8.

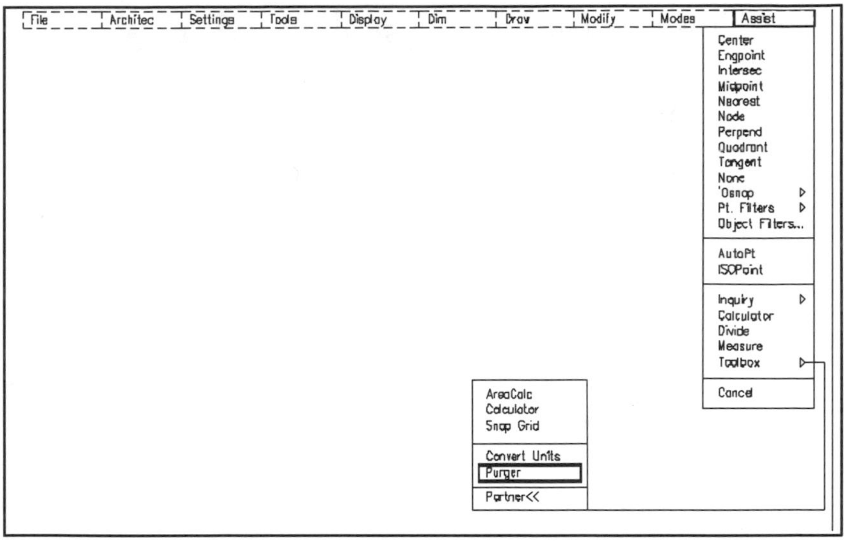

Figure 9.

6.   Purge these unused erased layers using the Purger command from the Assist pull-down menu under Toolbox as shown in Figure 9.

7.   Purger exits the current drawing editor, removes all unused layers, then reloads the same drawing.

Assist>Toolbox>Purger

> PURGER

> PURGE this drawing Yes/No <No:> **Y**

> Enter backup drawing name or . for none <.>: [**enter**]

Note: The command purges all the unused entities including layers, blocks, linetypes. It can also create a backup copy of the current drawing.

8.   The remaining layers should have the status shown below. Use the Layering Control dialog box to freeze the roof layers to get them out of the way before creating multiple floors.

Modes>Modify Layers>{Layering Control}

Layer Name	State
0	On
ARDOOR	On
ARGLAZING	On
ARHEADER	On
ARPARTITON	On
ARSTAIR3D	On
ARWALL	On
ARWALLCEN	On
ARWHEADER	On
ARWINDOW	On
FMCHAIR	On
FMMISC	On
FMTABLE	On
MPFIX2D	On
MPFIXTURE	On
RFFASCIA	Frozen
RFFRAME	Frozen
RFSOFFIT	Frozen
ROOFF3D	Frozen

Creating Vports

1. The display screen can be split into two vertical views with the AutoCAD Vports command or the Tiled Vports... option under Layout from the Display pul-ldown menu.

2. Enter the AutoCAD Vports command to create two vertical viewports on the display screen to help orient you while working on different levels.

   > Command: **VPORTS**

   > Save/Restore/Delete/Join/SIngle/?/2/<3>/4: **2**

   > Horizontal/<Vertical>: **Vertical**

   > Regenerating drawing

3. Activate the right viewport by picking it with your pointing device.

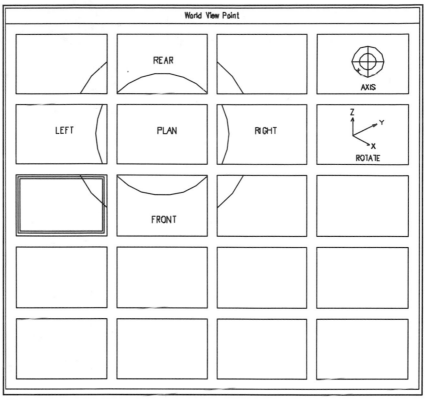

Figure 10.

4. Select the Vpoint icon menu, then pick the bottom left icon (displaying the extra frames) shown in Figure 10 to create an isometric view as shown in Figure 11.

Display>Viewpoint>**WorldVpt...** {World View Point}

Note: Entering the AutoCAD Vpoint command with the coordinates -1,-1,1 provides the same view as the bottom left icon .

Build Levels

1. Specify the first floor level of the multi-story building.

2. Create the level names and elevations using the Build Levels command under the Multi-Story pull-down menu as shown in Figure 12.

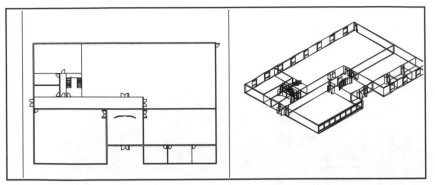

Figure 11.

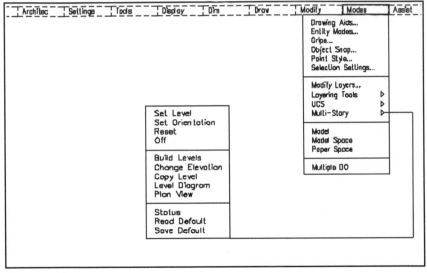

Figure 12.

3. Define the following major level names and elevations:

Floor level layer name	Elevation
FL01	0
FL02	10'
FL03	20'

Modes>Multi-Story>Build Levels

> DO

> Enter lowest level or ? <FL00>: **FL01**

> Enter absolute elevation of level FL01 or ? <0">: **0**

> Add another level Yes/No <Yes>: **Y**

> Last level set - FL01

> Enter next level or ?: **FL02**

> Enter absolute elevation of level FL02 or ? <0>: **10'**

> Add another level Yes/No <Yes>: **Y**

> Last level set - FL02

> Enter next level or ?: **FL03**

> Enter absolute elevation of level FL03 or ?/Relative <20'-0">: [**Enter**]

> Add another level Yes/No <Yes>: **N**

> Processing completed.

Set the Level

1. Some commands require that Multi-Story be ON. The Set Level command shown in Figure 12 will turn Multi-Story ON.

2. Set the current level to FL01 by selecting Set Level under Multi-Story in the Modes pull-down menu.

Modes>Multi-story>Set Level

> Multi-Story- ON

> Enter level or?: **FL01**

> Current level is FL01, Elevation is 0", Orientation is 0.0

Status

1. Select Status from the Multi-Story menu shown in Figure 12 to confirm and view the current level settings.

Modes>Multi-story>Status

2. The Status command identifies the name, elevation, orientation and next level as listed below:

NAME	ELEVATION	ORIENTATION	NEXT LEVEL
FL01	0"	0.0	10'-0" *CURRENT
FL02	10'-0"	0.0	10'-0"
FL03	20'-0"	0.0	

Save the Levels

1. Select Save Default under Multi-Story to save the current setup for future projects that are similar or in case you make changes and need to restore the original definitions.

2. Save the levels file to the name 3STORY.

> **Modes>Multi-story>Save Default**

> > Enter LEVELS (LVL) file to write, or Dir/Help/eXit <CORE>: **3STORY**

> > Writing default values...Default values written

> > Current level is FL01, Elevation is 0", Orientation is 0.0

> > Processing completed.

Copy Level

1. The Copy Level option of the Multi-story menu is a tool to change a single story structure to a multi-story building.

2. Begin creating the first of three levels by changing all layers except the roof layers to Level FL01. The roof layers should still be frozen. They will later be thawed and moved to third level.

3. Use the Copy Level command under Multi-Story shown in Figure 12 to create a new set of layers with a prefix, or Major name, called Level FL01 and add the set to the current layers.

4. The Copy Level command will copy all entities from the original layer name to a layer name with nodes. For example, if a line is drawn on layer ARWALL, a

duplicate line will also be created on FL01-ARWALL. (It does not rename the layer.) The original layers can be erased, then purged.

Modes>Multi-story>Copy Level

> DO

> Select layer(s) to COPY FROM **<enter name>:**

> Select objects: **W [click on the left viewport to activate it, if necessary]**

> First corner: Other corner: 563 found **[window the entire plan displayed in the left viewport]**

Note: The number of entities in your drawing or the number of layers copied may vary.

> Select objects: **[Enter]**

> COPY selected entities only? Yes/No: **N**

> 10 layer(s) selected

> Select objects: [**Enter**]

> Processing — please wait

> Select layer to COPY TO **<Enter name>:**

> Select objects:

> Enter MAJOR name or . for none <FL01>:**FL01**

> Enter MINOR-1 name or . for none <.>: [**Enter**]

> COPY 177 entities FROM ARWALL TO FL01-ARWALL.

> COPY 5 entities FROM ARWALLCEN TO FL01-ARWALLCEN.

> COPY 11 entities FROM ARPARTITION TO FL01-ARPARTITION.

Note: A number of these statements or similar ones will appear as the layers are processed. The number of entities may vary from those shown here.

> Current level is FL01, Elevation is 0", Orientation is 0.0.

5. The new list of layers, except for the roof layers, now consists of single node and two nodes names. For example, the wall layer is called FL01-ARWALL combining the Major name FL01 and the Basic (single node) name ARWALL. The current layer list reads as follows:

Note: Your list may differ slightly, especially if you have created new layers or inserted different symbols.

    0
    ARDOOR
    ARGLAZING
    ARHEADER
    ARPARTITON
    ARSTAIR3D
    ARWALL
    ARWALLCEN
    ARWHEADER
    ARWINDOW
    FL01-ARDOOR
    FL01-ARGLAZING
    FL01-ARHEADER
    FL01-ARPARTITON
    FL01-ARSTAIR3D
    FL01-ARWALL
    FL01-ARWALLCEN
    FL01-ARWHEADER
    FL01-FMCHAIR
    FL01-FMMISC
    FL01-FMTABLE
    FL01-MPFIX2D
    FL01-MPFIXTURE
    FMCHAIR
    FMMISC
    FMTABLE
    MPFIX2D
    MPFIXTURE
    RFFASCIA
    RFFRAME

RFSOFFIT

ROOFF3D

Note: Enter the AutoCAD List command with the C or crossing selection set option to list the wall lines; notice that two lines are selected: ARWALL and FL01-ARWALL.

Layer Freeze

1. Select the Layer Freeze command under Layering Tools in the Modes pull-down menu. The Layering Tools menu is shown in Figure 13.

2. Freeze all the FL01 layers and process them using FL01 as the Major name.

Modes>Layering Tools>Layer Freeze [freeze all FL01 layers]

> DO

> Select layer(s) to FREEZE **<enter name>:**

> Select objects: **[Enter]**

> Enter MAJOR name or . for none <FL01>: **FL01**

> Enter MINOR-1 name or . for none <.>: [**Enter**]

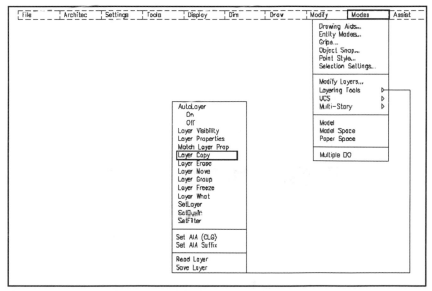

Figure 13.

> Enter BASIC name or . for none <ALL>: [**Enter**]

· > FL01-* entered. Accept Yes/No Yes: **Y**

> 14 layer(s) selected.

Note: The number of layers may differ slightly, especially if you have created new layers or inserted different symbols.

> Current level is FL01, Elevation is 0", Orientation is 0.0

3. With all the FL01 layers frozen, erase all line entities from the original floor plan by selecting the AutoCAD Erase command under the Modify pull-down menu and using the window selection set.

`Modify>Erase`

> Erase

> Select objects: **W**

> First corner: Other corner: **[place window around all entities in floor plan]**

> Select objects: **[Enter]**

Layer Visibility

1. Thaw all the FL01 layers to restore the line entities for first floor plan to the screen.

2. Thawing layers requires a regeneration as indicated by the prompt: Regeneration required to view results, proceed?

3. Select the Layer Visibility command from the Layering Tools menu, accepting the default FL01 as the Major name.

`Modes>Layering Tools>Layer Visibility`

> LYRVIS

> Freeze/Thaw/ON/OFF/Lock/Unlock **<Freeze>:T**

> Enter MAJOR name or . for none <FL01>: **FL01**

> Enter MINOR-1 name or . for none <.>: [**Enter**]

> Enter BASIC name or . for none <ALL>: [**Enter**]

> FL01-* entered. Accept Yes/No Yes: **Y**

> 14 layer(s) selected.

> Regen required to view results, proceed? Yes/No Yes: **Y**

> Process another layer Yes/No <No>: **N**

> Current level is FL01, Elevation is 0", Orientation is 0.0

Purge Layers

1. Purge the original single node layers that were previously erased.

2. Pick Purger from Toolbox under the Assist pull-down menu to remove all the unused layers from the drawing.

    Assist>Toolbox>Purger

    > PURGER

    > PURGE this drawing Yes/No <No:> **Y**

    > Enter backup drawing name or . for none <.>: [**Enter**]

3. Using the Modify Layers command from the Modes pull-down menu, peruse the remaining layers.

4. Some single node layers nested within the Storefront window block will still exist. However, the block reference layer is assigned to FL01-ARWALL.

    Modes>Modify Layers...{Layer Control}

Copy Layers – FL01 to FL02

1. Copy all FL01 layers, except the furniture layers, from the first floor to the second floor FL02 layers.

2. The first two characters of each layer name are distinct and represent their discipline. The Wall, Mechanical/Plumbing and Furniture layers, for example, are assigned the letter group: AR, MP and FM.

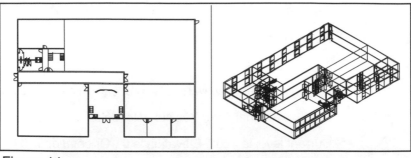

Figure 14.

3. Apply each of the discipline letter groups with the asterisk (*) wildcard to copy specific layers from FL01 to FL02.

4. The new layers will automatically be copied to the 10′ elevation set earlier by the Set Levels command as shown in Figure 14.

5. Select the Copy Level command from Multi-Story to create a level with the Major name FL02.

Modes>Multi-Story>Copy Level

> DO

> Select layer(s) to COPY FROM   **name:**

> Select objects: **[Enter]**

> Enter MAJOR name or . for none <FL01>: **FL01**

> Enter MINOR-1 name or . for none <.>: **[Enter]**

> Enter BASIC name or . for none <.>: **AR***

> FL01-AR* entered. Accept Yes/No <Yes>: **Y**

> Enter BASIC name or . for none <.>: **MP***

> FL01-MP* entered. Accept Yes/No Yes: **Y**

> Enter BASIC name or . for none <.>: **[Enter]**

> 10 layer(s) selected

> Select layer to COPY TO **<Enter name>:**

> Select object: **[Enter]**

> Enter MAJOR name or . or none <FL01>: **FL02**

Note: Select FL02 from side screen or enter FL02 at the command line.

> Enter MINOR-1 name or . for none .: **[Enter]**

> COPY 177 entities FROM FL01-ARWALL TO FL02-ARWALL

> COPY 5 entities FROM FL01-ARWALLCEN TO FL02-ARWALLCEN

> COPY 16 entities FROM FL01-ARDOOR TO FL02-ARDOOR

Note: A number of these statements or similar ones will appear as he layers are processed. The number of entities may vary from those shown here.

> Current level is FL01, Elevation is 0", Orientation is 0.0.

6. An enlarged isometric view of FL01 and FL02 is shown in Figure 15.

Set Level FL02

1. Before creating level FL03, the three exterior doors on Level FL02 shown in Figure 16 must be removed.

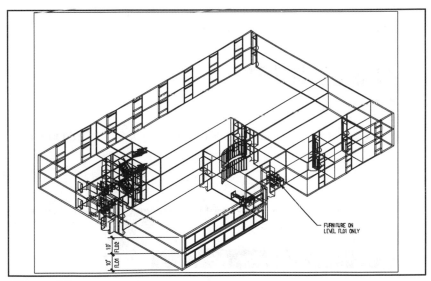

Figure 15.

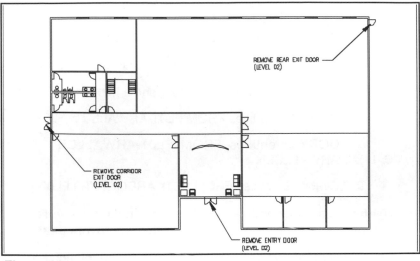

Figure 16.

2. Set the current working level to FL02 by selecting Set Level from Multi-Story under the Modes pull-down menu.

3. Although both levels are visible, the UCS (User Coordinate System) will be set to level FL02.

4. The Set Level command changes entities on the current level only and ignores all other levels. The purpose is to edit a specific floor level while all other levels are visible.

Modes>Multi-Story>Set Level

> Enter level or ? <FL01>: **FL02**

> Current level is FL02, Elevation is 10'-0", Orientation is 0.0

AutoLoad

1. If the Architectural module is not loaded, select AutoLoad from the side screen or File pull-down menu.

AutoLoad>Architec [from side screen menu]

or

> Select application name or . for none: C:\ASG6\ARCHITEC\
ARCHITEC

2. We will apply the Remove command in the Door/Window submenu to edit the doors on Level FL02.

Remove Doors

1. ASG's Remove Door command reconstructs the wall, automatically deleting the door and door header.

2. Zoom into the back corner of the building as shown in Figure 17 and remove the rear exit door.

3. Select the Remove command from the Door/Window submenu under the Tools pull-down menu. Pick the door to be removed. Figure 17 shows the door at level FL02 before removal, and Figure 18 after removal.

Tools>Door/Window>Remove

> DO

> Select windows and doors to remove: [**select rear exit door at upper left corner of plan as shown in Figure 17**]

> Select objects: 1 found

> Select objects: [**Enter**]

> Processing — please wait

> Current level is FL02, Elevation is 10'-0", Orientation is 0.0

4. Repeat the Remove command by highlighting Tools, then double clicking the status bar or the space bar. Remove the double swing entry door and exit door at the corridor on level FL02.

5. The entry door before and after removal is shown in Figures 19 and 20.

Tools>Door/Window>Remove

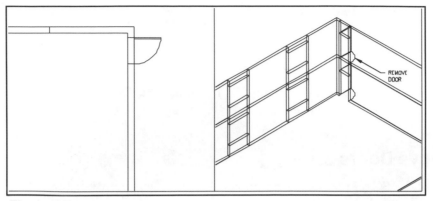

Figure 17.

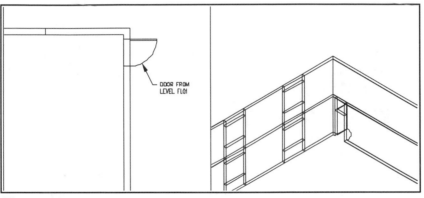

Figure 18.

Copy Level

1. To create level FL03 select the Copy Level command again from Multi-Story.

2. Level FL02 is copied to FL03 as shown in Figure 21 and Figure 22. (Figure 22 is an enlarged isometric view of Levels FL01, FL02 and FL03.)

    Modes>Multi-Story>Copy Level

    >   DO

    >   Select layer(s) to COPY FROM **<Enter name>:**

    >   Select objects: **[Enter]**

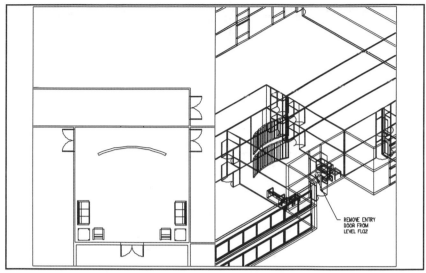

Figure 19.

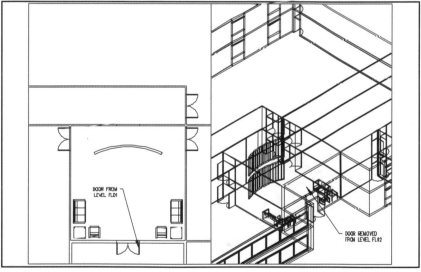

Figure 20.

> Enter MAJOR name or . for none <FL01>: **FL02**

> Enter MINOR-1 name or . for none <.>: **[Enter]**

> Enter BASIC name or . for none <.>: **[Enter]**

> FL02-AR* entered. Accept Yes/No <Yes>: **Y**

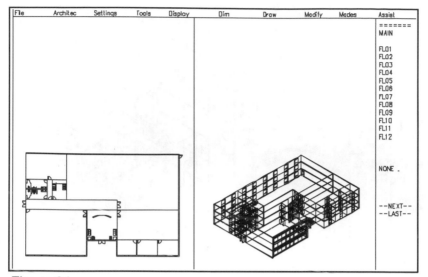

Figure 21.

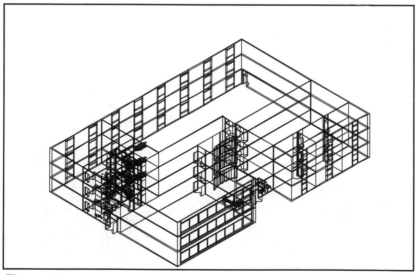

Figure 22.

> 10 layer(s) selected

> Select layer to COPY TO **<Enter name>:**

> Select object: **[Enter]**

> Enter MAJOR name or . or none <FL01>: **FL03**

Note: Select FL03 from side screen or enter FL03 at the command line.

> Enter MINOR-1 name or . for none <.>: **[Enter]**

> COPY 165 entities FROM FL02-ARWALL TO FL03-ARWALL

> COPY 5 entities FROM FL02-ARWALLCEN TO FL03-ARWALLCEN

> COPY 13 entities FROM FL02-ARDOOR TO FL03-ARDOOR.

Note: A number of these statements or similar ones will appear as the layers are processed. The number of entities may vary from those shown here.

> Current level is FL02, Elevation is 10'-0", Orientation is 0.0.

Move Layers

1. Relocate the building roof from the first level to the top of the third level.

2. Freeze all layers beginning with the letters FL0 and thaw the ROOFF3D, RFFRAME, RFFASCIA and RFSOFFIT layers, using the asterisk (*) as a wildcard.

3. The MAJOR name to freeze level layers is FL0* and the BASIC name to thaw roof layers is R*.

4. Select Layer Visibility from Layering Tools under the Modes pull-down menu.

Modes>Layering Tools>Layer Visibility

> LYRVIS

> Freeze/Thaw/ON/OFF/Lock/Unlock <Freeze>: **F**

> Select objects: **[Enter]**

> Enter MAJOR name or . for none <FL01>: **FL0***

> Enter MINOR-1 name or . for none <.>: **[Enter]**

> Enter BASIC name or . for none <ALL>: **[Enter]**

> FL01*-* entered. Accept Yes/No <Yes>: **Y**

> 34 layer(s) selected

> Process another layer: Yes/No <No>: **Y**

> Freeze/Thaw/ON/OFF/Lock/Unlock <Freeze>: **T**

> Enter MAJOR name or . for none <FL01>: **.**

Note: The command recognizes that no Minor-1 name exists from the previous prompt response.

> Enter BASIC name or . for none <ALL>: **R***

> R* entered. Accept Yes/No <Yes>: **Y**

> 5 layer(s) selected

> Regen required to view results, proceed? Yes/No <Yes>: **Y**

> Process another layer Yes/No <No>: **N**

> Current level is FL02, Elevation is 10'-0", Orientation is 0.0

5. The roof layers will appear in the active viewport only. To display the roof layers in the both viewports, as shown in Figure 23, enter AutoCAD's Regenall command at the command line.

> Command: **Regenall**

> Regenerating drawing

6. Move the roof layers from level FL01 to the top of level FL03.

Modes>Layering Tools>Multi-Story>Layer Move

> DO

> Select layer(s) to MOVE FROM <Enter Name>:

> Select objects: **[Enter]**

> Enter MAJOR name or . for none <FL01>: **.**

> Enter BASIC name or . for none <.>: **R***

> R* entered. Accept Yes/No <Yes>: **Y**

> 38 layer(s) selected

> Regen required to view results, proceed? Yes/No <Yes>: **Y**

> Process another layer Yes/No <No>: **N**

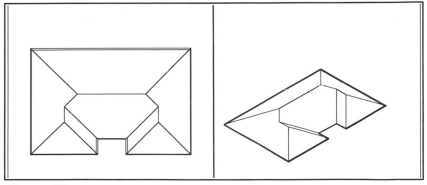

Figure 23.

> Current level is FL02, Elevation is 10'-0", Orientation is 0.0Enter BASIC name or . for none <.>: **[Enter]**

> 5 layer(s) selected.

> Select layer to MOVE TO <enter name>:

> Select object: **[Enter]**

> Enter MAJOR name or . or none <FL01>: **FL03**

Note: Select FL03 from side screen or enter FL03 at the command line.

> Enter MINOR-1 name or . for none <.>: **[Enter]**

> Retain basic layer names, or MOVE to a single layer?

> Retain/Single <Retain>: **R**

> MOVE 8 entities FROM RFFRAME TO FL03-RFFRAME.

> MOVE 34 entities FROM ROOFF3D TO FLO3-RFBLOCKS

> MOVE 8 entities FROM RFSOFFIT TO FL03-RFSOFFIT

> MOVE 8 entities FROM RFFASCIA TO FL03-RFFASCIA

Note: The Basic roof layers are renamed to Level FL03 as each is moved.

> Multi-Story is on, entities changed to proper elevation...

> Current level is FL02, Elevation is 10'-0", Orientation is 0..

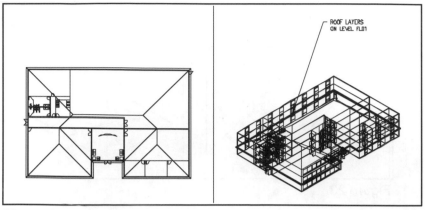

ROOF LAYERS
ON LEVEL FL01

Figure 24.

Note: The Current level is FL02, based on the last level set for removing the doors, and does not effect this process.

7.   Thaw all the layers using Layer Visibility from the Layering Tools submenu.

> Modes>Layering Tools>Layer Visibility

   >   LYRVIS

   >   Freeze/Thaw/ON/OFF/Lock/Unlock <Freeze>: **T**

   >   Enter MAJOR name or . for none <FL01>: *****

   >   Enter MINOR-1 name or . for none <.>: **[Enter]**

   >   Enter BASIC name or . for none <ALL>: **[Enter]**

   >   *-* entered. Accept Yes/No <Yes>: **Y**

   >

8.   Figure 24 shows the roof layers in relation to level FL01.

9.   Enter the AutoCAD Regenall command again to restore the layers in the other viewport.

   >   Command: **Regenall**

   >   Regenerating drawing

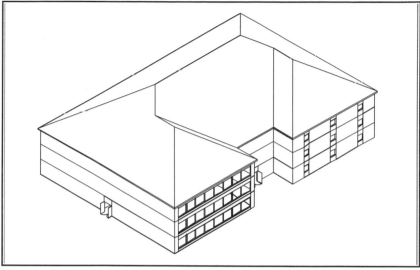

Figure 25.

10.   The completed three-story multi-story building is shown in Figure 25 (with the interior building walls hidden).

Level Diagram

1.   Activate the right viewport by picking it with your pointing device.

2.   Pick Zoom Window under the Display pull-down menu and zoom into right front corner of the building as shown in Figure 26.

3.   Add a diagram identifying floor level heights to the isometric view.

4.   Select Level Diagram from Multi-story and use the front right side of the building at level 0, as the insertion point as shown in Figure 26.

Modes>Multi-story>Level Diagram

>   DO

>   Place on an elevation plane Yes/No <Yes>: **Y**

>   Enter horizontal offset of dimension <4'-0">: **4'**

>   Add elevation notation Yes/No <Yes>: **Y**

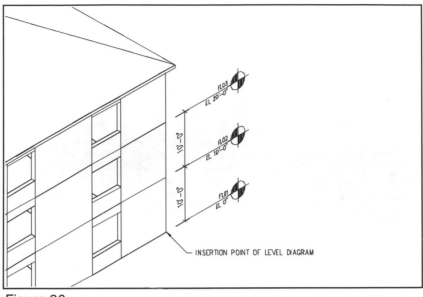

INSERTION POINT OF LEVEL DIAGRAM

Figure 26.

> Building block...

> Pick insertion point: **ENDP** of **[front right side of building as shown in Figure 26]**

> Elevation diagram block is named LEVEL-1...

> Current level is FL02, Elevation is 10'-0", Orientation is 0.0

Restore Viewport

1. Restore the plan drawing (in the left viewport) to a single plan viewport.

2. Pick the left viewport with your pointing device to make it active.

3. Select Tiled Vports under Layout from the Display pull-down menu to open the Tiled Vports Layout icon menu as shown in Figure 27.

4. Pick the icon at the upper left corner.

> **Display>Layout>Tiled Vports...{Tiled Vports Layout}[pick icon displaying a single viewport]**

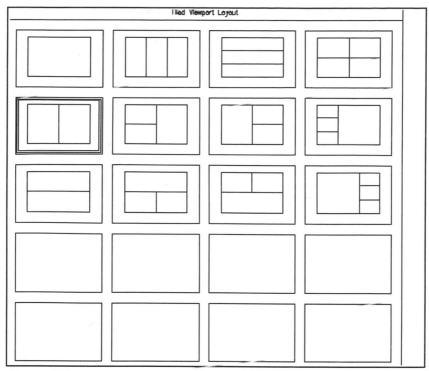

Figure 27.

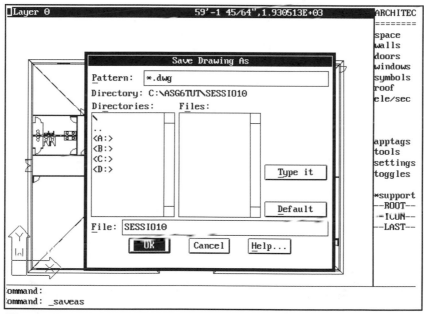

Figure 28.

Save As

1. This completes session 9.

2. Select Save from the File pulldown to save the current drawing. (Save executes the Qsave command and saves your drawing without being prompted for the current drawing name.)

3. Select Save As... to save the current drawing as SESSIO10 in the C:\ASG6TUT\ SESSIO10 directory as shown in Figure 28.

4. Save As... opens the Save Drawing As... dialog box to prompt for a directory path and new drawing name, making the new drawing current.

Session 10
Eye View

Overview

In this session we will use ASG's Eye commands to create quick perspective views of the multi-story building, as well as a Walk-Thru and Walk-Around.

First, you'll view the Entry Lobby in perspective, and then walk through the interior space with the Eye Walk command, which creates script files to walk from one point to another. You'll use the Eye Round command to make slide files, and then invoke AutoCAD's Script command to walk around the building, viewing exterior perspectives.

1. If you have remained in the drawing session, SESSIO10 should be the current drawing. If you have stopped after Session 9, open the SESSIO10 drawing saved to the C:\ASG6TUT\SESSIO10 directory.

2. Pick Open from the File pull-down menu to display the Drawing Modification dialog box and pick Discard Changes.

3. In the Open Drawing dialog box, select the SESSIO10 drawing as shown in Figure 1.

   File>Open{Drawing Modification dialog box}{Open Drawing dialog box}

   Note: Type in FL01 if the command line asks for Floor level.

4. Select Erase from the Modify pull-down menu and remove the Level Diagram tag created in Session 9 from the front right corner of the building.

   Modify>Erase

   > Erase

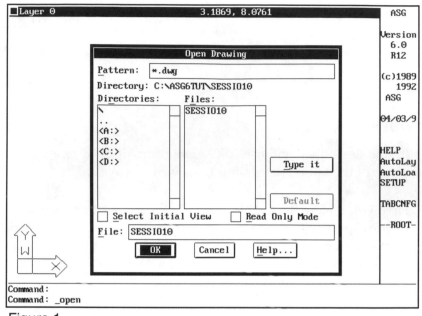

Figure 1.

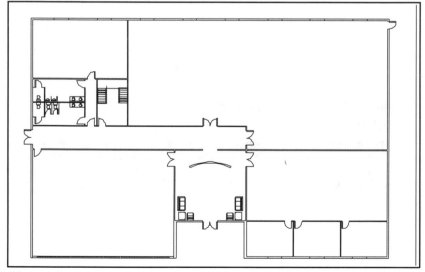

Figure 2.

>   Select objects: 1 found **[pick Level Diagram tag]**

>   Select objects: **[Enter]**

5. If your plan drawing looks like Figure 2, use the Modify Layers command on the Modes menu to turn on the roof layers.

Eye View Command Overview

1. Create a perspective view of the interior entry area looking from the custom curved wall to the front entry door.

2. The Eye command requires these for defining perspective views:

   Camera: This is the point or location where you are standing in the drawing.

   Target: You are looking through the camera toward this point.

   Lens: The lens controls the angle of vision. A small number widens the angle of vision and a large number narrows the angle of vision.

3. Verify that your level is set to FL01 before proceeding with the perspective view. Select Multi-Story from the Modes pull-down menu and pick Set Level.

   `Modes>Multi-Story>Set Level`

   > DO

   > Enter level or ? <FL01>: **FL01**

   > Current level is FL01, Elevation is 0", Orientation is 0.0

4. To simplify this exercise for the interior perspective of the first level, freeze layers on all floors except floor level one (FL01*).

5. Select Layer Visibility from the Modes pull-down menu under Layering Tools to process multiple Levels (FL02 and FL03).

   `Modes>Layering Tools>Layer Visibility`

   > LYRVIS

   > Freeze/Thaw/ON/OFF/Unlock: <Freeze>: **F**

   > Select layer(s) to FREEZE <Enter name>:

   > Select objects: **[Enter]**

   > Enter MAJOR name or . for none <FL01>: **FL02***

> Enter MINOR-1 name or . for none .: **[Enter]**

> Enter BASIC name or . for none All: **[Enter]**

> FL02-* entered. Accept Yes/No <Yes/No>: **Y**

> 11 layer(s) selected

> Process another layer? Yes/No <No>: **Y**

> Freeze/Thaw/ON/OFF/Unlock: <Freeze>: **F**

> Select layer(s) to FREEZE <enter name>:

> Select objects: **[Enter]**

> Enter MAJOR name or . for none <FL01>: **FL03***

> Enter MINOR-1 name or . for none <.>: **[Enter]**

> Enter BASIC name or . for none <All>: **[Enter]**

> FL03-* entered. Accept Yes/No <Yes/No>: **Y**

> 14 layer(s) selected

> Process another layer? Yes/No <No>: **N**

> Current level is FL01, Elevation is 0", Orientation is 0.0

Eye

1. Select the Eye submenu from the Display pull-down menu as shown in Figure 3.

2. Pick a target point near the entry door and a camera point near the center of the custom curved wall as shown in Figure 4.

3. Accept the defaults for eye level at 5'-6", target height at 5'-6" and lens at 30-mm to make the view as shown in Figure 5.

Display>Eye>Eye

> Command: EYE

> Eye level is 5'-6", target height is 5'-6", lens mm is 30.

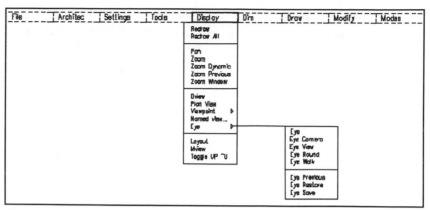

Figure 3.

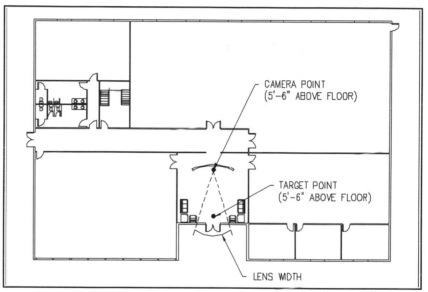

Figure 4.

> Pick target point in plan or Eye/Target/Lens: [**pick target point as shown in Figure 4**]

> Pick camera point in plan: [**pick camera point as shown in Figure 4**]

> Save this view for AutoShade Yes/No <No>:**NO**

Note: We will not be using AutoShade.

> Current level is FL01, Elevation is 0, Orientation is 0.0

Note: Since this drawing was saved from Session 9 using Multi-Story commands, the current level, elevation and orientation are provided. Otherwise, this information would not appear as part of the command.

4. The perspective view shown in Figure 5 is created by invoking AutoCAD's Hide command to display the interior perspective.

> Command: **HIDE**

> Regenerating drawing.

Adjusting the Lens

1. Return to the plan view by selecting Current UCS from the Display pull-down menu under Plan View.

Display>Plan View>Current UCS

> PLAN

> <Current UCS>/Ucs/World

> Regenerating drawing

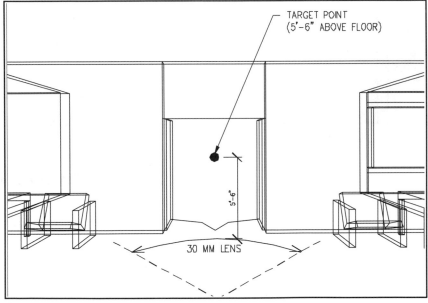

Figure 5.

2. Widen the view by adjusting the Lens option of the Eye command to 12 mm. Pick the same approximate target and camera positions.

3. Select Eye from the Display pull-down menu under the Eye submenu.

Display>Eye>Eye

> Command: EYE

> Eye level is 5'-6", target height is 5'-6", lens mm is 30

> Pick target point in plan or Eye/Target/Lens: **L**

> Enter lens mm <30>: **12**

> Eye level is 5'-6", target height is 5'-6", lens mm is 12.

> Pick target point in plan or Eye/Target/Lens: [**pick target point as shown in Figure 4**]

> Pick camera point in plan: [**pick camera point as shown in Figure 4**]

> Save this view for AutoShade Yes/No <No>:**NO**

> Current level is FL01, Elevation is 0, Orientation is 0.0

4. The adjusted view will appear wider, including more of the furniture and front entry elevation as shown in Figure 6.

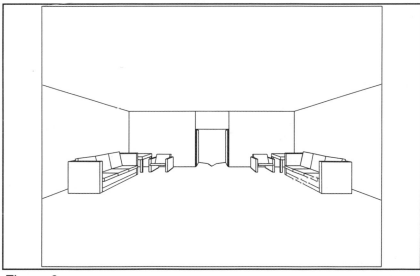

Figure 6.

Eye Camera

1. To save the current perspective view place a camera into the drawing by selecting the Eye Camera command while in the perspective view.

2. Select the Eye Camera command from the Eye submenu and assign the name VIEW1. The camera will appear as a horizontal line across the perspective view as shown in Figure 7.

    Display>Eye>Eye Camera

    > Command: EYECAM

    > Enter camera name: **VIEW1 [assign View1 as camera name]**

    > Current level is FL01, Elevation is 0, Orientation is 0.0

3. Return to the plan view by selecting Current UCS from the Plan View submenu under the Display pull-down menu.

    Display>Plan View>Current UCS

    > PLAN

    > <Current UCS>/Ucs/World

    > Regenerating drawing

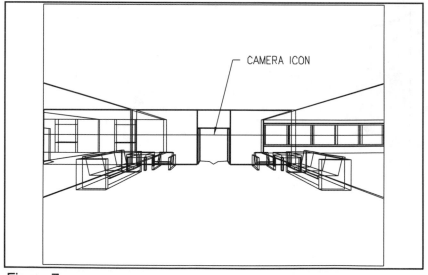

CAMERA ICON

Figure 7.

4. The camera icon appears in front of the custom curved wall. An enlarged view of the icon is shown in Figure 8.

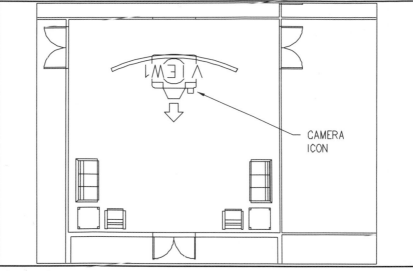

CAMERA
ICON

Figure 8.

Eye View

1. To restore the saved view, select Eye View from the Eye submenu shown in Figure 3.

2. Pick the camera icon named VIEW1 (saved with the previous Eye Camera command).

Display>Eye>Eye View

> Command: EYEVIEW

> Select Camera <none>: [**pick the camera icon in the drawing labeled VIEW1**]

> Processing-- please wait.

> Current level is FL01, Elevation is 0", Orientation is 0.0.

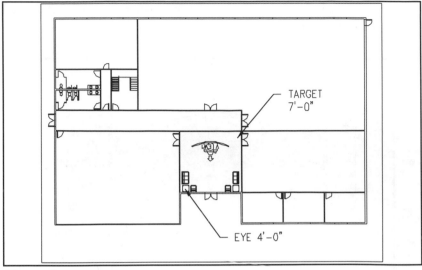

Figure 9.

Eye Walk

1. Pick Current UCS from Plan View and return to the plan view.

   Display>Plan View>Current UCS

   > PLAN

   > <Current UCS>/Ucs/World

   > Regenerating drawing

2. Make a new perspective selecting two new points at opposite ends of the entry area as shown in Figure 9.

3. Select the Eye command again and set eye level at 4′, target at 7′and lens at 15mm.

   Display>Eye>Eye

   > Command: EYE

   > Eye level is 5′-6", target height is 5′-6", lens is 12

   > Pick target point in plan or Eye/Target/Lens: **E**

   > Enter eye level (height) <5′-6">: **4′**

> Eye level is 4'-0", target height is 5'-6", lens is 12

> Pick target point in plan or Eye/Target/Lens: **T**

> Enter target height <5'-6">: **7'**

> Eye level is 4'-0", target height is 7'-0", lens is 12

> Pick target point in plan or Eye/Target/Lens: **L**

> Enter lens mm <12>: **15**

> Eye level is 4'-0", target height is 7'-0", lens is 15

> Pick target point in plan or Eye/Target/Lens: [**pick target point at front corner of entry**]

> Pick camera point in plan: [**pick camera point near door to Office-2**]

> Processing – please wait

> Save this view for AutoShade Yes/No <No>: **NO**

> Current level is FL01, Elevation is 0", Orientation if 0.0

4. After the new perspective view is generated as shown in Figure 10, a slide show can be made moving between the camera and the target points.

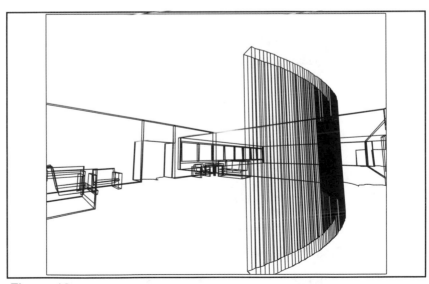

Figure 10.

5. Select Eye Walk from the Eye submenu to create a script file for the slide show with four steps and a prefix name of WLK, hiding each view, specifying a 1000 millisecond delay.

Display>Eye>Eye Walk

> Command: EYEWALK

> Enter number of steps from Camera to Target <distance>: **4**

> Enter view name prefix (1-3 characters): **WLK**

> Make slides of each view Yes/No <No>: **Y**

Note: The slides file names will be assigned a sequential number with the prefix.

> View type Hide/Shade <wireframe>: **H**

> Make Script file to display slides Yes/No <No>: **Y**

> Enter delay time in milliseconds <0>: **1000**

Note: The Script file name will be the same as the prefix WLK with a .SCR extension. It reads as follows:

        vslide wlk0
        delay 1000
        vslide wlk1
        delay 1000
        vslide wlk2
        delay 1000
        vslide wlk3
        delay 1000

> Processing – please wait

> Creating view wlk0

> Creating view wlk1

> Creating view wlk2

> Creating view wlk3

> Current level is FL01, Elevation is 0", Orientation if 0.0

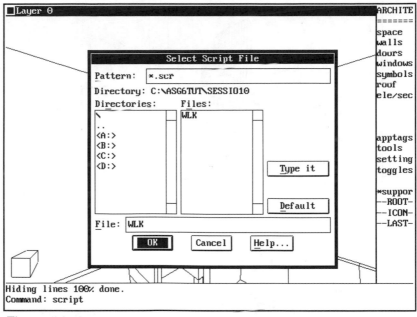

Figure 11.

6. The slide show as shown in Figure 11 can be viewed using AutoCAD's Script command and entering the name WLK.

7. Enter Script at the command line to display the Select Script File dialog box and select the WLK file as shown in Figure 12.

> Command: **Script {Select Script File}**

Note: The script file is executed alternately invoking the Vslide and Delay commands.

Eye Round

1. Thaw all the layers and make a slide show viewing all sides of the exterior of building.

2. Select Layer Visibility from the Layering Tools menu processing all Levels as FL0*.

> LYRVIS

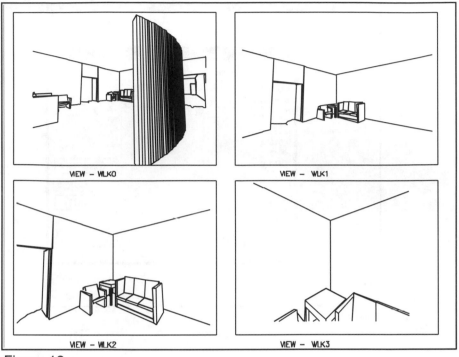

Figure 12.

> Freeze/Thaw/ON/OFF/Unlock <Freeze>: **T**

> Select layer(s) to FREEZE <enter name>:

> Enter MAJOR name or . for none <FL01>: **FL0***

> Enter MINOR-1 name or . for none .: **[Enter]**

> Enter BASIC name or . for none: **[Enter]**

> FL0*-* entered. Accept Yes/No <Yes/No>: **Y**

> 39 layer(s) selected

> Regen required to view results, proceed? Yes/No <Yes>: **Y**

> Process another layer? Yes/No <No>: **N**

> Current level is FL01, Elevation is 0", Orientation is 0.0

3. Return to the plan view again. Select Current UCS from Plan View.

Display>Plan View>Current UCS

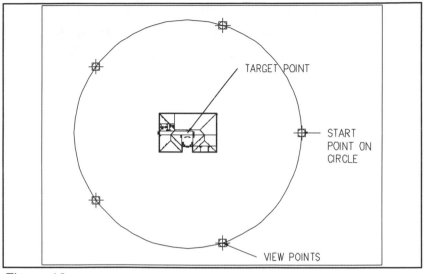

Figure 13.

4.   Zoom out to make the drawing appear smaller.

5.   Pick Zoom Scale(X) from the Display pull-down menu under Zoom and select 0.10x from the side screen menu.

Display>Zoom>Zoom Scale(X)

>   Command: Zoom

>   All/Center/Dynamic/Extents/Left/Previous/Vmax/Window/ Scale(X/XP): **.10x [automatic response from side screen menu]**

6.   Using the exterior building mass as the fixed point, make a slide show by selecting the Eye Round command from the Eye submenu.

7.   The Eye Round command generates a circle around the building as shown in Figure 13.

8.   Set the eye and target point at 5'-6", and 30 mm lens. Using six steps with the prefix file name RND, make a slide show using Hide, delaying each view 1000 milliseconds.

Display>Eye>Eye Round

> Command: EYEROUND

> Eye level is 4', target height is 7', lens mm is 15

> Pick target point in plan or Eye/Target/Lens: **E**

> Enter eye level (height) <4'>: **5'6"**

> Eye level is 5' 6", target height is 7', lens mm is 15

> Pick target point in plan or Eye/Target/Lens: **T**

> Enter target height <7'-0">: **5'6"**

> Eye level is 5' 6", target height is 5'6", lens mm is 15

> Pick target point in plan or Eye/Target/Lens: **L**

> Enter lens mm <15>: **30**

> Eye level is 5' 6", target height is 5'6", lens mm is 30

> Pick target point in plan or Eye/Target/Lens: [**select point at center of building as shown in Figure 13**]

> Pick start point on circle: [**select a point to create the circle as shown in Figure 13**]

Note: Create a circle with a large diameter similar to Figure 13 to view the building at a distance.

> Draw new circle Yes/No <No>: **N**

> Enter number of steps around the circle: **6**

> Enter view name prefix (1-3 characters): **RND**

> Make slides of each view Yes/No: **Y**

> View type Hide/Shade <wireframe>: **H**

> Make Script file to display slides Yes/No <No>: **Y**

> Enter delay time in milliseconds (0): **1000**

> Processing – please wait

> Creating view md0

> Creating view md1

> Creating view md2

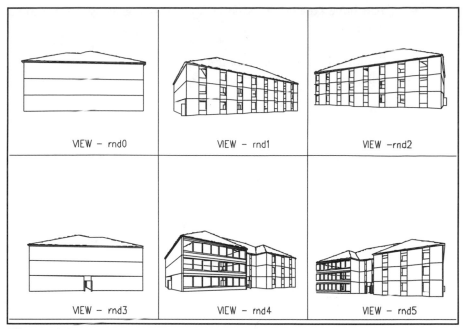

Figure 14.

> Creating view md3

> Creating view md4

> Creating view md5

> Current level is FL01, Elevation is 0", Orientation is 0.0

9. Enter Script at the command line to display the Select Script File dialog box and select RND as the file name.

> Command: **Script {Select Script File}**

10. The 6 views are shown in Figure 14.

End

1. To complete the ASG Architectural Tutorial, select Exit AutoCAD from the Files pull-down menu to save your drawing and end the drawing session.

`File>Exit AutoCAD`

2. You have created an Architectural drawing using only some of the features from ASG.

3. Explore the remaining commands, tools, settings, and toggles on your own, using this tutorial as a reference guide.

Index

More OnWord Press Titles

Pro/ENGINEER Books

INSIDE Pro/ENGINEER
Book $49.95 Includes Disk

The Pro/ENGINEER Quick Reference
Book $24.95

The Pro/ENGINEER Exercise Book
Book $39.95 Includes Disk

Mechanical CAD

Manager's Guide to Computer-Aided Engineering
Book $49.95

MicroStation Books

INSIDE MicroStation
Book $29.95 Optional Disk $14.95

INSIDE MicroStation Companion Workbook
Book $34.95 Includes Disk/Redline Drawings/Projects

INSIDE MicroStation Companion Workbook Instructor's Guide
Book $9.95 Includes Disk/Redline Drawings/Projects/Lesson Plans

MicroStation Reference Guide
Book $18.95 Optional Disk $14.95

The MicroStation Productivity Book
Book $39.95 Optional Disk $49.95

MicroStation Bible
Book $49.95 Optional Disk $49.95

Programming With MDL
Book $49.95 Optional Disk $49.95

Programming With User Commands
Book $65.00 Optional Disk $40.00

101 MDL Commands
Book $49.95 Optional Executable Disk $101.00 Optional Source Disks (6) $259.95

101 User Commands
Book $49.95 Optional Disk $101.00

Bill Steinbock's Pocket MDL Programmer's Guide
Book $24.95

MicroStation for AutoCAD Users
Book $29.95 Optional Disk $14.95

MicroStation for AutoCAD Users Tablet Menu
Tablet Menu $99.95

MicroStation 4.X Delta Book
Book $19.95

The MicroStation 3D Book
Book $39.95 Optional Disk $39.95

Managing and Networking MicroStation
Book $29.95 Optional Disk $29.95

The MicroStation Database Book
Book $29.95 Optional Disk $29.95

The MicroStation Rendering Book
Book $34.95 Includes Disk

INSIDE I/RAS B
Book $24.95 Includes Disk

The CLIX Workstation User's Guide
Book $34.95 Includes Disk

SunSoft Solaris Series

The SunSoft Solaris 2.* User's Guide
Book $29.95 Includes Disk

SunSoft Solaris 2.* for Managers and Administrators
Book $34.95 Optional Disk $29.95

The SunSoft Solaris 2.* Quick Reference
Book $18.95

Five Steps to SunSoft Solaris 2.*
Book $24.95 Includes Disk

One Minute SunSoft Solaris Manager
Book $14.95

SunSoft Solaris for Windows Users
Book $24.95

The Hewlett Packard HP-UX Series

The HP-UX User's Guide
Book $29.95 Includes Disk

HP-UX For Managers and Administrators
Book $34.95 Optional Disk $29.95

The HP-UX Quick Reference
Book $18.95

Five Steps to HP-UX
Book $24.95 Includes Disk

One Minute HP-UX Manager
Book $14.95

HP-UX for Windows Users
Book $24.95

CAD

INSIDE CADVANCE
Book $34.95 Includes Disk

Using Drafix Windows CAD
Book $34.95 Includes Disk

CAD and the Practice of Architecture: ASG Solutions
Book $39.95 Includes Disk

CAD Management

One Minute CAD Manager
Book $14.95

The CAD Rating Guide
Book $49.00

Geographic Information Systems

The GIS Book
Book $29.95

DTP/CAD Clip Art

1001 DTP/CAD Symbols Clip Art Library: Architectural
Book $29.95

MicroStation
DGN Disk $175.00   Book/Disk $195.00

AutoCAD
DWG Disk $175.00   Book/Disk $195.00

CAD/DTP

DXF Disk $175.00 Book/Disk $225.00
IGES Disk $195.00 Book/Disk $225.00
TIF Disk $195.00 Book/Disk $225.00
EPS Disk $195.00 Book/Disk $225.00
HPGL Disk $195.00 Book/Disk $225.00

CD ROM With All Formats
CD $275.00 Book/CD $295.00

Networking/LANtastic

Fantastic LANtastic
Book $29.95 Includes Disk

The LANtastic Quick Reference
Book $14.95

One Minute Network Manager
Book $14.95

DISK/CD ROM
INCLUDED

OnWord Press Distribution

End User/Corporate

OnWord Press books are available world-wide to end users and corporate accounts from your local bookseller or computer/software dealer or call 1-800-223-6397 or 505/473-5454.

Wholesale

Domestic Education

OnWord Press books are distributed to the US dom~~estic education m~~ ~~~~
Publishe
0301 or
Columbi

Domes

OnWord I
US domes
hold. Call 1

OnWo

or write Van Nostrand Reinhold at 115 Fifth Avenue, New York, NY 10003.

Europe, Middle East, and Africa

OnWord Press books are distributed in Europe, the Middle East, and Africa by International Thomson Publishing. Call 071-497-1422, Fax 071-497-1426 or write International Thomson Publishing at Berkshire House, 168-173 High Holborn, Lon-
~~~~ V 7AA, United Kingdom.

...cific, Hawaii, Puerto
...d South America

...ress books are distributed in
...acific, Puerto Rico, and South
... International Thomson Pub-
...Call 2-272-6497, Fax 2-272-6498
...rnational Thomson Publishing
...ian Road, #01-05, Kim Tian
...ore 0316.

...e, NM 87505 USA

DATE DUE

JUN 26 1996

OCT 15 1997

MAY 02 2002

HIGHSMITH   # 45220